BGP for Cisco Networks

A CCIE v5 guide to the Border Gateway Protocol

By Stuart Fordham

Copyright

Notice of Rights

Copyright © 2014 by Stuart Fordham

All rights reserved. This book or any portion thereof may not be reproduced or used in any manner whatsoever without the express written permission of the publisher except for the use of brief quotations in a book review.

Front cover image copyright of Studiojumpee / Shutterstock, Inc.

Notice of Liability

Although the author and publisher have made every effort to ensure that the information in this book was correct at press time, the author and publisher do not assume and hereby disclaim any liability to any party for any loss, damage, or disruption caused by errors or omissions, whether such errors or omissions result from negligence, accident, or any other cause.

Trademarks

CCNA, CCNP, CCIE and Cisco are registered trademarks of Cisco Systems, Inc.

To my sons Jake and Caleb, I hope you will understand that daddy works hard so you can have a good future.

To my dad, I always understood that you worked hard so I could have a good future.

I think I have it pretty damn good.

1. About 7
1.1 About the Author 7
1.2 About this book 7
1.3 Following this book 9
1.4 Cisco IOS basics 9

2. A brief history of BGP 11
2.1 BGP In a nutshell 11
2.2 From GGP to EGP 11
2.3 From EBP to BGP 11
2.4 What's your vector, Victor? 13
2.5 BGP AS Numbering 14

3. Topology 16

4. eBGP Peering 17
4.1 Differences between iBGP and eBGP 17
4.2 Basic eBGP Peers 17
4.3 BGP peer formation and neighbor states 19
4.4 Router IDs 21
4.5 Route advertisement using the network command 22
4.6 Message Types 24
4.7 Topology Tables 25
4.8 Some more eBGP peers 26

5. iBGP Peering 32
5.1 The rules of BGP 32
5.2 Basic iBGP Peers 33
5.3 IGPs and BGP 44

6. Advanced BGP Peering 53
6.1 eBGP peers and hops 53
6.2 Active vs. Passive 55
6.3 TTL Security and Connected checking 57
TTL Security 57
Disable-Connected-Check 59
6.4 Route Reflectors 59
6.5 Peer groups 67
Soft-reconfiguration and Route-Refresh 68
6.6 Confederations 71
6.7 Clusters 74
6.8 local-as 79

7. Communities and AS numbers 82

    7.1 Communities 82
    7.2 Extended Communities 93
    7.3 allowas-in 93
    7.4 remove-private-as 94
    7.5 4-Byte AS numbers 97

8. Advanced BGP Routing 99
    8.1 Default routes and static routes 99
                Static Redistribution 99
                The network command 100
                Default Originate 101
    8.2 Route summarization and aggregation 103
    8.3 as-set 106
    8.4 Suppress maps 106
    8.5 Unsuppress maps 108
    8.6 conditional advertisement 109
    8.7 Route Injection 114
    8.8 Outbound route filtering 117
    8.9 Distribute Lists 121

9. Making BGP easier 123
    9.1 Dynamic peers 123
    9.2 Peer templates 125
                Peer Session templates 125
                Peer Policy templates 127

10. Multiprotocol BGP and Address Families 131
    10.1 Address families 134

11. Attributes and Decisions 139
    11.1 BGP Attributes 139
    11.2 BGP Regular expressions 142
    11.3 BGP Best Path Selection Algorithm 150
                Valid next hop 150
                Highest weight 150
                Highest LOCAL_PREF 154
                Locally originated routes 156
                Shortest AS_PATH 158
                Lowest origin type 160
                Lowest MED 162
                eBGP vs. iBGP 164
                Lowest IGP metric 165
                Multiple paths 165

   Received first 167
   Lowest router ID 167
   Minimum cluster list length 167
   Lowest neighbor address 167
  11.4 mnemonics 167

12. BGP and IGPs 169
  12.1 BGP and IGP redistribution 170
  12.2 BGP Backdoors 176
  12.3 BGP Distance 182

13. Securing BGP 185
  13.1 S-BGP 185
  13.2 BGP Authentication 186

14. Tweaking BGP 189
  14.1 BGP Timers 189
   Keepalive and Hold-down 189
   Advertisement timer 191
   Scan-Timer 192
  14.2 Next-Hop Tracking 192
  14.3 Prefix independent convergence and add-path 196
  14.4 Dampening 203

15. Troubleshooting BGP 207
  15.1 Troubleshooting peering 207
   Troubleshooting Physical issues 207
   Troubleshooting Ports 209
   Troubleshooting BGP Configuration issues 209
   Troubleshooting route advertisement 214

16. This book and the CCIE v5 221

17. Further Reading 223
  General 223
  Secure BGP 223
  PIC and Additional Paths 223
  Troubleshooting 223
  BGP Looking glasses 223

1. About

1.1 About the Author

I have been working in IT for about 12 years, starting off in desktop support, moving up the chain to third line and more recently and specifically finding my "home" within networking. I have worked for a number of companies, including local health authorities, Hedge Funds, and software houses. My current role is looking after the global network for a SaaS company.

I studied Psychology at university, but at the end of the degree I really did not fancy spending years and years studying in order to progress up the ladder. So I moved into IT, and have spent years studying on order to progress up the ladder. I have a number of qualifications including; CCNP, CCNA, JNCIP, CEH, RHCSA, MCITP, MCSE, MCSA: Security, Network+, Security+, A+ and I think that's about it. I tend to collect certifications, some I have purposefully let lapse in order to concentrate more on the Cisco side of things, others are still current. I enjoy writing and have written a few reviews and articles that are out there on the Internet, but this is my biggest venture to date.

I am married with twin sons and I live in Bedfordshire in the UK.

I can be contacted at stu@802101.com. I am always willing to hear feedback and suggestions.

My website address is http://www.802101.com.

1.2 About this book

It seems that as the number of certifications being passed grows so does the recommended reading list of books that need to be purchased. For the CCNA it was two books, for the CCNP it's three books. The technical jump from CCNP to CCIE is vast, and with that so is the required reading list. The publicized reading list from Cisco is a whopping 21 books[1]. Even with judicious purchasing of second hand books via the likes of eBay or Amazon marketplace you would still end up paying in the region of $15 (if very lucky) or more, so buying the entire book list even at this minimum price would total about $300 (about £200). I have bought a large number of the books on the reading list, but a number of them will go untouched, and large portions of others will go unread, at

---

[1] http://www.802101.com/2013/05/ccie-book-list.html

least until I need to cover bits I have missed. With twenty-odd books time is a significant factor, if you figure at best you would be able to finish one book a month, that's still nearly two years to complete the reading list. Granted not all books are created equal in length, and some people have more time than others to go through the reading, but even so, there is still a lot of reading to be done. Let's face it; no one really wants to spend two years reading for one exam.

So finding a book that is affordable, contains all the relevant information, but at the same time can be precise and short enough (but without lacking the detail) to finish within a week or so, can be a bit of a mission.

After more than 10 years of being in this industry I have read a large number of computer books on a variety of subjects; from the very best to the very worst and there are a number of things that, in my mind, make for a good networking book. Networks are by their very nature constantly evolving. So by that token any book that teaches anything about networks should also follow this evolutionary path, it should build and scale as the book progresses in the same way that someone faced with a network will first start from the ground up, such as basic connectivity, before their own skills and knowledge grow as the network grows and additions to the network are added, such as more complex routing, access rules and redundancy. The types of books that don't present an evolutionary network to the reader are also, in my experience, one of two types. Type A is full of tables of commands with little actual examples of the commands and their results. Type B is slightly better and offers the commands within the context of a network, showing the results and effects of the commands. Generally type B uses singular examples, each is self-contained and example X bears no relevance to example Y. Therefore the reader cannot actually see the evolution of the network, how the intricacies of pathways are built and changed as the network grows.

With this in mind I decided to write one myself. Hopefully it will serve two purposes, the first being to solidify my own knowledge towards the CCIE certification, the second to start a series of Cisco-centric networking books that will:

- Be affordable
- Be easy to read within a couple of weeks
- Be of use at any level of networking competency
- Follow a topology to show how a network is built and evolves
- Allow the reader to follow using either physical or virtual (i.e. GNS3) equipment

1.3 Following this book

I have used GNS3 for the majority of the topology, primarily as this is the virtual environment that many people studying Cisco exams (after packet tracer of course) are familiar with. Some examples have required the use of IOU, but this is due to the later IOS releases needed.

Hopefully by the time this book is ready for publishing, Cisco will have released VIRL/CML, and if and when it is released I will rebuild the topology and publish the files on my website.

For more information on Cisco IOU and Cisco VIRL please have a look at my site:

http://www.802101.com/2013/06/getting-started-with-cisco-iou-ios-on.html
http://www.802101.com/2013/11/cisco-goes-virl.html

The initial router configurations can be downloaded from:

http://l.802101.com/802books

See chapter 3 for the topology that will be used through the majority of this book.

There are a couple of scenarios where I have had to move away from the main topology and set up smaller examples, although this goes against the evolutionary style that I hope to accomplish with this book, I hope you'll understand the reasoning behind not pushing it all into one topology.

There is also an inherent problem with using emulation, especially at the time of writing with the CCIE v5 exam set to replace the v4, in that it is harder to find software that supports the IOS or IOS-XR versions that will be in the exam (see chapter 16 for more information on the exam itself). Because of this some features that should be in this book have been (regretfully) omitted although they will be mentioned and briefly explained. Thankfully this is just limited to items on the written exam only and not the lab exam.

1.4 Cisco IOS basics

There is a lot of command truncation in this book. Although this book is aimed at CCIE level BGP I do hope that anyone at any level can pick it up and get going. So a few quick words about the commands used.

Most of the show commands will be truncated to "sh" and will use further truncation such as "neigh" being the short version of neighbor. I also use the output modifier a lot this is the bar, or pipe character "|" as well as "i" for include, "e" for exclude, "beg" for begin (at). If you have never even looked at the Cisco IOS before then there are plenty of guides around to get you going. If you know a bit about the Cisco IOS and are looking for a good BGP resource, then hopefully this is the right place for you.

When entering configuration mode IOS always adds "Enter configuration commands, one per line. End with CNTL/Z". I have removed these lines from all output.

2. A brief history of BGP

2.1 BGP In a nutshell

If you want a very brief over-view of BGP then have a read over the next paragraph, for a longer explanation of the history of BGP then read the rest of the chapter.

BGP is an inter-domain path-vector routing protocol that runs over TCP on port 179. It provides a reliable loop-free routing between different Autonomous Systems (ASs). The current version is BGP-4 which has support for CIDR, 4-byte AS numbers, and can carry IPv4, IPv6, VPNv4 (Virtual Private Networks version 4), CLNS (Connectionless Network Services), and L2VPN (Layer 2 VPN). BGP routers (called "Speakers") form peerings (also known as neighbor relationships) with other BGP peers, these can either be internal, therefore within the same AS (iBGP) or external, connecting two different ASs (eBGP).

2.2 From GGP to EGP

Way back in the early days of the Internet, in the 1980s, routing was very different to what it has now evolved to be. There were a small number of core routers, and these maintained a complete table about network reachability on the Internet. At the time the Internet was a very small place, limited to large institutions and the military.

These core routers used the Gateway-to-Gateway Protocol (GGP) to exchange information between them. GGP was an interior routing protocol, and operated much like RIP does nowadays; it was a distance-vector routing protocol that used hop count to find the best path to its intended destination. Beyond these core routers lay a larger number of non-core routers, and these routers used the Exterior Gateway Protocol (EGP) to exchange network reachability with the core routers. Picture it as a tree, the core routes forming a strong base, with the non-core routers being the branches.

2.3 From EBP to BGP

EGP fitted well with this tree-like structure, it was a relatively simple protocol (as protocols go), connecting to the Internet's core, or backbone. EGP worked well just so long as the basic rules were followed, the major rules being that traffic should only flow via the core. This did not scale or evolve well, and as the Internet became more and more decentralized, instead becoming a collection of internetworks composed of separate Autonomous Systems (ASs), EGP could not handle a topology based around interconnected ASs, and therefore BGP rose up to take the mantel as the routing protocol of the Internet.

BGP stands for Border Gateway Protocol. The current version is version 4, which has been used since around 1994. BGP is the successor to the Exterior Gateway Protocol (EGP), and is classed as an advanced distance vector protocol, but also as a path vector protocol. Each AS is given an autonomous system number (ASN). ASNs were originally a 16-bit number (referred to as the 2-byte AS number), these ASNs are numbered from 1 - 65535, with the last few (64512 - 65535) being reserved for private usage. These private usage ASNs are often assigned by an ISP, but will be stripped out (see section 7.4), as they are not routable on the Internet. This pool of 2-byte AS numbers were originally calculated to be fully depleted by 2011, and although these 2-byte numbers are still being handed out, the RIRs (Regional Internet Registry) that hand them out, are re-using old ones. Their preference now is to use 4-byte AS numbers, which puts the total number of AS numbers available around the 4 billion mark. BGP uses several path attributes in its routing decisions, which we will cover later on, but the closest to a default metric BGP has is the AS_PATH, which is a sequence of ASNs passed along with the route. As the route passes through an AS, that AS adds its own unique number to the sequence; this is also the primary method of loop avoidance within BGP. A router will not accept a route into its BGP table that contains its own AS number, unless we tell it to (see section 7.3).

As stated the current version is BGP-4. The first version was created back in 1989 under RFC 1105. It was similar to EGP with routers being more stringently aligned (up, down or horizontal).

BGP-2 came out in June 1990 under RFC 1163, and removed the up, down or horizontal alignment, paving the way for a protocol much more suited to arbitrary ASs. BGP-2 also added path attributes to BGP, which is the basis for the creation of the routing tables.

BGP-3 followed in October 1991 (RFC 1267), which optimized and simplified the way in which routing information is exchanged.

BGP-4 was standardized in March 1995 under RFC 1771 (after an initial standardizing under RFC 1654 in July 1994), adding CIDR (Classless Inter-Domain Routing) to its feature set. Since then BGP has not changed its version number, but has been through a string of changes, some of the major ones are listed below.

June 2000, RFC 2858, added support for IPv6 and IPX
May 2001, RFC 3107, added support for MPLS labels
January 2006, RFC 4271, made RFC 1771 obsolete
May 2007, RFC 4893, Adds support for four-octet AS Number Space

December 2008, RFC 5396, Added the decimal notation system for the AS numbers
June 2011, RFC 6286, Only AS-wide uniqueness of BGP identifiers is now required
May 2012, RFC 6608, defined sub-codes for the BGP Finite State Machine (FSM)
December 2012, RFC 6793, BGP now carries the AS numbers as four-octet entities

As protocols go, BGP gets updated very frequently, one would suggest that our reliance on it now means that it needs to stay and grow with us for a long time to come.

Will BGP every reach version 5? Yes, most likely, when that will be is anyone's guess, and what it will take the routing of the Internet to be is going to be very interesting.

2.4 What's your vector, Victor?

As already mentioned, BGP is a path vector protocol. The various routing protocols (both internal and external) all fall under three headings; path vector, distance vector, or link state. A path vector protocol maintains an entry in the routing table with the destination network, the next hop router and the path to the destination. BGP uses the AS number as its path vector, yet BGP also lies somewhere in between as it shares a number of features with distance vector protocols (such as RIP, RIPv2 and EIGRP); it informs neighbors of topology changes periodically. BGP holds its own table, which is updated with each change and uses a table version number to keep track of changes. Routes are stored in the Routing Information Bases (or RIBs), and these are the Adj-RIB-in, Adj-RIB-out and Loc-RIB. For a route to be advertised to a neighbor it must be present in the Adj-RIB-out. Routes advertised from a neighbor will be present in the Adj-RIB-in. local routes are placed in the Loc-RIB, and the next hop for these routes needs to be present in the Forwarding Information Base (FIB)

Distance vector

Referred to as Bellman-Ford protocols, distance vector protocols include RIPv2 and EIGRP. The name is derived from fact that the protocol includes a list of distances (based on hop-count or other metrics) associated with each destination prefix. Each node calculates the best path to each destination prefix. After selecting the best path, the router then sends the distance vectors to its neighbors, with the reachability and corresponding metrics. Each router then does this, until each has selected a best path to each destination. Once a common understanding has been reached the router are said to have "converged". A refresh timer is used to ensure that everyone has the best information in their routing tables. Convergence is sped up through the use of triggered updates whereby failures of a path are sent to neighbors before the refresh timer expires.

Link-state

Link-state protocols such as OSPF and IS-IS use a replicated distributed database. Routers exchange information, called link-states, about the links and nodes in the network. They do not exchange routing tables (like Distance vector protocols do) but they exchange information about neighbors and networks. This information is stored in the link-state database and calculations are based on the Dijkstra algorithm.

2.5 BGP AS Numbering

Autonomous System Numbers (ASNs) are unique to an organization. They must be unique as they are linked to IP addresses that are assigned by the ISP to the company using the ASN.

To obtain an ASN from a Regional Internet Registrar (RIR) the request must satisfy a number of requirements:

- You must be multi-homed (have connections to more than one ISP)
- You must specify the exterior routing protocol used to communicate with the ISP (which will be BGP)
- You must provide the ASNs of all your ISPs
- You may be asked to provide the IP addresses of your ISPs routers (your default gateways)
- Your ISP (and yourself) must already be on file in the RIR
- You must have blocks of IP addresses that need routing.

There are four RIRs; ARIN for the Americas and Africa, RIPE for Europe, APNIC for Asia and LACNIC for the Caribbean and Latin America.

The URLs for requesting ASNs are listed below:

https://www.arin.net/resources/request/asn.html
http://www.ripe.net/ripe/docs/asnrequestform.html
http://ftp.apnic.net/apnic/docs/asn-request
http://lacnic.net/templates/asn-template-sp.txt

Throughout this book the standard 2-byte or 16-bit numbering system will be used, this is the numbers 1 through 65,535 inclusive, though we will also look at the newer version as well.

Much like IP addresses there are public and private ranges of ASNs, as defined in RFC 1930. The pubic range is from 1 through to 64511, and the private range is from 64512 to 65535.

Because of the limited number of available ASNs, most new ASNs are now 32-bit, which is also called AS-dot notation.

If you are following the examples in this book, then it is important to remember that as we are using valid public ASNs that you should not try this on production equipment. Either try it out in a lab environment or on virtualized equipment (such as GNS3, or Cisco's CML/VIRL).

3. Topology

The topology we will be using is:

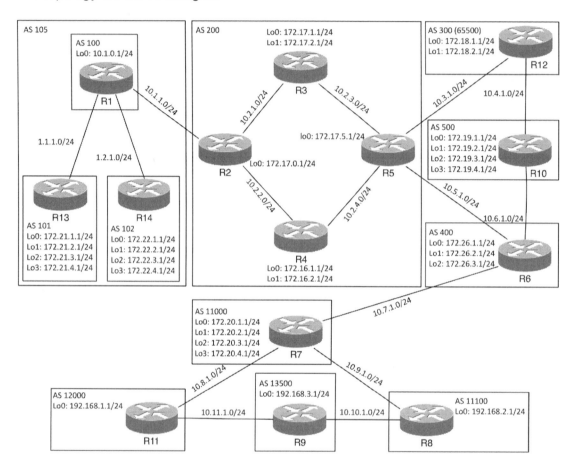

We have a number of separate ASs, each containing one router, and another AS (200) containing four routers, which we will use when we look at iBGP. It is far from a complex topology, but will enable us to cover all that we need to learn.

With that said, let's start creating our first peers.

4. eBGP Peering

As we have already discussed BGP connects autonomous systems (AS) together, and this is where we are going to jump right in, by setting up a BGP neighbor relationship between two ASs. Once we have finished our first practical example, we will then look into how the relationships form, and at the message types used with BGP messages.

4.1 Differences between iBGP and eBGP

Before we start configuring our first peering, let's have a quick look at the differences between iBGP and eBGP peers.

Other than the fact that one connects routers within one AS and the other connects two different ASs together, what, are the other differences between iBGP and eBGP?

The differences are in what attributes are taken into consideration when deciding on how that information affects our routing tables.

We will cover the different BGP attributes in greater depth later on, but for the moment we should know that Local Preference is used by iBGP only, whereas AS_PATH is used by eBGP only. eBGP peers will change the NEXT_HOP attribute, whereas iBGP will not (and this will be important later on). TTLs are also handled differently; with eBGP the TTL is set to 1, with iBGP the TTL is able to go to the maximum of 255. BGP offers loop prevention between ASs based on the AS_PATH attribute, because this is not used within iBGP, loop prevention must rely on the split horizon rule; that a route learned via iBGP will not be advertised to another iBGP speaker, unless it's learned through an IGP. This would indicate that all iBGP speakers should be be in a full mesh, which sometimes is not convenient for the network in question, but we can use confederations and route reflectors (both covered later) to overcome this.

So let's kick off by setting up a neighbor relationship between R1 in AS 100 and R2 in AS 200, which will be our first eBGP relationship. I have shut down the s0/0 interface on R2 in order that when we are ready we can turn on the interface, and hopefully capture some good traffic.

4.2 Basic eBGP Peers

With any BGP relationship, whether it be external or internal, we start with the command "router bgp" followed by an AS number:

```
R1#conf t
R1(config)#router bgp ?
  <1-65535>  Autonomous system number

R1(config)#router bgp 100
R1(config-router)#
```

Once we have entered our command and AS number, we are taken into the routing protocol sub-prompt. It is here that we start to define to whom, and how, we are connecting.

From the config-router command prompt we type in "neighbor" followed by the IP address of the neighbor we wish to peer to. It's important (to point out the obvious) that we must already have connectivity to this neighbor for the relationship to form. Before we press enter we must also specify which AS they are in using the command "remote-as", this command is the same whether we are configuring an eBGP relationship or an iBGP relationship.

The commands we will use are therefore:

```
R1(config-router)#neighbor 10.1.1.2 remote-as 200
```

The full command sequence for R1 would be:

```
R1(config)#router bgp 100
R1(config-router)#neighbor 10.1.1.2 remote-as 200
```

The commands we need to enter on R2 are very similar, and once entered we will see our neighbor relationship form when we get the neighbor up message:

```
R2#conf t
R2(config)#router bgp 200
R2(config-router)#neighbor 10.1.1.1 remote-as 100
R2(config-router)#
%BGP-5-ADJCHANGE: neighbor 10.1.1.1 Up
R2(config-router)#exit
```

So there we have how to create a BGP relationship in a few lines. We can confirm that R1 and R2 are neighbors, using the "sh ip bgp neighbors" command and below is some of the output from this:

```
R1#sh ip bgp neighbors
BGP neighbor is 10.1.1.2,  remote AS 200, external link
  BGP version 4, remote router ID 172.17.0.1
```

```
      BGP state = Established, up for 00:00:52
    Last read 00:00:21, last write 00:00:21, hold time is 180,
keepalive interval is 60 seconds
    Neighbor capabilities:
      Route refresh: advertised and received(old & new)
      Address family IPv4 Unicast: advertised and received
    Message statistics:
      InQ depth is 0
      OutQ depth is 0
                              Sent            Rcvd
      Opens:                   1               1
      Notifications:           0               0
      Updates:                 0               0
      Keepalives:              2               2
      Route Refresh:           0               0
      Total:                   3               3
    Default minimum time between advertisement runs is 30 seconds
<truncated>
Connection state is ESTAB, I/O status: 1, unread input bytes: 0
Connection is ECN Disabled, Minimum incoming TTL 0, Outgoing TTL 1
Local host: 10.1.1.1, Local port: 29372
Foreign host: 10.1.1.2, Foreign port: 179
```

We can see the following useful information, firstly, that the relationship is an external one, and secondly that the router ID advertised by R2 is 172.17.0.1. Our BGP state is established, and has been for a little under a minute. In that time we have sent two keepalive messages, which we will cover in 4.6. Lastly, we can see that the connection is using port 179 on R2 and 29372 on R1, indicating that R2 is the active peer of the relationship.

Before we move on to the mechanics of how connections are formed, it needs to be pointed out that if the router receives a connection request on port 179 from a source address not explicitly listed in its configuration (by using the neighbor command) then the request will be ignored, we'll be needing this later on.

4.3 BGP peer formation and neighbor states

Before I set up the BGP connection on R2, I shut down the interface connecting it to R1, so that when ready we can turn on the interface and capture the traffic. There are number of ways to accomplish this. If we are using GNS3 then we can right click on the link between the two routers and select "Start Capturing", alternatively we can use IOS and issue the command "debug bgp all".

From the IOS debug output we get the following:

```
BGP: 10.1.1.2 passive open to 10.1.1.1
BGP: 10.1.1.2 went from Active to Idle
BGP: 10.1.1.2 went from Idle to Connect
BGP: 10.1.1.2 rcv message type 1, length (excl. header) 26
BGP: 10.1.1.2 rcv OPEN, version 4, holdtime 180 seconds
BGP: 10.1.1.2 went from Connect to OpenSent
BGP: 10.1.1.2 sending OPEN, version 4, my as: 100, holdtime 180
seconds
BGP: 10.1.1.2 rcv OPEN w/ OPTION parameter len: 16
BGP: 10.1.1.2 rcvd OPEN w/ optional parameter type 2 (Capability) len
6
BGP: 10.1.1.2 OPEN has CAPABILITY code: 1, length 4
BGP: 10.1.1.2 OPEN has MP_EXT CAP for afi/safi: 1/1
BGP: 10.1.1.2 rcvd OPEN w/ optional parameter type 2 (Capability) len
2
BGP: 10.1.1.2 OPEN has CAPABILITY code: 128, length 0
BGP: 10.1.1.2 OPEN has ROUTE-REFRESH capability(old) for all address-
families
BGP: 10.1.1.2 rcvd OPEN w/ optional parameter type 2 (Capability) len
2
BGP: 10.1.1.2 OPEN has CAPABILITY code: 2, length 0
BGP: 10.1.1.2 OPEN has ROUTE-REFRESH capability(new) for all address-
families
BGP: 10.1.1.2 rcvd OPEN w/ remote AS 200
BGP: 10.1.1.2 went from OpenSent to OpenConfirm
BGP: 10.1.1.2 send message type 1, length (incl. header) 45
BGP: 10.1.1.2 went from OpenConfirm to Established
%BGP-5-ADJCHANGE: neighbor 10.1.1.2 Up
```

We can see that the router goes through a number of states. From an initial Active it goes to Idle, from there it goes to Connect. From Connect it goes to OpenSent, and then to OpenConfirm, before finally becoming Established. These states are known as the BGP Finite-State Machine.

Idle is the initial state when the routing process is enabled, or when the device is reset. The device waits to receive a connection request from a remote peer, this request is shown as the passive open message in the output above. Once we get the connection request we then move to the **Connect** state, where the BGP process detects that a peer is attempting to connect and set up a TCP session. The router then tries to establish the TCP session with a peer. If the session is successful we then go into the **OpenSent** state, where the connection is established and an OPEN message is sent. Hopefully we should hear back from the remote peer, at which stage we would then move to the **OpenConfirm** state. Here, once we receive the OPEN message from the remote peer, we then wait for an initial keepalive message to be received. Once received we then transition to the **Established** state, at which point we can safely say that peering is now fully operational.

Both routers will try and initiate the connection process, but once the OPEN process is completed, the routers will see that there is no need for both sessions to run in order to create the peering; so one session will be terminated. It is the router with the highest ID whose session will remain active.

These are not the only messages sent by the peers. Once the relationship is in the Established state, the peers exchange keepalives to make sure that the remote peer is still available. The keepalive messages are sent, by default, every 60 seconds, and if no reply is heard within the holdtime (default 180 seconds), the router declares the peer to be dead.

The other messages used are Update and Notification messages. Before we go through these though, we need to revisit our topology and make a slight modification.

4.4 Router IDs

Having a router id is a requirement of BGP. If you do not set one yourself using the command "bgp router-id <router-id>" (such as "bgp router-id 1.1.1.1"), then the router will select one for you. The router will first try to use the highest IP address of any loopback interface, and, if none are found, then the highest IP address of any physical interface.

If you do not have any IP addresses configured and try to configure a BGP routing process, you will get the following message:

```
Router(config)#router bgp 100
Router(config-router)#
%BGP-4-NORTRID: BGP could not pick a router-id. Please configure manually.
Router(config-router)#
```

During this book I will be using the same format for all of the BGP router IDs, which will be the router number four times, separated by dots (like an IP address). R1 (router 1) would be 1.1.1.1, R2 will be 2.2.2.2, and so on. If the router-id is not explicitly shown during initial configuration examples, please assume that it has been done, we don't want to reply on potluck, and we should control this.

We need to enter the bgp process again using the "router bgp <as number>" command, and then specify a router id using the command "bgp router-id <router-id>":

```
R1(config)#router bgp 100
R1(config-router)#bgp router-id 1.1.1.1
R1(config-router)#
%BGP-5-ADJCHANGE: neighbor 10.1.1.2 Down Router ID changed
R1(config-router)#
%BGP-5-ADJCHANGE: neighbor 10.1.1.2 Up
R1(config-router)#

R2(config)#router bgp 200
R2(config-router)#bgp router-id 2.2.2.2
R2(config-router)#
%BGP-5-ADJCHANGE: neighbor 10.1.1.1 Down Router ID changed
R2(config-router)#
%BGP-5-ADJCHANGE: neighbor 10.1.1.1 Up
R2(config-router)#
```

We can see our neighbor relationship come down, and get re-established. Now if we look at the bgp neighbor details on R1 we can confirm that R2 has the correct router-id:

```
R1#sh ip bgp neigh
BGP neighbor is 10.1.1.2,  remote AS 200, external link
  BGP version 4, remote router ID 2.2.2.2
  BGP state = Established, up for 00:00:22
```

So now we have corrected our router-id, but a BGP network is pretty useless unless we can route traffic over it.

4.5 Route advertisement using the network command

In order to advertise routes into an eBGP relationship we have a couple of options. The simplest of which is to use the network command:

```
R1#conf t
R1(config)#router bgp 100
R1(config-router)#network 10.1.0.0 mask 255.255.255.0
```

This will cause an UPDATE message to be passed over to R2, and R2 will then add this network first into its BGP table and then, if deemed both valid and best, it will then add the route into its routing table:

```
R2#sh ip bgp
```

```
BGP table version is 2, local router ID is 2.2.2.2
Status codes: s suppressed, d damped, h history, * valid, > best, i -
internal, r RIB-failure, S Stale
Origin codes: i - IGP, e - EGP, ? - incomplete

   Network          Next Hop           Metric LocPrf Weight Path
*> 10.1.0.0/24      10.1.1.1                0              0 100 i
R2#sh ip route | b Gate
Gateway of last resort is not set

     10.0.0.0/24 is subnetted, 3 subnets
C       10.2.1.0 is directly connected, Serial0/1
                 is directly connected, Serial0/2
C       10.1.1.0 is directly connected, Serial0/0
B       10.1.0.0 [20/0] via 10.1.1.1, 00:00:33
R2#ping 10.1.0.1

Type escape sequence to abort.
Sending 5, 100-byte ICMP Echos to 10.1.0.1:
!!!!!
Success rate is 100 percent (5/5)
R2#
```

We can see that R2 has learnt of the 10.1.0.0/24 network through BGP (B), that it has come from AS 100 (as shown in the path), and that we have reachability (it is valid, as indicated by the *), through the next hop ip address of 10.1.1.1. Because it is the only route to this destination, it is also "best", as indicated by the ">".

This presents a good place to step back to BGP message types and have a look at UPDATE and NOTIFICATION messages.

4.6 Message Types

When we started to advertise the 10.1.0.0/24 network into BGP, it triggered an UPDATE message from R1 to R2, and below is the exact contents of that UPDATE message.

```
▽ Border Gateway Protocol - UPDATE Message
      Marker: ffffffffffffffffffffffffffffffff
      Length: 52
      Type: UPDATE Message (2)
      Unfeasible routes length: 0 bytes
      Total path attribute length: 25 bytes
   ▽ Path attributes
      ▷ ORIGIN: IGP (4 bytes)
      ▷ AS_PATH: 100 (7 bytes)
      ▷ NEXT_HOP: 10.1.1.1 (7 bytes)
      ▷ MULTI_EXIT_DISC: 0 (7 bytes)
   ▽ Network layer reachability information: 4 bytes
      ▽ 10.1.0.0/24
            NLRI prefix length: 24
            NLRI prefix: 10.1.0.0 (10.1.0.0)
```

In this packet we can see that we are informed that the AS_PATH is AS 100, the NEXT_HOP is 10.1.1.1, and the NLRI (Network Layer Reachability Information) is for the prefix 10.1.0.0/24. This is not the only information that the UPDATE message contains, but we will cover some of the other information later on.

The other message type we have left to cover is a NOTIFICATION message; hopefully we won't see any of these as these are used to signal that something is wrong with a BGP session. Such a message will be sent if an unsupported option is sent in an OPEN message, or if a peer fails to send an UPDATE or KEEPALIVE message. If an error is detected then the BGP session is closed. A table of the error codes found within a NOTIFICATION message is next.

Error Code	Error Type	Error Subcode
1	Message header Error	1 - Connection Not Synchronized 2 - Bad Message Length 3 - Bad Message Type
2	OPEN message Error	1 - Unsupported Version 2 - Bad Peer AS 3 - Bad BGP Identifier 4 - Unsupported Optional Parameter 5 - Authentication Failure 6 - Unacceptable Hold Time
3	UPDATE message Error	1 - Malformed Attribute List 2 - Unrecognized well-know attribute 3 - Missing Well-Known Attribute 4 - Attribute Flags Error 5 - Attribute Length Error 6 - Invalid Origin Attribute 7 - AS Routing Loop 8 - Invalid NEXT_HOP attribute 9 - Optional Attribute Error 10 - Invalid Network Field
4	Hold Timer Expired	
5	Finite State Error	
6	Cease	

4.7 Topology Tables

Now that we know how the 10.1.0.0/24 network reached R2, we need to know what R2 actually did with the information in the UPDATE message.

BGP uses tables called RIBs (short for Routing Information Base). When the UPDATE message informed R2 about the additional network this was placed into the RIB, and from there populated the ip routing table on R2:

```
R2#sh ip bgp
BGP table version is 2, local router ID is 2.2.2.2
Status codes: s suppressed, d damped, h history, * valid, > best, i -
internal,
              r RIB-failure, S Stale
Origin codes: i - IGP, e - EGP, ? - incomplete

   Network          Next Hop            Metric LocPrf Weight Path
*> 10.1.0.0/24      10.1.1.1                 0             0 100 i
```

The output above shows that the route through 10.1.1.1 to the 10.1.0.0 network is both valid and best (we will see cases of multiple routes later on). Its AS_PATH is through AS 100 (again we will see examples of longer paths later on). We can also see some information such as Metric, LocPrf (standing for Local Preference) and weight, which we will cover in chapter 11.

4.8 Some more eBGP peers

The connections between the other routers are, at this early stage, no different in execution than that between R1 and R2. As an example, the configurations for R5, R6, R10 and R12 are listed below. We will leave the other routers unconfigured for the moment.

R5:

```
R5#sh run | section bgp
router bgp 200
 no synchronization
 bgp router-id 5.5.5.5
 bgp log-neighbor-changes
 network 172.17.5.0 mask 255.255.255.0
 neighbor 10.3.1.2 remote-as 300
 neighbor 10.5.1.2 remote-as 400
 no auto-summary
R5#
```

R6

```
R6#sh run | section bgp
router bgp 400
 no synchronization
 bgp router-id 6.6.6.6
 bgp log-neighbor-changes
 network 172.26.1.0 mask 255.255.255.0
```

```
  network 172.26.2.0 mask 255.255.255.0
  network 172.26.3.0 mask 255.255.255.0
  neighbor 10.5.1.1 remote-as 200
  neighbor 10.6.1.2 remote-as 500
  no auto-summary
R6#
```

R10

```
R10#sh run | section bgp
router bgp 500
 no synchronization
 bgp router-id 10.10.10.10
 bgp log-neighbor-changes
 network 172.19.1.0 mask 255.255.255.0
 network 172.19.2.0 mask 255.255.255.0
 network 172.19.3.0 mask 255.255.255.0
 network 172.19.4.0 mask 255.255.255.0
 neighbor 10.4.1.1 remote-as 300
 neighbor 10.6.1.1 remote-as 400
 no auto-summary
R10#
```

R12

```
R12#sh run | section bgp
router bgp 300
 no synchronization
 bgp router-id 12.12.12.12
 bgp log-neighbor-changes
 network 172.18.1.0 mask 255.255.255.0
 network 172.18.2.0 mask 255.255.255.0
 neighbor 10.3.1.1 remote-as 200
 neighbor 10.4.1.2 remote-as 500
 no auto-summary
R12#
```

Now that we have a fairly good set of peers set up, we will have a quick look at their routing tables before we try and join AS 100 to the other side of the network through the use of an iBGP peering in the next chapter.

We will look more closely at the BGP decision process in chapter 11, but it is important to touch on a few things now, mainly to get a feel for how the Path metric (AS_PATH) is changed as the network expands.

Firstly, here are the BGP routing tables and IP routing tables from the routers we have just set up:

```
R5#sh ip bgp | beg Network
   Network          Next Hop         Metric LocPrf Weight Path
*> 172.17.5.0/24    0.0.0.0               0         32768 i
*> 172.18.1.0/24    10.3.1.2              0             0 300 i
*> 172.18.2.0/24    10.3.1.2              0             0 300 i
*  172.19.1.0/24    10.3.1.2                            0 300 500 i
*>                  10.5.1.2                            0 400 500 i
*  172.19.2.0/24    10.3.1.2                            0 300 500 i
*>                  10.5.1.2                            0 400 500 i
*  172.19.3.0/24    10.3.1.2                            0 300 500 i
*>                  10.5.1.2                            0 400 500 i
*  172.19.4.0/24    10.3.1.2                            0 300 500 i
*>                  10.5.1.2                            0 400 500 i
*  172.26.1.0/24    10.3.1.2                            0 300 500 400 i
*>                  10.5.1.2              0             0 400 i
*  172.26.2.0/24    10.3.1.2                            0 300 500 400 i
*>                  10.5.1.2              0             0 400 i
*  172.26.3.0/24    10.3.1.2                            0 300 500 400 i
*>                  10.5.1.2              0             0 400 i
R5#sh ip route | beg Gateway
Gateway of last resort is not set

     172.17.0.0/24 is subnetted, 1 subnets
C       172.17.5.0 is directly connected, Loopback0
     172.19.0.0/24 is subnetted, 4 subnets
B       172.19.4.0 [20/0] via 10.5.1.2, 00:02:29
B       172.19.3.0 [20/0] via 10.5.1.2, 00:02:29
B       172.19.2.0 [20/0] via 10.5.1.2, 00:02:29
B       172.19.1.0 [20/0] via 10.5.1.2, 00:02:29
     172.18.0.0/24 is subnetted, 2 subnets
B       172.18.2.0 [20/0] via 10.3.1.2, 00:02:47
B       172.18.1.0 [20/0] via 10.3.1.2, 00:02:47
     172.26.0.0/24 is subnetted, 3 subnets
B       172.26.2.0 [20/0] via 10.5.1.2, 00:02:29
B       172.26.3.0 [20/0] via 10.5.1.2, 00:02:29
B       172.26.1.0 [20/0] via 10.5.1.2, 00:02:29
     10.0.0.0/24 is subnetted, 4 subnets
C       10.3.1.0 is directly connected, Serial0/3
C       10.2.3.0 is directly connected, Serial0/0
C       10.2.4.0 is directly connected, Serial0/1
C       10.5.1.0 is directly connected, Serial0/2
R5#
```

```
R6#sh ip bgp | beg Network
   Network          Next Hop         Metric LocPrf Weight Path
*  172.17.5.0/24    10.6.1.2                        0 500 300 200 i
*>                  10.5.1.1              0         0 200 i
*  172.18.1.0/24    10.6.1.2                        0 500 300 i
*>                  10.5.1.1                        0 200 300 i
*  172.18.2.0/24    10.6.1.2                        0 500 300 i
*>                  10.5.1.1                        0 200 300 i
*> 172.19.1.0/24    10.6.1.2              0         0 500 i
*> 172.19.2.0/24    10.6.1.2              0         0 500 i
*> 172.19.3.0/24    10.6.1.2              0         0 500 i
*> 172.19.4.0/24    10.6.1.2              0         0 500 i
*> 172.26.1.0/24    0.0.0.0               0     32768 i
*> 172.26.2.0/24    0.0.0.0               0     32768 i
*> 172.26.3.0/24    0.0.0.0               0     32768 i
R6#sh ip route | beg Gateway
Gateway of last resort is not set

     172.17.0.0/24 is subnetted, 1 subnets
B       172.17.5.0 [20/0] via 10.5.1.1, 00:03:16
     172.19.0.0/24 is subnetted, 4 subnets
B       172.19.4.0 [20/0] via 10.6.1.2, 00:03:16
B       172.19.3.0 [20/0] via 10.6.1.2, 00:03:16
B       172.19.2.0 [20/0] via 10.6.1.2, 00:03:16
B       172.19.1.0 [20/0] via 10.6.1.2, 00:03:16
     172.18.0.0/24 is subnetted, 2 subnets
B       172.18.2.0 [20/0] via 10.5.1.1, 00:03:16
B       172.18.1.0 [20/0] via 10.5.1.1, 00:03:16
     172.26.0.0/24 is subnetted, 3 subnets
C       172.26.2.0 is directly connected, Loopback1
C       172.26.3.0 is directly connected, Loopback2
C       172.26.1.0 is directly connected, Loopback0
     10.0.0.0/24 is subnetted, 3 subnets
C       10.7.1.0 is directly connected, Serial0/2
C       10.6.1.0 is directly connected, Serial0/1
C       10.5.1.0 is directly connected, Serial0/0
R6#

R10#sh ip bgp | beg Network
   Network          Next Hop         Metric LocPrf Weight Path
*  172.17.5.0/24    10.6.1.1                        0 400 200 i
*>                  10.4.1.1                        0 300 200 i
*  172.18.1.0/24    10.6.1.1                        0 400 200 300 i
*>                  10.4.1.1              0         0 300 i
*  172.18.2.0/24    10.6.1.1                        0 400 200 300 i
*>                  10.4.1.1              0         0 300 i
*> 172.19.1.0/24    0.0.0.0               0     32768 i
```

```
 *> 172.19.2.0/24      0.0.0.0            0            32768 i
 *> 172.19.3.0/24      0.0.0.0            0            32768 i
 *> 172.19.4.0/24      0.0.0.0            0            32768 i
 *> 172.26.1.0/24      10.6.1.1           0                0 400 i
 *> 172.26.2.0/24      10.6.1.1           0                0 400 i
 *> 172.26.3.0/24      10.6.1.1           0                0 400 i
R10#sh ip route | beg Gateway
Gateway of last resort is not set

     172.17.0.0/24 is subnetted, 1 subnets
B       172.17.5.0 [20/0] via 10.4.1.1, 00:03:52
     172.19.0.0/24 is subnetted, 4 subnets
C       172.19.4.0 is directly connected, Loopback3
C       172.19.3.0 is directly connected, Loopback2
C       172.19.2.0 is directly connected, Loopback1
C       172.19.1.0 is directly connected, Loopback0
     172.18.0.0/24 is subnetted, 2 subnets
B       172.18.2.0 [20/0] via 10.4.1.1, 00:03:52
B       172.18.1.0 [20/0] via 10.4.1.1, 00:03:52
     172.26.0.0/24 is subnetted, 3 subnets
B       172.26.2.0 [20/0] via 10.6.1.1, 00:03:52
B       172.26.3.0 [20/0] via 10.6.1.1, 00:03:52
B       172.26.1.0 [20/0] via 10.6.1.1, 00:03:52
     10.0.0.0/24 is subnetted, 2 subnets
C       10.6.1.0 is directly connected, Serial0/1
C       10.4.1.0 is directly connected, Serial0/0
R10#

R12#sh ip bgp | beg Network
   Network          Next Hop      Metric LocPrf Weight Path
 *> 172.17.5.0/24    10.3.1.1           0                0 200 i
 *> 172.18.1.0/24    0.0.0.0            0            32768 i
 *> 172.18.2.0/24    0.0.0.0            0            32768 i
 *  172.19.1.0/24    10.3.1.1                            0 200 400 500 i
 *>                  10.4.1.2           0                0 500 i
 *  172.19.2.0/24    10.3.1.1                            0 200 400 500 i
 *>                  10.4.1.2           0                0 500 i
 *  172.19.3.0/24    10.3.1.1                            0 200 400 500 i
 *>                  10.4.1.2           0                0 500 i
 *  172.19.4.0/24    10.3.1.1                            0 200 400 500 i
 *>                  10.4.1.2           0                0 500 i
 *  172.26.1.0/24    10.3.1.1                            0 200 400 i
 *>                  10.4.1.2                            0 500 400 i
 *  172.26.2.0/24    10.3.1.1                            0 200 400 i
 *>                  10.4.1.2                            0 500 400 i
 *  172.26.3.0/24    10.3.1.1                            0 200 400 i
 *>                  10.4.1.2                            0 500 400 i
```

```
R12#sh ip route | beg Gateway
Gateway of last resort is not set

     172.17.0.0/24 is subnetted, 1 subnets
B       172.17.5.0 [20/0] via 10.3.1.1, 00:04:43
     172.19.0.0/24 is subnetted, 4 subnets
B       172.19.4.0 [20/0] via 10.4.1.2, 00:04:24
B       172.19.3.0 [20/0] via 10.4.1.2, 00:04:24
B       172.19.2.0 [20/0] via 10.4.1.2, 00:04:24
B       172.19.1.0 [20/0] via 10.4.1.2, 00:04:24
     172.18.0.0/24 is subnetted, 2 subnets
C       172.18.2.0 is directly connected, Loopback1
C       172.18.1.0 is directly connected, Loopback0
     172.26.0.0/24 is subnetted, 3 subnets
B       172.26.2.0 [20/0] via 10.4.1.2, 00:04:24
B       172.26.3.0 [20/0] via 10.4.1.2, 00:04:24
B       172.26.1.0 [20/0] via 10.4.1.2, 00:04:24
     10.0.0.0/24 is subnetted, 2 subnets
C       10.3.1.0 is directly connected, Serial0/0
C       10.4.1.0 is directly connected, Serial0/1
R12#
```

We can start to see the build up of the route information that is held by our routers. We are not going to affect any of the decisions that BGP has made at this stage, instead we will just highlight them, as food for thought. To show a couple of examples, R5 has received two routes for the 172.19.1.0/24 network, one from R12, and one from R6. But it is the route from R6 that gets installed in the routing table. Similarly R6 has received two routes for the 172.18.1.0/24 network, one from R10, and the other from R5. It is the route from R5 that is installed into the routing table. We see the same again for R10 and R12, however R12 is the clearest example though of how BGP makes its decision process. Taking the 172.17.5.0/24 network as the example, we can go in two directions, either through AS 500, into AS 400, and then finally into AS 200, or directly to AS 200. Clearly the shortest route makes more sense. If we look at the same route on R10 we see that the 172.17.5.0/24 network has the same number of autonomous systems in its AS_PATH, but favors one over the other. We will find out why in chapter 11. For now let's try and connect up AS 100 to AS 300 and 400, through AS 200, which is our first example of iBGP peering.

5. iBGP Peering

Although BGP was designed to connect different Autonomous Systems (eBGP), it can also be used within an AS (iBGP). In this chapter, we will create iBGP peers for AS 200, looking at the rules that govern iBGPs, as well as ways around these, such as using an IGP within our BGP for connectivity and routing.

5.1 The rules of BGP

There are a few "golden" rules within BGP, and these very much influence how we will set up BGP. We haven't covered them yet, as our first peering, between R1 and R2 followed all the rules. When we start expanding our network out, we can see that rules are meant to be broken (or, at least, slightly mis-shaped to fit our purpose). When we start configuring AS 200 we encounter "The Rule of Synchronization" which to quote directly from Cisco:

If your AS passes traffic from another AS to a third AS, BGP should not advertise a route before all routers in your AS learn about the route via IGP. BGP waits until IGP propagates the route within the AS and then advertises it to external peers. A BGP router with synchronization enabled does not install iBGP learned routes into its routing table if it is not able to validate those routes in its IGP.[2]

So what does this actually mean? Well, it's probably best to re-word it referencing our topology:

If AS 200 passes traffic from AS 100 into AS 300 then BGP will not advertise a route before routers R2, R3, R4 and R5 have learned about the route via a routing protocol such as EIGRP, RIP, or OSPF. Only once all routers within the AS have this route will it be advertised to AS 300. But we can turn this off by disabling synchronization.

Now depending on what version of IOS you are running, synchronization may already be turned off, in fact this is the default behavior since 12.2(8)T. Nonetheless we need to understand it, as we will see that we are still affected by it.

We will configure our iBGP peers in AS 200 with some basics, and make sure that we can see the 10.1.0.0/24 network (being advertised by R1) throughout. Firstly we will try

---

[2]

http://www.cisco.com/en/US/tech/tk365/technologies_q_and_a_item09186a00800949e8.shtml#nineteen and prove or disprove the need for an IGP, and then, as we progress through the book, we will look at the other options available to us.

Because of the nature of iBGP peers within an AS, there is greater scope for configuring redundancy as you see fit. Because you are able (through an IGP or static routes) to advertise loopback addresses (which generally have private IP addresses and are therefore not routable on the internet), often you will see iBGP peers bound to a particular loopback interface, in order to form stable and resilient peer relationships, and it is loopback addresses that we will use within AS 200.

5.2 Basic iBGP Peers

We will be starting with the link between R2 and R3 in detail, and, because the other links within this AS are all very similar, the configuration of the other links will be only shown through an export of the standard "sh run" command.

Before we can set up the peer relationship, we need to ensure that we can reach all the loopback interfaces on the other routers in the AS, and to do that we are going to (for the moment) just use some simple static route commands:

R2:

```
R2#sh run | i route
router bgp 200
 bgp router-id 2.2.2.2
ip route 172.16.1.0 255.255.255.0 10.2.2.2
ip route 172.17.1.0 255.255.255.0 10.2.1.2
```

R3:

```
R3#sh run | i route
ip route 172.17.0.0 255.255.255.0 10.2.1.1
ip route 172.17.5.0 255.255.255.0 10.2.3.2
```

R4:

```
R4#sh run | i route
ip route 172.17.0.0 255.255.255.0 10.2.2.1
ip route 172.17.5.0 255.255.255.0 10.2.4.1
```

R5:

```
R5#sh run | i route
```

```
ip route 172.16.1.0 255.255.255.0 10.2.4.2
ip route 172.17.1.0 255.255.255.0 10.2.3.1
```

Now we are ready to configure AS 200. Creating an iBGP relationship really is no different to how we created our eBGP relationship. The AS stays the same; we still use the remote-as command, even though it is an internal relationship. Below are the initial commands to start configuring our R2 to R3 peer relationship:

```
R2#conf t
R2(config)#router bgp 200
R2(config-router)#neighbor 172.17.1.1 remote-as 200
R2(config-router)#exit
R2(config)#exit

R3#conf t
R3(config)#router bgp 200
R3(config-router)#bgp router-id 3.3.3.3
R3(config-router)#neighbor 172.17.0.1 remote-as 200
R3(config-router)#exit
R3(config)#exit
```

When a peer relationship is formed, we can confirm that our peer is up using the command "sh ip bgp neighbor" along with the remote peers address. For a healthy peer, as we have seen in section 4.3, we would expect the state to be "Established"

```
R2#sh ip bgp neigh 172.17.1.1
BGP neighbor is 172.17.1.1,  remote AS 200, internal link
  BGP version 4, remote router ID 0.0.0.0
  BGP state = Active

R3#sh ip bgp neigh 172.17.0.1
BGP neighbor is 172.17.0.1,  remote AS 200, internal link
  BGP version 4, remote router ID 0.0.0.0
  BGP state = Active
```

Here our state is "Active" meaning that our attempts to form a peer relationship between the two have been unsuccessful. So why is this? We can confirm that synchronization is turned off:

```
R3#sh run | section bgp
router bgp 200
 no synchronization
 bgp router-id 3.3.3.3
 bgp log-neighbor-changes
 neighbor 172.17.0.1 remote-as 200
 no auto-summary
```

R3#

So this is not the problem. So where, then, does the issue stem from? Let's have a look at the logs, using the command "clear ip bgp <ip address or remote peer>" to perform a complete reset of the BGP peer connection, and make sure that we can capture the logs that we need:

```
R3#debug ip bgp
BGP debugging is on for address family: IPv4 Unicast
R3#
BGP: 172.17.0.1 open active, local address 10.2.1.2
BGP: 172.17.0.1 open failed: Connection refused by remote host, open
active delayed 28930ms (35000ms max, 28% jitter)
R3#clear ip bgp *
R3#
BGPNSF state: 172.17.0.1 went from nsf_not_active to nsf_not_active
BGP: 172.17.0.1 went from Active to Idle
BGP: 172.17.0.1 went from Idle to Active
BGP: 172.17.0.1 open active delayed 27449ms (35000ms max, 28% jitter)
BGP: 172.17.0.1 open active, local address 10.2.1.2
BGP: 172.17.0.1 open failed: Connection refused by remote host, open
active delayed 26926ms (35000ms max, 28% jitter)
R3#
```

Looking at the configuration and debug log, we know that R3 should be trying to connect to 172.17.01. From the logs we can see that R3 is attempting to connect to the correct IP address, but that the remote host (R2) is refusing the connection. We know that we can reach the Loopback interface on R2:

```
R3#ping 172.17.0.1

Type escape sequence to abort.
Sending 5, 100-byte ICMP Echos to 172.17.0.1:
!!!!!
Success rate is 100 percent (5/5)
R3#traceroute 172.17.0.1

Type escape sequence to abort.
Tracing the route to 172.17.0.1

  1 10.2.1.1 20 msec 12 msec 24 msec
R3#
```

Returning to the debug log, we can see that the local address being used is 10.2.1.2, but both sides are connecting to each other's loopback0 interface IP address. We also know, from when we created our eBGP peer, that if a request to peer comes in from an IP address that is not specified within a neighbor statement, then the request will be dropped. So now we know the cause. What we need to do is make our router send the BGP connection requests, and all subsequent BGP traffic via its loopback interface, instead of the interface nearest the destination, which is the default. To do this we specify an update source:

```
R3(config)#router bgp 200
R3(config-router)#neighbor 172.17.0.1 update-source lo0

R2(config)#router bgp 200
R2(config-router)#neighbor 172.17.1.1 update-source lo0
R2(config-router)#exit
R2(config)#exit
R2#
%BGP-5-ADJCHANGE: neighbor 172.17.1.1 Up
R2#

R3#sh ip bgp neigh 172.17.0.1
BGP neighbor is 172.17.0.1,  remote AS 200, internal link
  BGP version 4, remote router ID 2.2.2.2
  BGP state = Established, up for 00:04:03
```

And with that one line command we have our first iBGP peer. The commands are no different to add the rest of the routers to this network. Once all the other neighbor and network statements have been entered, the BGP configurations for AS 200 look like this:

```
R2#sh run | section bgp
router bgp 200
 no synchronization
 bgp router-id 2.2.2.2
 bgp log-neighbor-changes
 network 172.17.0.0 mask 255.255.255.0
 neighbor 10.1.1.1 remote-as 100
 neighbor 172.16.1.1 remote-as 200
 neighbor 172.16.1.1 update-source Loopback0
 neighbor 172.17.1.1 remote-as 200
 neighbor 172.17.1.1 update-source Loopback0
 no auto-summary
R2#

R3#sh run | section bgp
router bgp 200
 no synchronization
 bgp router-id 3.3.3.3
 bgp log-neighbor-changes
```

```
  network 172.17.1.0 mask 255.255.255.0
  network 172.17.2.0 mask 255.255.255.0
  neighbor 172.17.0.1 remote-as 200
  neighbor 172.17.0.1 update-source Loopback0
  neighbor 172.17.5.1 remote-as 200
  neighbor 172.17.5.1 update-source Loopback0
  no auto-summary
R3#

R4#sh run | section bgp
router bgp 200
 no synchronization
 bgp log-neighbor-changes
 network 172.16.1.0 mask 255.255.255.0
 network 172.16.2.0 mask 255.255.255.0
 neighbor 172.17.0.1 remote-as 200
 neighbor 172.17.0.1 update-source Loopback0
 neighbor 172.17.5.1 remote-as 200
 neighbor 172.17.5.1 update-source Loopback0
 no auto-summary
R4#

R5#sh run | section bgp
router bgp 200
 no synchronization
 bgp router-id 5.5.5.5
 bgp log-neighbor-changes
 network 172.17.5.0 mask 255.255.255.0
 neighbor 10.3.1.2 remote-as 300
 neighbor 10.5.1.2 remote-as 400
 neighbor 172.16.1.1 remote-as 200
 neighbor 172.16.1.1 update-source Loopback0
 neighbor 172.17.1.1 remote-as 200
 neighbor 172.17.1.1 update-source Loopback0
 no auto-summary
R5#
```

With the basics plumbed in, we can start to see the beginnings of a pretty well connected topology.

```
R2#sh ip bgp neighbors | i ID | Established
  BGP version 4, remote router ID 1.1.1.1
  BGP state = Established, up for 00:25:55
  BGP version 4, remote router ID 4.4.4.4
  BGP state = Established, up for 00:00:32
  BGP version 4, remote router ID 3.3.3.3
  BGP state = Established, up for 00:10:25
```

R2#

```
R5#sh ip bgp neighbors | i ID | Established
  BGP version 4, remote router ID 12.12.12.12
  BGP state = Established, up for 00:26:32
  BGP version 4, remote router ID 6.6.6.6
  BGP state = Established, up for 00:26:36
  BGP version 4, remote router ID 4.4.4.4
  BGP state = Established, up for 00:00:50
  BGP version 4, remote router ID 3.3.3.3
  BGP state = Established, up for 00:03:08
R5#
```

We have some basic communication within our iBGP network at the moment, but it is not without its issues. Let's take a look at R3 for example:

```
R3#sh ip bgp
BGP table version is 7, local router ID is 3.3.3.3
Status codes: s suppressed, d damped, h history, * valid, > best, i -
internal,
              r RIB-failure, S Stale
Origin codes: i - IGP, e - EGP, ? - incomplete

   Network          Next Hop         Metric LocPrf Weight Path
*  i10.1.0.0/24     10.1.1.1              0    100      0 100 i
r>i172.17.0.0/24    172.17.0.1            0    100      0 i
*>  172.17.1.0/24   0.0.0.0               0         32768 i
*>  172.17.2.0/24   0.0.0.0               0         32768 i
r>i172.17.5.0/24    172.17.5.1            0    100      0 i
*  i172.18.1.0/24   10.3.1.2              0    100      0 300 i
*  i172.18.2.0/24   10.3.1.2              0    100      0 300 i
*  i172.19.1.0/24   10.5.1.2              0    100      0 400 500 i
*  i172.19.2.0/24   10.5.1.2              0    100      0 400 500 i
*  i172.19.3.0/24   10.5.1.2              0    100      0 400 500 i
*  i172.19.4.0/24   10.5.1.2              0    100      0 400 500 i
*  i172.26.1.0/24   10.5.1.2              0    100      0 400 i
*  i172.26.2.0/24   10.5.1.2              0    100      0 400 i
*  i172.26.3.0/24   10.5.1.2              0    100      0 400 i
R3#
```

We can see that it is aware of all the networks that its directly connected peers (R1 and R5) are also aware of, such as the 172.18, 19, and 26 networks, as well as the 10.1.0.0/24 network that is attached to R1. The routes are marked as "valid" as denoted by a *, but not as "best" (denoted by a ">"). When we look at the routing table we can see that they have not been added:

```
R3#sh ip route | beg Gateway
Gateway of last resort is not set

     172.17.0.0/24 is subnetted, 4 subnets
S       172.17.5.0 [1/0] via 10.2.3.2
C       172.17.1.0 is directly connected, Loopback0
S       172.17.0.0 [1/0] via 10.2.1.1
C       172.17.2.0 is directly connected, Loopback1
     10.0.0.0/24 is subnetted, 2 subnets
C       10.2.1.0 is directly connected, Serial0/0
C       10.2.3.0 is directly connected, Serial0/1
R3#
```

We are also missing quite a few routes, such as the loopback interfaces on R4. So how do we get the full and proper routing table that we need? We can start by looking at what R3 is being passed from R2 and R5:

```
R2#sh ip bgp neigh 172.17.1.1 advertised-routes
BGP table version is 9, local router ID is 2.2.2.2
Status codes: s suppressed, d damped, h history, * valid, > best, i -
internal,
              r RIB-failure, S Stale
Origin codes: i - IGP, e - EGP, ? - incomplete

   Network          Next Hop        Metric LocPrf Weight Path
*> 10.1.0.0/24      10.1.1.1             0             0 100 i
*> 172.17.0.0/24    0.0.0.0              0         32768 i

Total number of prefixes 2
R2#

R5#sh ip bgp neigh 172.17.1.1 advertised-routes
BGP table version is 17, local router ID is 5.5.5.5
Status codes: s suppressed, d damped, h history, * valid, > best, i -
internal,
              r RIB-failure, S Stale
Origin codes: i - IGP, e - EGP, ? - incomplete

   Network          Next Hop        Metric LocPrf Weight Path
*> 172.17.5.0/24    0.0.0.0              0         32768 i
*> 172.18.1.0/24    10.3.1.2             0             0 300 i
*> 172.18.2.0/24    10.3.1.2             0             0 300 i
*> 172.19.1.0/24    10.5.1.2                           0 400 500 i
*> 172.19.2.0/24    10.5.1.2                           0 400 500 i
*> 172.19.3.0/24    10.5.1.2                           0 400 500 i
*> 172.19.4.0/24    10.5.1.2                           0 400 500 i
*> 172.26.1.0/24    10.5.1.2             0             0 400 i
```

```
*> 172.26.2.0/24      10.5.1.2               0              0 400 i
*> 172.26.3.0/24      10.5.1.2               0              0 400 i

Total number of prefixes 10
R5#
```

There is nothing wrong with what we see being advertised to R3 by its peers. We can, however, see that the routes passed to R3 are installed into its BGP table unchanged, which is that the next-hop is a router to which it has no connection. The route is deemed valid, even though R3 has no route to 10.3.1.2 or 10.5.1.2. This is again one of the rules of iBGP peers; the next-hop address does not get changed as the route is passed to neighbors. We can fix this by instructing our BGP speakers to modify the next hop IP address:

```
R2#conf t
R2(config)#router bgp 200
R2(config-router)#neigh 172.17.1.1 next-hop-self
R2(config-router)#neigh 172.16.1.1 next-hop-self

R3#conf t
R3(config)#router bgp 200
R3(config-router)#neigh 172.17.0.1 next-hop-self
R3(config-router)#neigh 172.17.5.1 next-hop-self

R4#conf t
R4(config)#router bgp 200
R4(config-router)#neigh 172.17.0.1 next-hop-self
R4(config-router)#neigh 172.17.5.1 next-hop-self

R5#conf t
R5(config)#router bgp 200
R5(config-router)#neigh 172.17.1.1 next-hop-self
R5(config-router)#neigh 172.16.1.1 next-hop-self
R5(config-router)#
```

Now, if we check R3's BGP table, we can see that it is looking much healthier:

```
R3#sh ip bgp | beg Network
   Network           Next Hop        Metric LocPrf Weight Path
*>i10.1.0.0/24       172.17.0.1            0    100      0 100 i
r>i172.17.0.0/24     172.17.0.1            0    100      0 i
*>  172.17.1.0/24    0.0.0.0               0             32768 i
*>  172.17.2.0/24    0.0.0.0               0             32768 i
r>i172.17.5.0/24     172.17.5.1            0    100      0 i
*>i172.18.1.0/24     172.17.5.1            0    100      0 300 i
*>i172.18.2.0/24     172.17.5.1            0    100      0 300 i
```

```
*>i172.19.1.0/24      172.17.5.1              0       100        0 400 500 i
*>i172.19.2.0/24      172.17.5.1              0       100        0 400 500 i
*>i172.19.3.0/24      172.17.5.1              0       100        0 400 500 i
*>i172.19.4.0/24      172.17.5.1              0       100        0 400 500 i
*>i172.26.1.0/24      172.17.5.1              0       100        0 400 i
*>i172.26.2.0/24      172.17.5.1              0       100        0 400 i
*>i172.26.3.0/24      172.17.5.1              0       100        0 400 i
R3#
```

The routes that were considered valid, but not "best", are now considered both valid and best, as well as showing as being generated internally (within the same AS). Consequently the routing table also looks full and healthy:

```
R3#sh ip route | beg Gateway
Gateway of last resort is not set

        172.17.0.0/24 is subnetted, 4 subnets
S          172.17.5.0 [1/0] via 10.2.3.2
C          172.17.1.0 is directly connected, Loopback0
S          172.17.0.0 [1/0] via 10.2.1.1
C          172.17.2.0 is directly connected, Loopback1
        172.19.0.0/24 is subnetted, 4 subnets
B          172.19.4.0 [200/0] via 172.17.5.1, 00:02:32
B          172.19.3.0 [200/0] via 172.17.5.1, 00:02:32
B          172.19.2.0 [200/0] via 172.17.5.1, 00:02:32
B          172.19.1.0 [200/0] via 172.17.5.1, 00:02:32
        172.18.0.0/24 is subnetted, 2 subnets
B          172.18.2.0 [200/0] via 172.17.5.1, 00:02:32
B          172.18.1.0 [200/0] via 172.17.5.1, 00:02:32
        172.26.0.0/24 is subnetted, 3 subnets
B          172.26.2.0 [200/0] via 172.17.5.1, 00:02:32
B          172.26.3.0 [200/0] via 172.17.5.1, 00:02:32
B          172.26.1.0 [200/0] via 172.17.5.1, 00:02:32
        10.0.0.0/24 is subnetted, 3 subnets
C          10.2.1.0 is directly connected, Serial0/0
C          10.2.3.0 is directly connected, Serial0/1
B          10.1.0.0 [200/0] via 172.17.0.1, 00:03:39
R3#
```

However, R3 is still unaware of R4, and similarly R2 is unaware of anything beyond R3 or R4.

So, how do we get the two sides talking? The obvious way would be to connect, through serial or Ethernet means, R3 and R4, and R2 and R5, directly together, but for the purposes of this we will assume that this option is not available.

We have a number of other options available. As mentioned earlier, one of the differences between iBGP and eBGP is the TTL (the number of hops a packet can take before it dies), with iBGP we have a TTL of 255 so we are not hampered there, but they need to be able to see the routes in order to establish a peer relationship.

First of all let's try advertising the physical networks:

```
R3(config)#router bgp 200
R3(config-router)#network 10.2.1.0 mask 255.255.255.0
R3(config-router)#network 10.2.3.0 mask 255.255.255.0

R4(config)#router bgp 200
R4(config-router)#network 10.2.2.0 mask 255.255.255.0
R4(config-router)#network 10.2.4.0 mask 255.255.255.0
```

Now can R3 and R2 see the loopback IP addresses of R4 and R5 respectively?

```
R2#sh ip bgp | beg Network
   Network          Next Hop         Metric LocPrf Weight Path
*> 10.1.0.0/24      10.1.1.1              0            0 100 i
r>i10.2.1.0/24      172.17.1.1            0    100     0 i
r>i10.2.2.0/24      172.16.1.1            0    100     0 i
*>i10.2.3.0/24      172.17.1.1            0    100     0 i
*>i10.2.4.0/24      172.16.1.1            0    100     0 i
r>i172.16.1.0/24    172.16.1.1            0    100     0 i
*>i172.16.2.0/24    172.16.1.1            0    100     0 i
*> 172.17.0.0/24    0.0.0.0               0         32768 i
r>i172.17.1.0/24    172.17.1.1            0    100     0 i
*>i172.17.2.0/24    172.17.1.1            0    100     0 i
R2#

R3#sh ip bgp | beg Network
   Network          Next Hop         Metric LocPrf Weight Path
*>i10.1.0.0/24      172.17.0.1            0    100     0 100 i
*> 10.2.1.0/24      0.0.0.0               0         32768 i
*> 10.2.3.0/24      0.0.0.0               0         32768 i
r>i172.17.0.0/24    172.17.0.1            0    100     0 i
*> 172.17.1.0/24    0.0.0.0               0         32768 i
*> 172.17.2.0/24    0.0.0.0               0         32768 i
r>i172.17.5.0/24    172.17.5.1            0    100     0 i
*>i172.18.1.0/24    172.17.5.1            0    100     0 300 i
*>i172.18.2.0/24    172.17.5.1            0    100     0 300 i
*>i172.19.1.0/24    172.17.5.1            0    100     0 400 500 i
*>i172.19.2.0/24    172.17.5.1            0    100     0 400 500 i
*>i172.19.3.0/24    172.17.5.1            0    100     0 400 500 i
*>i172.19.4.0/24    172.17.5.1            0    100     0 400 500 i
```

```
*>i172.26.1.0/24      172.17.5.1              0       100       0 400 i
*>i172.26.2.0/24      172.17.5.1              0       100       0 400 i
*>i172.26.3.0/24      172.17.5.1              0       100       0 400 i
R3#
```

No, they can't. Concentrating still on R3, we have found that advertising any routes we can think of doesn't always achieve what we require, so let's see what R2 and R5 are actually sending it:

```
R2#sh ip bgp neigh 172.17.1.1 advertised-routes
BGP table version is 15, local router ID is 2.2.2.2
Status codes: s suppressed, d damped, h history, * valid, > best, i -
internal,
              r RIB-failure, S Stale
Origin codes: i - IGP, e - EGP, ? - incomplete

   Network          Next Hop            Metric LocPrf Weight Path
*> 10.1.0.0/24      10.1.1.1                 0             0 100 i
*> 172.17.0.0/24    0.0.0.0                  0         32768 i

Total number of prefixes 2
R2#

R5#sh ip bgp neigh 172.17.1.1 advertised-routes
BGP table version is 23, local router ID is 5.5.5.5
Status codes: s suppressed, d damped, h history, * valid, > best, i -
internal,
              r RIB-failure, S Stale
Origin codes: i - IGP, e - EGP, ? - incomplete

   Network          Next Hop            Metric LocPrf Weight Path
*> 172.17.5.0/24    0.0.0.0                  0         32768 i
*> 172.18.1.0/24    10.3.1.2                 0             0 300 i
*> 172.18.2.0/24    10.3.1.2                 0             0 300 i
*> 172.19.1.0/24    10.5.1.2                               0 400 500 i
*> 172.19.2.0/24    10.5.1.2                               0 400 500 i
*> 172.19.3.0/24    10.5.1.2                               0 400 500 i
*> 172.19.4.0/24    10.5.1.2                               0 400 500 i
*> 172.26.1.0/24    10.5.1.2                 0             0 400 i
*> 172.26.2.0/24    10.5.1.2                 0             0 400 i
*> 172.26.3.0/24    10.5.1.2                 0             0 400 i

Total number of prefixes 10
R5#
```

We can see that although both R2 and R5 have the 172.16.1.0/24 and 172.16.2.0/24 networks in their routing tables, they are not even attempting to pass these to R3.

Herein lies the issue, to avoid routing loops inside an AS, BGP will not advertise to another peer routes learned from another peer within the same AS. Therefore, we either need a full BGP mesh, set up an IGP such as RIP, OSPF, or EIGRP, or use other means such as confederations or route-reflectors, both of which we will cover in a later chapter. For the moment though we will set up an IGP.

5.3 IGPs and BGP

We can set up any IGP in order to get our routes advertised, each works, certainly for our purposes, as well as another. For this section I have chosen EIGRP, not for any particular reason, but most network people have a favorite IGP, often for reasons they can't justify. It's important to briefly note that if you are using OSPF, then your OSPF router ID <u>must</u> match your bgp router ID.

I won't go into EIGRP in too much detail here, this will be saved for a later volume, but setting up and EIGRP process is fairly straight forward. You start in configuration mode with the command "router eigrp" followed by the eigrp autonomous system number. Then you add your networks, and you end up with something like this:

```
R2#sh run | section eigrp
router eigrp 100
 network 10.2.1.0 0.0.0.255
 network 10.2.2.0 0.0.0.255
 network 172.17.0.0 0.0.0.255
 no auto-summary
R2#

R3#sh run | section eigrp
router eigrp 100
 network 10.2.1.0 0.0.0.255
 network 10.2.3.0 0.0.0.255
 network 172.17.1.0 0.0.0.255
 network 172.17.2.0 0.0.0.255
 no auto-summary
R3#

R4#sh run | section eigrp
router eigrp 100
 network 10.2.2.0 0.0.0.255
 network 10.2.4.0 0.0.0.255
 network 172.16.1.0 0.0.0.255
```

```
    network 172.16.2.0 0.0.0.255
    no auto-summary
R4#

R5#sh run | section eigrp
router eigrp 100
    network 10.2.3.0 0.0.0.255
    network 10.2.4.0 0.0.0.255
    network 172.17.5.0 0.0.0.255
    no auto-summary
R5#
```

And, just for fun, let's remove our static routes; after all, static routes are *verboten* in the CCIE exam, so why use them here, unless we explicitly need to?

```
R2#conf t
R2(config)#no ip route 172.16.1.0 255.255.255.0 10.2.2.2
R2(config)#no ip route 172.17.1.0 255.255.255.0 10.2.1.2
R2(config)#

R3#conf t
R3(config)#no ip route 172.17.5.0 255.255.255.0 10.2.3.2
R3(config)#no ip route 172.17.0.0 255.255.255.0 10.2.1.1
R3(config)#

R4#conf t
R4(config)#no ip route 172.17.0.0 255.255.255.0 10.2.2.1
R4(config)#no ip route 172.17.5.0 255.255.255.0 10.2.4.1
R4(config)#

R5#conf t
R5(config)#no ip route 172.16.1.0 255.255.255.0 10.2.4.2
R5(config)#no ip route 172.17.1.0 255.255.255.0 10.2.3.1
R5(config)#
```

So how do the routing tables on R2 and R3 look now? More specifically, do we have reachability?

```
R2#sh ip route | beg Gateway
Gateway of last resort is not set

     172.17.0.0/24 is subnetted, 4 subnets
D       172.17.5.0 [90/2809856] via 10.2.2.2, 00:03:34, Serial0/2
                   [90/2809856] via 10.2.1.2, 00:03:34, Serial0/1
D       172.17.1.0 [90/2297856] via 10.2.1.2, 00:05:06, Serial0/1
C       172.17.0.0 is directly connected, Loopback0
```

```
D          172.17.2.0 [90/2297856] via 10.2.1.2, 00:16:54, Serial0/1
     172.16.0.0/24 is subnetted, 2 subnets
D          172.16.1.0 [90/2297856] via 10.2.2.2, 00:05:15, Serial0/2
D          172.16.2.0 [90/2297856] via 10.2.2.2, 00:15:43, Serial0/2
     10.0.0.0/24 is subnetted, 6 subnets
C          10.2.1.0 is directly connected, Serial0/1
C          10.2.2.0 is directly connected, Serial0/2
C          10.1.1.0 is directly connected, Serial0/0
D          10.2.3.0 [90/2681856] via 10.2.1.2, 00:14:48, Serial0/1
B          10.1.0.0 [20/0] via 10.1.1.1, 00:57:05
D          10.2.4.0 [90/2681856] via 10.2.2.2, 00:14:50, Serial0/2
R2#ping 172.17.5.1

Type escape sequence to abort.
Sending 5, 100-byte ICMP Echos to 172.17.5.1:
!!!!!
Success rate is 100 percent (5/5)
R2#

R3#sh ip route | beg Gateway
Gateway of last resort is not set

     172.17.0.0/24 is subnetted, 4 subnets
D          172.17.5.0 [90/2297856] via 10.2.3.2, 00:01:57, Serial0/1
C          172.17.1.0 is directly connected, Loopback0
D          172.17.0.0 [90/2297856] via 10.2.1.1, 00:01:51, Serial0/0
C          172.17.2.0 is directly connected, Loopback1
     172.16.0.0/24 is subnetted, 2 subnets
D          172.16.1.0 [90/2809856] via 10.2.3.2, 00:01:27, Serial0/1
                     [90/2809856] via 10.2.1.1, 00:01:27, Serial0/0
D          172.16.2.0 [90/2809856] via 10.2.3.2, 00:02:37, Serial0/1
                     [90/2809856] via 10.2.1.1, 00:02:37, Serial0/0
     172.19.0.0/24 is subnetted, 4 subnets
B          172.19.4.0 [200/0] via 172.17.5.1, 00:33:59
B          172.19.3.0 [200/0] via 172.17.5.1, 00:33:59
B          172.19.2.0 [200/0] via 172.17.5.1, 00:33:59
B          172.19.1.0 [200/0] via 172.17.5.1, 00:33:59
     172.18.0.0/24 is subnetted, 2 subnets
B          172.18.2.0 [200/0] via 172.17.5.1, 00:33:59
B          172.18.1.0 [200/0] via 172.17.5.1, 00:34:01
     172.26.0.0/24 is subnetted, 3 subnets
B          172.26.2.0 [200/0] via 172.17.5.1, 00:34:01
B          172.26.3.0 [200/0] via 172.17.5.1, 00:34:01
B          172.26.1.0 [200/0] via 172.17.5.1, 00:34:03
     10.0.0.0/24 is subnetted, 5 subnets
C          10.2.1.0 is directly connected, Serial0/0
D          10.2.2.0 [90/2681856] via 10.2.1.1, 00:02:41, Serial0/0
```

```
C          10.2.3.0 is directly connected, Serial0/1
B          10.1.0.0 [200/0] via 172.17.0.1, 00:35:07
D          10.2.4.0 [90/2681856] via 10.2.3.2, 00:02:41, Serial0/1
R3#ping 172.16.1.1

Type escape sequence to abort.
Sending 5, 100-byte ICMP Echos to 172.16.1.1:
!!!!!
Success rate is 100 percent (5/5)
R3#
```

We can see that by running an IGP within our BGP AS, the routes are passed into the routing tables (through the IGP though, not through BGP). Now, what will happen if we peer R2 and R5 together and R3 and R4 together?

```
R2(config)#router bgp 200
R2(config-router)#neigh 172.17.5.1 remote-as 200
R2(config-router)#neigh 172.17.5.1 update-source lo0
R2(config-router)#neigh 172.17.5.1 next-hop-self


R5(config)#router bgp 200
R5(config-router)#neigh 172.17.0.1 remote-as 200
R5(config-router)#neigh 172.17.0.1 update-source lo0
%BGP-5-ADJCHANGE: neighbor 172.17.0.1 Up
R5(config-router)#neigh 172.17.0.1 next-hop-self
```

R2 and R5 both have knowledge of networks outside of their own AS, which are advertised by the other peer:

```
R2#sh ip bgp | beg Network
   Network          Next Hop        Metric LocPrf Weight Path
*> 10.1.0.0/24      10.1.1.1             0             0 100 i
r>i10.2.1.0/24      172.17.1.1           0    100      0 i
r>i10.2.2.0/24      172.16.1.1           0    100      0 i
r>i10.2.3.0/24      172.17.1.1           0    100      0 i
r>i10.2.4.0/24      172.16.1.1           0    100      0 i
r>i172.16.1.0/24    172.16.1.1           0    100      0 i
r>i172.16.2.0/24    172.16.1.1           0    100      0 i
*> 172.17.0.0/24    0.0.0.0              0         32768 i
r>i172.17.1.0/24    172.17.1.1           0    100      0 i
r>i172.17.2.0/24    172.17.1.1           0    100      0 i
r>i172.17.5.0/24    172.17.5.1           0    100      0 i
*>i172.18.1.0/24    172.17.5.1           0    100      0 300 i
*>i172.18.2.0/24    172.17.5.1           0    100      0 300 i
*>i172.19.1.0/24    172.17.5.1           0    100      0 400 500 i
*>i172.19.2.0/24    172.17.5.1           0    100      0 400 500 i
```

```
*>i172.19.3.0/24      172.17.5.1         0    100      0 400 500 i
*>i172.19.4.0/24      172.17.5.1         0    100      0 400 500 i
*>i172.26.1.0/24      172.17.5.1         0    100      0 400 i
*>i172.26.2.0/24      172.17.5.1         0    100      0 400 i
*>i172.26.3.0/24      172.17.5.1         0    100      0 400 i
R2#

R5#sh ip bgp | beg Network
   Network            Next Hop       Metric LocPrf Weight Path
*>i10.1.0.0/24        172.17.0.1         0    100      0 100 i
r>i10.2.1.0/24        172.17.1.1         0    100      0 i
r>i10.2.2.0/24        172.16.1.1         0    100      0 i
r>i10.2.3.0/24        172.17.1.1         0    100      0 i
r>i10.2.4.0/24        172.16.1.1         0    100      0 i
r>i172.16.1.0/24      172.16.1.1         0    100      0 i
r>i172.16.2.0/24      172.16.1.1         0    100      0 i
r>i172.17.0.0/24      172.17.0.1         0    100      0 i
r>i172.17.1.0/24      172.17.1.1         0    100      0 i
r>i172.17.2.0/24      172.17.1.1         0    100      0 i
*>  172.17.5.0/24     0.0.0.0            0         32768 i
*>  172.18.1.0/24     10.3.1.2           0             0 300 i
*>  172.18.2.0/24     10.3.1.2           0             0 300 i
*   172.19.1.0/24     10.3.1.2                         0 300 500 i
*>                    10.5.1.2                         0 400 500 i
*   172.19.2.0/24     10.3.1.2                         0 300 500 i
*>                    10.5.1.2                         0 400 500 i
*   172.19.3.0/24     10.3.1.2                         0 300 500 i
*>                    10.5.1.2                         0 400 500 i
*   172.19.4.0/24     10.3.1.2                         0 300 500 i
*>                    10.5.1.2                         0 400 500 i
*   172.26.1.0/24     10.3.1.2                         0 300 500 400 i
*>                    10.5.1.2           0             0 400 i
*   172.26.2.0/24     10.3.1.2                         0 300 500 400 i
*>                    10.5.1.2           0             0 400 i
*   172.26.3.0/24     10.3.1.2                         0 300 500 400 i
*>                    10.5.1.2           0             0 400 i
R5#
```

Let's do the same with R3 and R4:

```
R3(config)#router bgp 200
R3(config-router)#neigh 172.16.1.1 remote-as 200
R3(config-router)#neigh 172.16.1.1 update-source lo0
R3(config-router)#neigh 172.16.1.1 next-hop-self

R4(config)#router bgp 200
R4(config-router)#neigh 172.17.1.1 remote-as 200
```

```
R4(config-router)#neigh 172.17.1.1 update-source lo0
R4(config-router)#neigh 172.17.1.1 next-hop-self
```

Now our iBGP AS has a complete mesh, courtesy of an IGP, and because of this R1's BGP table is also looking full and healthy:

```
R1#sh ip bgp | beg Network
   Network              Next Hop         Metric LocPrf Weight Path
*> 10.1.0.0/24          0.0.0.0               0         32768 i
*> 10.2.1.0/24          10.1.1.2                            0 200 i
*> 10.2.2.0/24          10.1.1.2                            0 200 i
*> 10.2.3.0/24          10.1.1.2                            0 200 i
*> 10.2.4.0/24          10.1.1.2                            0 200 i
*> 172.16.1.0/24        10.1.1.2                            0 200 i
*> 172.16.2.0/24        10.1.1.2                            0 200 i
*> 172.17.0.0/24        10.1.1.2              0             0 200 i
*> 172.17.1.0/24        10.1.1.2                            0 200 i
*> 172.17.2.0/24        10.1.1.2                            0 200 i
*> 172.17.5.0/24        10.1.1.2                            0 200 i
*> 172.18.1.0/24        10.1.1.2                            0 200 300 i
*> 172.18.2.0/24        10.1.1.2                            0 200 300 i
*> 172.19.1.0/24        10.1.1.2                            0 200 400 500 i
*> 172.19.2.0/24        10.1.1.2                            0 200 400 500 i
*> 172.19.3.0/24        10.1.1.2                            0 200 400 500 i
*> 172.19.4.0/24        10.1.1.2                            0 200 400 500 i
*> 172.26.1.0/24        10.1.1.2                            0 200 400 i
*> 172.26.2.0/24        10.1.1.2                            0 200 400 i
*> 172.26.3.0/24        10.1.1.2                            0 200 400 i
R1#
```

There is one issue though, which is with the last few networks. Everything looks fine, but if we try to ping the loopback interfaces on R10 and R12 we can see that it fails:

```
R1#ping 172.19.1.1

Type escape sequence to abort.
Sending 5, 100-byte ICMP Echos to 172.19.1.1:
.....
Success rate is 0 percent (0/5)
```

If however we change our source, it works fine:

```
R1#ping 172.19.1.1 source loopback0

Type escape sequence to abort.
Sending 5, 100-byte ICMP Echos to 172.19.1.1:
```

```
Packet sent with a source address of 10.1.0.1
!!!!!
Success rate is 100 percent (5/5)
R1#
```

The reason for this should hopefully be fairly obvious once we look at the routing table of R10:

```
R10#sh ip bgp | beg Network
   Network          Next Hop        Metric LocPrf Weight Path
*  10.1.0.0/24      10.4.1.1                          0 300 200 100 i
*>                  10.6.1.1                          0 400 200 100 i
*  10.2.1.0/24      10.6.1.1                          0 400 200 i
*>                  10.4.1.1                          0 300 200 i
*  10.2.2.0/24      10.4.1.1                          0 300 200 i
*>                  10.6.1.1                          0 400 200 i
```

I have truncated the output a bit here, but we have captured the relevant section. Without specifying a source for the ping, it will come, by default, from the closest interface to the destination (10.1.1.1). R10 has no concept of the 10.1.1.0/24 network, because it is not being advertised by either R1 or R2.

We can easily fix this using the network command:

```
R1#conf t
R1(config)#router bgp 100
R1(config-router)#network 10.1.1.0 mask 255.255.255.0
```

If we check R10, we can see that route in its BGP and routing tables:

```
R10#sh ip bgp | beg Network
   Network          Next Hop        Metric LocPrf Weight Path
*  10.1.0.0/24      10.4.1.1                          0 300 200 100 i
*>                  10.6.1.1                          0 400 200 100 i
*  10.1.1.0/24      10.6.1.1                          0 400 200 100 i
*>                  10.4.1.1                          0 300 200 100 i
*  10.2.1.0/24      10.6.1.1                          0 400 200 i
*>                  10.4.1.1                          0 300 200 i
*  10.2.2.0/24      10.4.1.1                          0 300 200 i
*>                  10.6.1.1                          0 400 200 i
```

So far so good...

```
R10#sh ip route | beg Gateway
Gateway of last resort is not set
```

```
         172.17.0.0/24 is subnetted, 4 subnets
B           172.17.5.0 [20/0] via 10.4.1.1, 01:36:28
B           172.17.1.0 [20/0] via 10.4.1.1, 01:06:32
B           172.17.0.0 [20/0] via 10.6.1.1, 00:15:05
B           172.17.2.0 [20/0] via 10.4.1.1, 01:06:01
         172.16.0.0/24 is subnetted, 2 subnets
B           172.16.1.0 [20/0] via 10.4.1.1, 01:05:31
B           172.16.2.0 [20/0] via 10.4.1.1, 01:05:31
         172.19.0.0/24 is subnetted, 4 subnets
C           172.19.4.0 is directly connected, Loopback3
C           172.19.3.0 is directly connected, Loopback2
C           172.19.2.0 is directly connected, Loopback1
C           172.19.1.0 is directly connected, Loopback0
         172.18.0.0/24 is subnetted, 2 subnets
B           172.18.2.0 [20/0] via 10.4.1.1, 01:36:28
B           172.18.1.0 [20/0] via 10.4.1.1, 01:36:28
         172.26.0.0/24 is subnetted, 3 subnets
B           172.26.2.0 [20/0] via 10.6.1.1, 01:36:28
B           172.26.3.0 [20/0] via 10.6.1.1, 01:36:28
B           172.26.1.0 [20/0] via 10.6.1.1, 01:36:28
         10.0.0.0/24 is subnetted, 8 subnets
B           10.2.1.0 [20/0] via 10.4.1.1, 00:43:21
B           10.2.2.0 [20/0] via 10.6.1.1, 00:42:50
B           10.1.1.0 [20/0] via 10.4.1.1, 00:02:41
B           10.2.3.0 [20/0] via 10.6.1.1, 00:42:50
B           10.1.0.0 [20/0] via 10.6.1.1, 00:15:07
B           10.2.4.0 [20/0] via 10.6.1.1, 00:42:50
C           10.6.1.0 is directly connected, Serial0/1
C           10.4.1.0 is directly connected, Serial0/0
R10#
```

Now can we ping from R1 to R10, without needing to specify the source:

```
R1#ping 172.19.1.1

Type escape sequence to abort.
Sending 5, 100-byte ICMP Echos to 172.19.1.1:
!!!!!
Success rate is 100 percent (5/5)
R1#
```

We need to make similar changes to R6 and R12, as pings from them to R1, without specifying the source of loopback 0, will also fail - as shown below:

```
R6#ping 10.1.0.1
```

```
Type escape sequence to abort.
Sending 5, 100-byte ICMP Echos to 10.1.0.1:
.....
Success rate is 0 percent (0/5)
R6#ping 10.1.0.1 so lo0

Type escape sequence to abort.
Sending 5, 100-byte ICMP Echos to 10.1.0.1:
Packet sent with a source address of 172.26.1.1
!!!!!
Success rate is 100 percent (5/5)
```

So let's fix that quickly:

```
R6#conf t
R6(config)#router bgp 400
R6(config-router)#network 10.6.1.0 mask 255.255.255.0
R6(config-router)#network 10.5.1.0 mask 255.255.255.0

R12#conf t
R12(config)#router bgp 300
R12(config-router)#network 10.3.1.0 mask 255.255.255.0
R12(config-router)#network 10.4.1.0 mask 255.255.255.0
```

And now our pings from these routers do not need to specify a source interface:

```
R6#ping 10.1.0.1

Type escape sequence to abort.
Sending 5, 100-byte ICMP Echos to 10.1.0.1:
!!!!!
Success rate is 100 percent (5/5)
R6#
```

Hopefully, this has helped indicate what we can check, to make sure that we have both visibility <u>and</u> reachability.

The use of an IGP, such as EIGRP, makes sense from a configurational standpoint, as most companies will run an IGP within their network and use BGP only on the connections to the Internet. That is not to say, however, that we cannot use BGP alone within our network. As previously stated we could have used confederations or route reflectors instead of setting up an IGP, and this is something we will cover as we move into chapter 6 and look at some more advanced BGP peering techniques. We will come back to look at iBGP's in greater detail in chapter 12 when we look at the intricacies of redistributing IGPs into BGP.

6. Advanced BGP Peering

There are still a few aspects of BGP peering that we need to cover. In this chapter we will look at how to control which peer starts the process of forming a neighbor relationship, then we will move on to removing our EIGRP set up in AS 200 and replace it with an all-BGP configuration, using route reflectors. We will also cover how we can ease the number of configuration commands required, by the use of peer groups. We will then move on to an alternative to route-reflectors and set up a community, before we end this chapter with a look at how routing loops, within a cluster of route-reflectors, are avoided, as well as how to be one AS, yet advertise ourselves as another AS.

Most of what we have done so far, has taken all the default behaviors of BGP, but there is so much that we can tweak to make BGP run faster, be more secure and to follow the directions we tell it to take.

As we have seen when we created the peering between R1 and R2, both speakers will try and initiate the connection process, with whoever has the highest router-id winning the competition. We can, however, change the rules here, and set one to be passive (meaning it will wait for a connection request from the other peer), allowing us to dictate which of the pair will be the one doing all the talking. This brings us along nicely to start configuring the other side of our network.

For this we will set R6 as the active and R7 as the passive speaker in the peering, using the neighbor command "transport connection-mode <active|passive>". We will also make these two use their loopback interfaces for the connection. When we set up AS 200 we used the loopback addresses, and we only required one extra command after the neighbor statement, and that was to specify the update source. This worked fine with iBGP, as the router will recognize that the peer is in the same AS, and will set a TTL of 255. This alone is not enough with eBGP. Peers using loopbacks, as the update-source will still have the default TTL set to 1, therefore the peers must be directly connected.

Let's get started with eBGP peers and loopback addresses.

6.1 eBGP peers and hops

Firstly on R6 and R7 we need to add static routes to the neighbor peers loopback interface:

```
R6#conf t
R6(config)#ip route 172.20.1.0 255.255.255.0 10.7.1.2
```

```
R7#conf t
R7(config)#ip route 172.26.1.0 255.255.255.0 10.7.1.1
R7(config)#do ping 172.26.1.1
Type escape sequence to abort.
Sending 5, 100-byte ICMP Echos to 172.26.1.1:
!!!!!
Success rate is 100 percent (5/5)
R7(config)#
```

With R6 and R7 having reachability to the other neighbor's loopback, it is time to start configuring R7:

```
R7(config)#router bgp 11000
R7(config-router)#bgp router-id 7.7.7.7
R7(config-router)#neigh 172.26.1.1 remote-as 400
```

Once we turn on debugging, and return to our BGP process to add the update source, we can start to see some errors:

```
R7#debug bgp all
BGP debugging is on for all address families
R7#conf t
R7(config)#router bgp 11000
R7(config-router)#
BGP: topo global:IPv4 Unicast:base Scanning routing tables
BGP: topo global:IPv4 Multicast:base Scanning routing tables
BGP: 172.26.1.1 Active open failed - update-source NULL is not
available, open active delayed 8192ms (35000ms max, 60% jitter)
R7(config-router)#neigh 172.26.1.1 update-source lo0
R7(config-router)#
BGP: 172.26.1.1 Active open failed - no route to peer, open active
delayed 8192ms (35000ms max, 60% jitter)
R7(config-router)#
```

Already we are informed that "update-source NULL is not available", a good indicator that we are talking from the wrong interface. After adding the update source (in bold above), we can see a different error message; "no route to peer", which is a good indicator that either we do not have a route (which we know we do due to the static routes we added a few moments ago), or that something about the peer is not falling in line with the rules of BGP. We need to specify that the destination is more than the default of one hop away, and we do this using the ebgp-multihop keyword, specifying the number of hops we would expect it to take to reach the destination. Once we have done this, the peers come up:

```
R7(config-router)#neigh 172.26.1.1 ebgp-multihop 2
R7(config-router)#
```

```
%BGP-5-ADJCHANGE: neighbor 172.26.1.1 Up
```

R6's neighbor configuration for R7 looks like this:

```
neighbor 172.20.1.1 remote-as 11000
neighbor 172.20.1.1 ebgp-multihop 2
neighbor 172.20.1.1 update-source Loopback0
```

The two have now established an adjacency, using their loopback interfaces, and we have proved that when we connect two eBGP peers, and do not use the directly connected interfaces, we need to change the default hop value.

Now let's move on to active and passive connections.

6.2 Active vs. Passive

During the formation of a BGP peering, both sides will try to initiate the connection. It is the router with the highest bgp router-id that will be the one that is connected to. We can, however, control the initial "discussion" between the two peers, and make one wait to be spoken to, instead of both talking at once. We will add the connection mode command to R7, making it the passive peer, clear the connection and then watch the communication between the two routers:

```
R7(config-router)#neigh 172.26.1.1 transport connection-mode passive
R7(config-router)#do clear ip bgp 172.26.1.1
```

Looking at the logs from R6 and R7, we can easily see if one side is set to passive:

```
R7(config-router)#d - TCP session must be opened passively
R7(config-router)#
BGP: topo global:IPv4 Unicast:base Scanning routing tables
BGP: topo global:IPv4 Multicast:base Scanning routing tables
BGP: 172.26.1.1 passive open to 172.20.1.1
BGP: 172.26.1.1 passive went from Idle to Connect
BGP: ses global 172.26.1.1 (0x69B7FC98:0) pas Setting open delay
timer to 60 seconds.
BGP: 172.26.1.1 passive rcv message type 1, length (excl. header) 26
BGP: ses global 172.26.1.1 (0x69B7FC98:0) pas Receive OPEN
BGP: 172.26.1.1 passive rcv OPEN, version 4, holdtime 180 seconds
BGP: 172.26.1.1 passive rcv OPEN w/ OPTION parameter len: 16
BGP: 172.26.1.1 passive rcvd OPEN w/ optional parameter type 2
(Capability) len 6
BGP: 172.26.1.1 passive OPEN has CAPABILITY code: 1, length 4
BGP: 172.26.1.1 passive OPEN has MP_EXT CAP for afi/safi: 1/1
```

```
BGP: 172.26.1.1 passive rcvd OPEN w/ optional parameter type 2
(Capability) len 2
BGP: 172.26.1.1 passive OPEN has CAPABILITY code: 128, length 0
BGP: 172.26.1.1 passive OPEN has ROUTE-REFRESH capability(old) for
all address-families
BGP: 172.26.1.1 passive rcvd OPEN w/ optional parameter type 2
(Capability) len 2
BGP: 172.26.1.1 passive OPEN has CAPABILITY code: 2, length 0
BGP: 172.26.1.1 passive OPEN has ROUTE-REFRESH capability(new) for
all address-families
BGP: nbr global 172.26.1.1 neighbor does not have IPv4 MDT topology
activated
BGP: 172.26.1.1 passive rcvd OPEN w/ remote AS 400
BGP: ses global 172.26.1.1 (0x69B7FC98:0) pas Adding topology IPv4
Unicast:base
BGP: ses global 172.26.1.1 (0x69B7FC98:0) pas Send OPEN
BGP: 172.26.1.1 passive went from Connect to OpenSent
BGP: 172.26.1.1 passive sending OPEN, version 4, my as: 11000,
holdtime 180 seconds, ID 7070707
BGP: 172.26.1.1 passive went from OpenSent to OpenConfirm
BGP: 172.26.1.1 passive went from OpenConfirm to Established
BGP: ses global 172.26.1.1 (0x69B7FC98:1) pas Assigned ID
BGP: ses global 172.26.1.1 (0x69B7FC98:1) Up
%BGP-5-ADJCHANGE: neighbor 172.26.1.1 Up

R6(config-router)#
BGP: 172.20.1.1 open active, local address 172.26.1.1
BGP: 172.20.1.1 went from Active to OpenSent
BGP: 172.20.1.1 sending OPEN, version 4, my as: 400, holdtime 180
seconds
BGP: 172.20.1.1 send message type 1, length (incl. header) 45
BGP: 172.20.1.1 rcv message type 1, length (excl. header) 34
BGP: 172.20.1.1 rcv OPEN, version 4, holdtime 180 seconds
BGP: 172.20.1.1 rcv OPEN w/ OPTION parameter len: 24
BGP: 172.20.1.1 rcvd OPEN w/ optional parameter type 2 (Capability)
len 6
BGP: 172.20.1.1 OPEN has CAPABILITY code: 1, length 4
BGP: 172.20.1.1 OPEN has MP_EXT CAP for afi/safi: 1/1
BGP: 172.20.1.1 rcvd OPEN w/ optional parameter type 2 (Capability)
len 2
BGP: 172.20.1.1 OPEN has CAPABILITY code: 128, length 0
BGP: 172.20.1.1 OPEN has ROUTE-REFRESH capability(old) for all
address-families
BGP: 172.20.1.1 rcvd OPEN w/ optional parameter type 2 (Capability)
len 2
BGP: 172.20.1.1 OPEN has CAPABILITY code: 2, length 0
```

```
BGP: 172.20.1.1 OPEN has ROUTE-REFRESH capability(new) for all
address-families
BGP: 172.20.1.1 rcvd OPEN w/ optional parameter type 2 (Capability)
len 6
BGP: 172.20.1.1 OPEN has CAPABILITY code: 65, length 4
BGP: 172.20.1.1 unrecognized capability code: 65 - ingored
BGP: 172.20.1.1 rcvd OPEN w/ remote AS 11000
BGP: 172.20.1.1 went from OpenSent to OpenConfirm
BGP: 172.20.1.1 went from OpenConfirm to Established
%BGP-5-ADJCHANGE: neighbor 172.20.1.1 Up
```

We can see that R7 waits for the connection to be initiated by R6. Now we have an eBGP peering, using loopbacks, specifying the number of hops, as well as specifying that one will be passive.

6.3 TTL Security and Connected checking

There are other ways to achieve the connection between two eBGP peers using loopbacks, without using the ebgp-multihop keyword, and that is to use the ttl-security keyword, or to disable BGP's one-hop check instead.

TTL Security

It is relatively easy for an attacker to spoof the TTL value in a packet, making it seem as though they are a directly connected peer. TTL Security reverses the behavior of eBGP multihop, which starts at 0 and increments per hop. With TTL security it starts at 255, and a TTL of 255 would ensure that the peer is actually one hop away. Using the ttl-security method is also useful if, for any reason (i.e., during the CCIE exam), you need to peer but are not allowed to use the ebgp-multihop command.

Using the ttl-security command controls the expected incoming TTL value for an eBGP peer, setting the value at 255 minus the value you specify. If you use the command "neighbor 1.1.1.1 ttl-security hops 2" the minimum expected TTL value will be 253 and the router will only accept packets with a TTL count greater or equal to 253. This is the reverse of using ebgp-multihops where the expected value would be 2.

If we look at some of the details of an eBGP connection, using the ebgp-multihop option, as is currently set between R6 and R7 we can see the following (and, no, the misspelling of Minimum is not my fault, spelling mileage varies from IOS release to IOS release):

```
R6#sh ip bgp neig 172.20.1.1 | i TTL
  Connection is ECN Disabled, Mininum incoming TTL 0, Outgoing TTL 2
```

```
R6#

R7#sh ip bgp neigh 172.26.1.1 | i TTL
Connection is ECN Disabled, Mininum incoming TTL 0,. Outgoing TTL 2
R7#
```

Now let's switch R6 and R7 to use ttl-security, in order to do this we must remove the ebgp-multihop command first:

```
R7(config)#router bgp 11000
R7(config-router)#no neigh 172.26.1.1 ebgp-multihop 2
R7(config-router)#neigh 172.26.1.1 ttl-security hops 2
R7(config-router)#

R6(config)#router bgp 400
R6(config-router)#no neigh 172.20.1.1 ebgp-multihop 2
R6(config-router)#neigh 172.20.1.1 ttl-security hops 2
R6(config-router)#
```

We then clear the bgp connection between the two, and have another look at what TTL values were are seeing:

```
R6#clear ip bgp 172.20.1.1
R6#
%BGP-5-ADJCHANGE: neighbor 172.20.1.1 Down User reset
%BGP-5-ADJCHANGE: neighbor 172.20.1.1 Up
R6#sh ip bgp neig 172.20.1.1 | i TTL
Connection is ECN Disabled, Mininum incoming TTL 253, Outgoing TTL 255
R6#

R7# sh ip bgp neigh 172.26.1.1 | i TTL
Connection is ECN Disabled, Mininum incoming TTL 253, Outgoing TTL 255
R7#
```

So, we can now see why both sides either need ebgp-multihop or ttl-security, and we can't mix and match.

Disable-Connected-Check

As mentioned, the other option is to disable parts of BGP. Using the neighbor command "disable-connected-check" we can tell BGP that we are not concerned that our neighbor is more than one hop away.

Firstly, let's remove the ttl-security commands we put in a moment ago:

    R6(config-router)#no neighbor 172.20.1.1 ttl-security hops 2

    R7(config-router)#no neighbor 172.26.1.1 ttl-security hops 2

And clear the peering:

    R6#clear ip bgp 172.20.1.1

With the BGP peering down we can now use the command "neighbor <neighbor ip address> disable-connected-check", in order to bring the peering back up again:

    R6(config-router)#neighbor 172.20.1.1 disable-connected-check

    R7(config-router)#neighbor 172.26.1.1 disable-connected-check

Sure enough the peer relationship becomes established once again:

    R6(config-router)#
    %BGP-5-ADJCHANGE: neighbor 172.20.1.1 Up
    R6(config-router)#

There we have two more ways to establish a peer relationship between two routers that are not directly connected.

Once we have advertised our loopbacks and our 10.7.1.0/24 network on R7 we are ready to move on.

6.4 Route Reflectors

As mentioned at the start of this chapter, one of our goals is to remove our IGP within AS 200, and to replace it with an all-BGP set up. We will do this using route-reflectors, and see that, as we move into this structure, our BGP configuration starts to get pretty long and repetitive. Peer groups are a way of simplifying BGP connections, where multiple peers share common features, like route-reflector clients do. In our topology the two will go very well together.

In order that we can test that AS 200, and indeed that the full topology still works without the need for EIGRP, we will first discuss route reflectors, and then apply the configuration within peer groups.

So far R1 has a pretty good view of the world:

```
R1#sh ip bgp | beg Network
   Network            Next Hop         Metric LocPrf Weight Path
*> 10.1.0.0/24        0.0.0.0               0         32768 i
*> 10.1.1.0/24        0.0.0.0               0         32768 i
*> 10.2.1.0/24        10.1.1.2                            0 200 i
*> 10.2.2.0/24        10.1.1.2                            0 200 i
*> 10.2.3.0/24        10.1.1.2                            0 200 i
*> 10.2.4.0/24        10.1.1.2                            0 200 i
*> 10.3.1.0/24        10.1.1.2                            0 200 300 i
*> 10.4.1.0/24        10.1.1.2                            0 200 300 i
*> 10.5.1.0/24        10.1.1.2                            0 200 400 i
*> 10.6.1.0/24        10.1.1.2                            0 200 400 i
*> 172.16.1.0/24      10.1.1.2                            0 200 i
*> 172.16.2.0/24      10.1.1.2                            0 200 i
*> 172.17.0.0/24      10.1.1.2              0             0 200 i
*> 172.17.1.0/24      10.1.1.2                            0 200 i
*> 172.17.2.0/24      10.1.1.2                            0 200 i
*> 172.17.5.0/24      10.1.1.2                            0 200 i
*> 172.18.1.0/24      10.1.1.2                            0 200 300 i
*> 172.18.2.0/24      10.1.1.2                            0 200 300 i
*> 172.19.1.0/24      10.1.1.2                            0 200 400 500 i
*> 172.19.2.0/24      10.1.1.2                            0 200 400 500 i
*> 172.19.3.0/24      10.1.1.2                            0 200 400 500 i
*> 172.19.4.0/24      10.1.1.2                            0 200 400 500 i
*> 172.26.1.0/24      10.1.1.2                            0 200 400 i
*> 172.26.2.0/24      10.1.1.2                            0 200 400 i
*> 172.26.3.0/24      10.1.1.2                            0 200 400 i
R1#
```

R1's plentiful BGP table is thanks to the IGP running within AS 200. Although this would be the normal method within a network, reserving the BGP speakers for connections to the ISP, we can actually have an all-BGP network and achieve the same result that R1 sees, without having an IGP within it. This is through the "reflecting" of routes between peers. We will have two different "reflectors" and these will be R3 and R4, and we will begin by removing the entire EIGRP configuration from R2, R3, R4 and R5. This is done simply by entering the command "no router eigrp 100" on each of the routers within configuration mode. We also need to remove the neighbor relationship between R2 and R5, using the command "no neighbor 172.17.0.1" on R5 and "no neighbor 172.17.5.1" on R2, and similarly the neighbor relationship between R3 and R4. Once this is done we can see that R1 has a very limited view of the world now:

```
R1#sh ip bgp | beg Network
   Network          Next Hop        Metric LocPrf Weight Path
*> 10.1.0.0/24      0.0.0.0              0         32768 i
*> 10.1.1.0/24      0.0.0.0              0         32768 i
*> 172.17.0.0/24    10.1.1.2             0             0 200 i
R1#
```

This again highlights the reliance on an IGP within an AS, in order to propagate routes to eBGP peers.

Starting with R3, there is very little we need to do to configure our first route reflector, but recall that when we implemented our IGP we also removed the static routes to the loopback addresses of our neighbors, so we will add these back in now:

```
R2(config)#ip route 172.17.1.0 255.255.255.0 10.2.1.2
R2(config)#ip route 172.16.1.0 255.255.255.0 10.2.2.2

R3(config)#ip route 172.17.5.0 255.255.255.0 10.2.3.2
R3(config)#ip route 172.17.0.0 255.255.255.0 10.2.1.1

R4(config)#ip route 172.17.0.0 255.255.255.0 10.2.2.1
R4(config)#ip route 172.17.5.0 255.255.255.0 10.2.4.1

R5(config)#ip route 172.17.1.0 255.255.255.0 10.2.3.1
R5(config)#ip route 172.16.1.0 255.255.255.0 10.2.4.2
```

As soon as our peers come up R1 has a slightly expanded view of the world:

```
R1#sh ip bgp | beg Network
   Network          Next Hop        Metric LocPrf Weight Path
*> 10.1.0.0/24      0.0.0.0              0         32768 i
*> 10.1.1.0/24      0.0.0.0              0         32768 i
*> 10.2.1.0/24      10.1.1.2                           0 200 i
*> 10.2.2.0/24      10.1.1.2                           0 200 i
*> 10.2.3.0/24      10.1.1.2                           0 200 i
*> 10.2.4.0/24      10.1.1.2                           0 200 i
*> 172.16.1.0/24    10.1.1.2                           0 200 i
*> 172.16.2.0/24    10.1.1.2                           0 200 i
*> 172.17.0.0/24    10.1.1.2             0             0 200 i
*> 172.17.1.0/24    10.1.1.2                           0 200 i
```

```
*> 172.17.2.0/24    10.1.1.2                      0 200 i
R1#
```

In order to best understand how the route reflectors work, let's narrow this down and focus on one particular route. Which will be the 172.20.1.0/24 network, advertised by R7.

R3 knows about it, and has reachability:

```
R3#sh ip bgp 172.20.1.0/24
BGP routing table entry for 172.20.1.0/24, version 42
Paths: (1 available, best #1, table Default-IP-Routing-Table)
  Not advertised to any peer
  400 11000
    172.17.5.1 from 172.17.5.1 (5.5.5.5)
      Origin IGP, metric 0, localpref 100, valid, internal, best
R3#ping 172.20.1.1

Type escape sequence to abort.
Sending 5, 100-byte ICMP Echos to 172.20.1.1:
!!!!!
Success rate is 100 percent (5/5)
R3#
```

However R2 does not have this listed in any of its tables:

```
R2#sh ip bgp 172.20.1.0/24
% Network not in table
R2#
```

This is because R3 is not advertising it to R2:

```
R3#sh ip bgp neigh 172.17.0.1 advertised-routes
BGP table version is 43, local router ID is 3.3.3.3
Status codes: s suppressed, d damped, h history, * valid, > best, i -
internal,
           r RIB-failure, S Stale
Origin codes: i - IGP, e - EGP, ? - incomplete

   Network          Next Hop         Metric LocPrf Weight Path
*> 10.2.1.0/24      0.0.0.0               0         32768 i
*> 10.2.3.0/24      0.0.0.0               0         32768 i
*> 172.17.1.0/24    0.0.0.0               0         32768 i
*> 172.17.2.0/24    0.0.0.0               0         32768 i

Total number of prefixes 4
R3#
```

So the purpose here is that in an internal autonomous system, which is not fully meshed, or does not run an IGP, we need to forward (reflect) the routes from one router (the "server") to another (the "client"). We can set R2 as a client of R3 using the command:

```
R3(config-router)#neighbor 172.17.0.1 route-reflector-client
R3(config-router)#
%BGP-5-ADJCHANGE: neighbor 172.17.0.1 Down RR client config change
R3(config-router)#
%BGP-5-ADJCHANGE: neighbor 172.17.0.1 Up
R3(config-router)#
```

The peering drops, and, after a short period, becomes established again. Now let's have another look at what R3 is sending to R2 and, sticking with the 172.20.1.0/24 network, see how R2 is treating it:

```
R3#sh ip bgp neigh 172.17.0.1 advertised-routes | beg Network
   Network          Next Hop        Metric LocPrf Weight Path
*>  10.2.1.0/24     0.0.0.0              0         32768 i
*>  10.2.3.0/24     0.0.0.0              0         32768 i
*>i10.3.1.0/24     172.17.5.1            0    100      0 300 i
*>i10.4.1.0/24     172.17.5.1            0    100      0 300 i
*>i10.5.1.0/24     172.17.5.1            0    100      0 400 i
*>i10.6.1.0/24     172.17.5.1            0    100      0 400 i
*>i10.7.1.0/24     172.17.5.1            0    100      0 400 11000 i
*>  172.17.1.0/24   0.0.0.0              0         32768 i
*>  172.17.2.0/24   0.0.0.0              0         32768 i
r>i172.17.5.0/24   172.17.5.1            0    100      0 i
*>i172.18.1.0/24   172.17.5.1            0    100      0 300 i
*>i172.18.2.0/24   172.17.5.1            0    100      0 300 i
*>i172.19.1.0/24   172.17.5.1            0    100      0 300 500 i
*>i172.19.2.0/24   172.17.5.1            0    100      0 300 500 i
*>i172.19.3.0/24   172.17.5.1            0    100      0 300 500 i
*>i172.19.4.0/24   172.17.5.1            0    100      0 300 500 i
*>i172.20.1.0/24   172.17.5.1            0    100      0 400 11000 i
*>i172.20.2.0/24   172.17.5.1            0    100      0 400 11000 i
*>i172.20.3.0/24   172.17.5.1            0    100      0 400 11000 i
*>i172.20.4.0/24   172.17.5.1            0    100      0 400 11000 i
*>i172.26.1.0/24   172.17.5.1            0    100      0 400 i
*>i172.26.2.0/24   172.17.5.1            0    100      0 400 i
*>i172.26.3.0/24   172.17.5.1            0    100      0 400 i

Total number of prefixes 23
R3#

R2#sh ip bgp 172.20.1.0/24
```

```
  BGP routing table entry for 172.20.1.0/24, version 0
  Paths: (1 available, no best path)
    Not advertised to any peer
    400 11000
      172.17.5.1 (inaccessible) from 172.17.1.1 (3.3.3.3)
        Origin IGP, metric 0, localpref 100, valid, internal
        Originator: 5.5.5.5, Cluster list: 3.3.3.3
  R2#
```

R2 now has the route in its BGP table, but the route is not considered valid, as the next hop (R5's loopback interface) is unreachable. Previously, we saw this we could fix it by changing the next-hop as we passed the route over, using the "next-hop self" option. We still have this configured in our neighbor statement, so we can see that it now does not have the desired effect. This is because when we implement route-reflectors the next-hop-self command only modifies the next-hop attribute for routes learned from an eBGP peer, so in this instance the next-hop-self command will not have the desired effect. Instead we must use an outbound route-map[3].

As we progress through the coming chapters we will encounter route-maps in more detail, but for the time being we will set up one on R3 and R4 to get R2 visibility of routes originating from R5, by properly setting the next-hop address. We will also set R2 to be a route-reflector client of R4, R5 to be a client of R3 and R4, and use the same route-map to set the next-hop for routes going into R5 from R3 and R4.

First we will start by completing our route-reflector configurations:

```
  R3#conf t
  R3(config)#router bgp 200
  R3(config-router)#neigh 172.17.5.1 route-reflector-client
  %BGP-5-ADJCHANGE: neighbor 172.17.5.1 Down RR client config change
  %BGP-5-ADJCHANGE: neighbor 172.17.5.1 Up
  R3(config-router)#

  R4#conf t
  R4(config)#router bgp 200
  R4(config-router)#neigh 172.17.0.1 route-reflector-client
  %BGP-5-ADJCHANGE: neighbor 172.17.0.1 Down RR client config change
  %BGP-5-ADJCHANGE: neighbor 172.17.0.1 Up
  R4(config-router)#neigh 172.17.5.1 route-reflector-client
  %BGP-5-ADJCHANGE: neighbor 172.17.5.1 Down RR client config change
  %BGP-5-ADJCHANGE: neighbor 172.17.5.1 Up
  R4(config-router)#
```

---

[3] http://www.cisco.com/en/US/docs/ios/12_2s/feature/guide/fs_bgpnh.html#wp1043334

Now, let's create our first route-map. Route-maps are very powerful, and we will use them quite a bit as we progress, but in essence they follow an IF-THEN login. If a clause is matched (which can be an access-list, or a prefix-list for example), then set an attribute. Because we know that no matter what, R2 and R5 must always see the next hop as the address it peers from (the loopback interface) we can create a very simple route-map, missing out the IF part completely and skipping straight to the THEN part.

```
R3(config)#route-map SET-NEXT-HOP
R3(config-route-map)#set ip next-hop peer-address
R3(config-route-map)#exit
R3(config)#
```

There are a few options when setting the ip next-hop - we could specify an IP address, but for this instance we will choose the peer-address, which will use the loopback interface IP address. If we were using different interfaces for R2 and R5 this would achieve the same goal. We next apply this route-map to our neighbors:

```
R3(config)#router bgp 200
R3(config-router)#neighbor 172.17.0.1 route-map SET-NEXT-HOP out
R3(config-router)#neighbor 172.17.5.1 route-map SET-NEXT-HOP out
R3(config-router)#exit
```

We can now check that R2 has a valid route to the 172.20.1.0/24 network (if the change does not show up quickly enough use the "clear ip bgp 172.17.1.1" command on R2):

```
R2# sh ip bgp  | beg 172.20.1.0
*>i172.20.1.0/24    172.17.1.1          0      100       0 400 11000 i
* i                 172.17.5.1          0      100       0 400 11000 i
*>i172.20.2.0/24    172.17.1.1          0      100       0 400 11000 i
* i                 172.17.5.1          0      100       0 400 11000 i
*>i172.20.3.0/24    172.17.1.1          0      100       0 400 11000 i
* i                 172.17.5.1          0      100       0 400 11000 i
*>i172.20.4.0/24    172.17.1.1          0      100       0 400 11000 i
* i                 172.17.5.1          0      100       0 400 11000 i
```

So things are starting to improve here, the route from R3 is being added into the routing table. Now, we just need to fix the routes from R4:

```
R4(config)#route-map SET-NEXT-HOP
R4(config-route-map)#set ip next-hop peer-address
R4(config-route-map)#exit
R4(config)#router bgp 200
R4(config-router)#neigh 172.17.0.1 route-map SET-NEXT-HOP out
R4(config-router)#neigh 172.17.5.1 route-map SET-NEXT-HOP out
R4(config-router)#do clear ip bgp *
```

```
R4(config-router)#
%BGP-5-ADJCHANGE: neighbor 172.17.0.1 Down User reset
%BGP-5-ADJCHANGE: neighbor 172.17.5.1 Down User reset
R4(config-router)#
%BGP-5-ADJCHANGE: neighbor 172.17.0.1 Up
%BGP-5-ADJCHANGE: neighbor 172.17.5.1 Up
R4(config-router)#
```

And now R2 can see the following:

```
R2# sh ip bgp  | beg 172.20.1.0
*>i172.20.1.0/24    172.16.1.1          0     100      0 400 11000 i
* i                 172.17.1.1          0     100      0 400 11000 i
*>i172.20.2.0/24    172.16.1.1          0     100      0 400 11000 i
* i                 172.17.1.1          0     100      0 400 11000 i
*>i172.20.3.0/24    172.16.1.1          0     100      0 400 11000 i
* i                 172.17.1.1          0     100      0 400 11000 i
*>i172.20.4.0/24    172.16.1.1          0     100      0 400 11000 i
* i                 172.17.1.1          0     100      0 400 11000 i
```

We have valid routes from both our route-reflector servers. Similarly it's working well for R5, and the first couple of entries are shown below:

```
R5#sh ip bgp | beg Network
   Network          Next Hop         Metric LocPrf Weight Path
*>i10.1.0.0/24      172.16.1.1          0     100      0 100 i
* i                 172.17.1.1          0     100      0 100 i
*>i10.1.1.0/24      172.16.1.1          0     100      0 100 i
* i                 172.17.1.1          0     100      0 100 i
```

Now we have a very redundant iBGP AS using route-reflectors. We can see that R2 and R5 have alternative paths through to the other networks, and will go through either R3 or R4, depending on which route is considered best and gets installed into the routing table. We will cover the BGP decision process (why one route is preferred over another) in chapter 11.

Depending on the requirements in front of you (especially in the CCIE lab), it is probably quicker and easier to set up an IGP, such as EIGRP as we did earlier, but if IGPs are not an option, then route-reflectors work well in this scenario.

Route-reflectors do, however, leave a lot of command duplication in the configuration, and this is where peer groups can make our configurations easier.

6.5 Peer groups

Looking at R3 and R4, we can see a number of neighbor commands that are very similar; we will concentrate on R3 for the moment:

```
R3#sh run | section bgp
router bgp 200
 no synchronization
 bgp router-id 3.3.3.3
 bgp log-neighbor-changes
 network 10.2.1.0 mask 255.255.255.0
 network 10.2.3.0 mask 255.255.255.0
 network 172.17.1.0 mask 255.255.255.0
 network 172.17.2.0 mask 255.255.255.0
 neighbor 172.17.0.1 remote-as 200
 neighbor 172.17.0.1 update-source Loopback0
 neighbor 172.17.0.1 route-reflector-client
 neighbor 172.17.0.1 next-hop-self
 neighbor 172.17.0.1 route-map SET-NEXT-HOP out
 neighbor 172.17.5.1 remote-as 200
 neighbor 172.17.5.1 update-source Loopback0
 neighbor 172.17.5.1 route-reflector-client
 neighbor 172.17.5.1 next-hop-self
 neighbor 172.17.5.1 route-map SET-NEXT-HOP out
 no auto-summary
R3#

R4#sh run | section bgp
router bgp 200
 no synchronization
 bgp router-id 4.4.4.4
 bgp log-neighbor-changes
 network 10.2.2.0 mask 255.255.255.0
 network 10.2.4.0 mask 255.255.255.0
 network 172.16.1.0 mask 255.255.255.0
 network 172.16.2.0 mask 255.255.255.0
 neighbor 172.17.0.1 remote-as 200
 neighbor 172.17.0.1 update-source Loopback0
 neighbor 172.17.0.1 route-reflector-client
 neighbor 172.17.0.1 next-hop-self
 neighbor 172.17.0.1 route-map SET-NEXT-HOP out
 neighbor 172.17.5.1 remote-as 200
 neighbor 172.17.5.1 update-source Loopback0
 neighbor 172.17.5.1 route-reflector-client
 neighbor 172.17.5.1 next-hop-self
 neighbor 172.17.5.1 route-map SET-NEXT-HOP out
```

```
    no auto-summary
R4#
```

There are 5 commands that are identical, and one that is missing (although this is not impeding our topology, and should really be added just for usefulness). Using a peer group we can combine these commands and simplify our configuration.

We start by creating our peer group using the command "neighbor <peer-group-name> peer-group", and then we assign the variables (such as remote-as) as we would for any neighbor, but instead of using an IP address, we specify the peer group name:

```
R3(config)#router bgp 200
R3(config-router)#neighbor AS200-PEERGROUP peer-group
R3(config-router)#neighbor AS200-PEERGROUP remote-as 200
R3(config-router)#neighbor AS200-PEERGROUP route-reflector-client
R3(config-router)#neighbor AS200-PEERGROUP update-source lo0
R3(config-router)#neighbor AS200-PEERGROUP soft-reconfiguration inbound
R3(config-router)#neighbor AS200-PEERGROUP route-map SET-NEXT-HOP out
R3(config-router)#
```

I have added the "soft-reconfiguration inbound" statement, as it's very useful to have from a troubleshooting perspective, but should only really be used for troubleshooting, as will be explained next, before we return to setting up the route-reflectors.

Soft-reconfiguration and Route-Refresh

We have already seen what routes are being advertised to a peer, by the use of the "advertised-routes" keyword. Soft-reconfiguration inbound allows us to see what routes were received, or to refresh the routes sent, or received by us, to a particular neighbor using the command "clear ip bgp <ip address> soft [in|out], such as "clear ip bgp 10.1.1.1 soft in", to refresh our BGP table with the latest information from that particular neighbor. We don't strictly have to enable soft-reconfiguration inbound to use the clear command, as it is already available in the route refresh capability. The route refresh capability, which is negotiated when peers form relationships and enabled by default, works differently to soft-reconfiguration. We can confirm that the route-refresh capability is available by looking at the peers' capabilities:

```
R2#sh ip bgp neigh 172.17.1.1 | s Neighbor capabilities
  Neighbor capabilities:
    Route refresh: advertised and received(old & new)
    Address family IPv4 Unicast: advertised and received
R2#
```

If we do not enable soft-reconfiguration, and run the command "clear ip bgp 10.1.1.1 in" on R2, then R2 will send a ROUTE-REFRESH message to R1, and R1 will send back a standard UPDATE message. Once we enable soft-reconfiguration, BGP will start to keep a copy of received routes in the adj-RIB-in table. These are normally discarded after they are passed to the loc-RIB table. Because of this soft-reconfiguration can use more memory that route-refresh, but route-refresh will use more bandwidth. The command "soft-reconfiguration inbound" will effectively turn off the route-refresh capability, which can actually cause a large issue, if the adj-RIB-in table becomes corrupted, the router must be completely reset. Using route refresh, on the other hand, if the loc-RIB gets corrupted then the routes can be refreshed without a major loss of service. For our topology this is fine, but even Cisco state that it really shouldn't be used outside of troubleshooting *"Clearing the BGP session using the neighbor soft-reconfiguration command has a negative effect on network operations and should only be used as a last resort"*[4].

To test soft-reconfiguration on R2, we will enable it for one peer but not another:

```
R2(config)#router bgp 200
R2(config-router)#neigh 10.1.1.1 soft-reconfiguration inbound
R2(config-router)#exit
R2(config)#exit
R2#sh ip bgp neigh 10.1.1.1 received-routes
BGP table version is 542, local router ID is 2.2.2.2
Status codes: s suppressed, d damped, h history, * valid, > best, i -
internal,
              r RIB-failure, S Stale
Origin codes: i - IGP, e - EGP, ? - incomplete

   Network          Next Hop        Metric LocPrf Weight Path
*> 10.1.0.0/24      10.1.1.1             0             0 100 i
r> 10.1.1.0/24      10.1.1.1             0             0 100 i

Total number of prefixes 2
R2#sh ip bgp neigh 172.17.1.1 received-routes
% Inbound soft reconfiguration not enabled on 172.17.1.1
R2#
```

Returning to our route-reflectors, we then assign the neighbor to the peer group. The majority of our existing statements will automatically be removed when we add the neighbor to the peer group, but we might see one or two linger:

---

[4] http://www.cisco.com/en/US/docs/ios-xml/ios/iproute_bgp/command/bgp-m1.html#wp2269702887

```
R3(config-router)#neigh 172.17.5.1 peer-group AS200-PEERGROUP
R3(config-router)#
%BGP-5-ADJCHANGE: neighbor 172.17.5.1 Down RR client config change
R3(config-router)#
%BGP-5-ADJCHANGE: neighbor 172.17.5.1 Up
R3(config-router)#neigh 172.17.0.1 peer-group AS200-PEERGROUP
R3(config-router)#
%BGP-5-ADJCHANGE: neighbor 172.17.0.1 Down RR client config change
R3(config-router)#
%BGP-5-ADJCHANGE: neighbor 172.17.0.1 Up
```

Our configuration on R3 now looks like this:

```
R3(config-router)#do sh run | section bgp
router bgp 200
 no synchronization
 bgp router-id 3.3.3.3
 bgp log-neighbor-changes
 network 10.2.1.0 mask 255.255.255.0
 network 10.2.3.0 mask 255.255.255.0
 network 172.17.1.0 mask 255.255.255.0
 network 172.17.2.0 mask 255.255.255.0
 neighbor AS200-PEERGROUP peer-group
 neighbor AS200-PEERGROUP remote-as 200
 neighbor AS200-PEERGROUP update-source Loopback0
 neighbor AS200-PEERGROUP route-reflector-client
 neighbor AS200-PEERGROUP soft-reconfiguration inbound
 neighbor AS200-PEERGROUP route-map SET-NEXT-HOP out
 neighbor 172.17.0.1 peer-group AS200-PEERGROUP
 neighbor 172.17.0.1 update-source Loopback0
 neighbor 172.17.5.1 peer-group AS200-PEERGROUP
 neighbor 172.17.5.1 update-source Loopback0
 no auto-summary
R3(config-router)#
```

Everything looks much tidier!

We can check on the peer group membership using the command "sh ip bgp peer-group <peer-group-name>", which shows us what peers are within the peer group, as well as the remote AS, and the rest of the settings we have configured:

```
R3#sh ip bgp peer-group AS200-PEERGROUP
BGP peer-group is AS200-PEERGROUP,  remote AS 200
  BGP version 4
  Default minimum time between advertisement runs is 0 seconds
```

```
  For address family: IPv4 Unicast
  BGP neighbor is AS200-PEERGROUP, peer-group internal, members:
  172.17.0.1 172.17.5.1
   Index 0, Offset 0, Mask 0x0
   Route-Reflector Client
   Inbound soft reconfiguration allowed
   Route map for outgoing advertisements is SET-NEXT-HOP
   Update messages formatted 0, replicated 0
   Number of NLRIs in the update sent: max 0, min 0
R3#
```

As we have seen we did not need to remove all our individual neighbor statements, as these were removed automatically. The ones that are removed are ones that cannot be specific to one peer, such as the route-map; members of a peer-group cannot have a separate route-map, but they can have different update sources, as we can see because this command has been left in. If we tried to change the route-map for R2 we would get the following error:

```
R3(config)#router bgp 200
R3(config-router)#neighbor 172.17.0.1 route-map 172.17.0.1-ROUTE-MAP out
% Invalid command for a peer-group member
R3(config-router)#
```

Now, we have a working route-reflector configuration, as well as peer groups, and (more importantly) we have visibility and reachability.

6.6 Confederations

Have a look back at our topology, R1 (AS 100) is connected to R13 (AS 101) and R14 (AS 102), yet, instead of a series of simple eBGP peerings, we have them contained within one AS (AS 105). Routes from R13 and R14 will be advertised from R1, but the routes from R1, R13 and R14 will all appear to R2 as AS 105. This is what is known as a confederation.

We start with R1, firstly setting up the confederation AS, then specifying the peers that are to be included within the federation. Lastly we add the peers as we would normally:

```
R1(config)#router bgp 100
R1(config-router)#bgp confederation identifier 105
R1(config-router)#bgp confederation peers 101 102
R1(config-router)#neighbor 1.1.1.2 remote-as 101
R1(config-router)#neighbor 1.2.1.2 remote-as 102
```

At this stage you will probably start seeing some errors on R2 as R1 is now identifying itself as AS 105 (See Chapter 15 on Troubleshooting for the errors that were displayed). So we need to inform R2 that the AS for R1 is now 105:

```
R2(config)#router bgp 200
R2(config-router)#neigh 10.1.1.1 remote-as 105
R2(config-router)#
%BGP-5-ADJCHANGE: neighbor 10.1.1.1 Down Remote AS changed
R2(config-router)#
%BGP-5-ADJCHANGE: neighbor 10.1.1.1 Up
R2(config-router)#
```

Moving on to R13, we again add it to the confederation, and then tell it what its peers are:

```
R13(config)#router bgp 101
R13(config-router)#bgp router-id 13.13.13.13
R13(config-router)#bgp confederation identifier 105
R13(config-router)#bgp confederation peers 100
R13(config-router)#network 1.1.1.0 mask 255.255.255.0
R13(config-router)#network 172.21.1.0 mask 255.255.255.0
R13(config-router)#network 172.21.2.0 mask 255.255.255.0
R13(config-router)#network 172.21.3.0 mask 255.255.255.0
R13(config-router)#network 172.21.4.0 mask 255.255.255.0
R13(config-router)#neighbor 1.1.1.1 remote-as 100
R13(config-router)#
%BGP-5-ADJCHANGE: neighbor 1.1.1.1 Up
R13(config-router)#
```

And similarly for R14:

```
R14(config)#router bgp 102
R14(config-router)#bgp router-id 14.14.14.14
R14(config-router)#bgp confederation identifier 105
R14(config-router)#bgp confederation peers 100
R14(config-router)#network 1.2.1.0 mask 255.255.255.0
R14(config-router)#network 172.22.1.0 mask 255.255.255.0
R14(config-router)#network 172.22.2.0 mask 255.255.255.0
R14(config-router)#network 172.22.3.0 mask 255.255.255.0
R14(config-router)#network 172.22.4.0 mask 255.255.255.0
R14(config-router)#neigh 1.2.1.1 remote-as 100
R14(config-router)#
%BGP-5-ADJCHANGE: neighbor 1.2.1.1 Up
R14(config-router)#
```

We can check R2 to make sure that the new routes are being advertised, what AS they are being advertised as, and confirm reachability:

```
R2#sh ip bgp | i 105
 *> 1.1.1.0/24       10.1.1.1                          0 105 i
 *> 1.2.1.0/24       10.1.1.1                          0 105 i
 *> 10.1.0.0/24      10.1.1.1        0                 0 105 i
 r> 10.1.1.0/24      10.1.1.1        0                 0 105 i
 *> 172.21.1.0/24    10.1.1.1                          0 105 i
 *> 172.21.2.0/24    10.1.1.1                          0 105 i
 *> 172.21.3.0/24    10.1.1.1                          0 105 i
 *> 172.21.4.0/24    10.1.1.1                          0 105 i
 *> 172.22.1.0/24    10.1.1.1                          0 105 i
 *> 172.22.2.0/24    10.1.1.1                          0 105 i
 *> 172.22.3.0/24    10.1.1.1                          0 105 i
 *> 172.22.4.0/24    10.1.1.1                          0 105 i
R2#ping 172.21.1.1

Type escape sequence to abort.
Sending 5, 100-byte ICMP Echos to 172.21.1.1:
!!!!!
Success rate is 100 percent (5/5)
R2#
```

So, we can see that although the R13 and R14 routers are in their own AS, we can make them members of a confederation, and, as such, advertise their networks as the confederation AS number, rather than their own. If we look at the BGP table of R1 we see that the R13 and R14 routers are passing their advertised networks to R1 with their correct AS number, but it is in brackets, indicating that it is a member of a confederation:

```
R1#sh ip bgp | i \(1
 r> 1.1.1.0/24       1.1.1.2         0      100        0 (101) i
 r> 1.2.1.0/24       1.2.1.2         0      100        0 (102) i
 *> 172.21.1.0/24    1.1.1.2         0      100        0 (101) i
 *> 172.21.2.0/24    1.1.1.2         0      100        0 (101) i
 *> 172.21.3.0/24    1.1.1.2         0      100        0 (101) i
 *> 172.21.4.0/24    1.1.1.2         0      100        0 (101) i
 *> 172.22.1.0/24    1.2.1.2         0      100        0 (102) i
 *> 172.22.2.0/24    1.2.1.2         0      100        0 (102) i
 *> 172.22.3.0/24    1.2.1.2         0      100        0 (102) i
 *> 172.22.4.0/24    1.2.1.2         0      100        0 (102) i
R1#
```

Just to mention the include command above - because our BGP table is getting pretty large, it's a good idea to keep the outputs as concise as possible. Because we know that a confederation peer will advertise its AS within a bracket, and we know that the expected AS numbers will start with a 1, then searching for "(1" would be a good place to start, however the bracket treats the include statement as a regular expression (regex):

```
R1#sh ip bgp | i (1
% unmatched ()
% Failed to compile regular expression.
R1#
```

Using the slash mark in front of the query escapes the first character, so that IOS will treat it literally, and not attempt to use a regular expression. We will cover pattern matching through regex in chapter 11.

6.7 Clusters

Clusters are implemented along with Route Reflectors; they provide a way to ensure loop-free topologies. Every Route Reflector adds its own cluster ID to the cluster list, and if the router receives a route with its own cluster ID in the cluster list, it will be discarded, as it sees this as a loop in the network.

Our main topology does not actually lend itself very well to a good example of how Cluster-IDs are used to prevent loops, so let's step away from our topology for a few moments and set up a new network to briefly illustrate this:

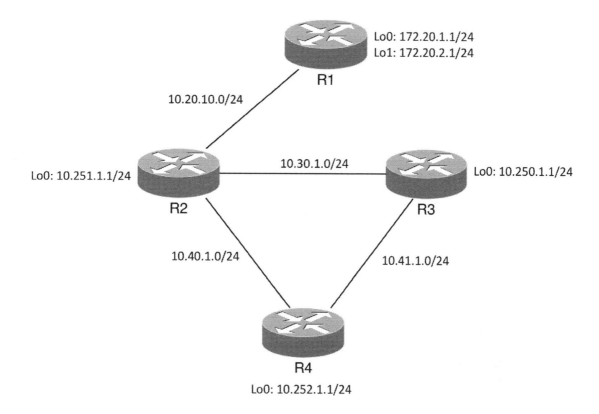

We have a single AS (200), with R2 and R3 acting as route-reflectors for R4. The BGP configurations are below:

```
R1#sh run | section bgp
router bgp 200
 no synchronization
 bgp log-neighbor-changes
 network 172.20.1.0 mask 255.255.255.0
 network 172.20.2.0 mask 255.255.255.0
 neighbor 10.20.10.2 remote-as 200
 no auto-summary
R1#

R2#sh run | section bgp
router bgp 200
 no synchronization
 bgp cluster-id 200.200.200.200
 bgp log-neighbor-changes
 network 10.20.10.0 mask 255.255.255.0
 network 10.30.1.0 mask 255.255.255.0
 network 10.40.1.0 mask 255.255.255.0
```

```
  network 10.251.1.0 mask 255.255.255.0
  neighbor 10.20.10.1 remote-as 200
  neighbor 10.20.10.1 route-reflector-client
  neighbor 10.20.10.1 next-hop-self
  neighbor 10.30.1.2 remote-as 200
  neighbor 10.30.1.2 next-hop-self
  neighbor 10.40.1.2 remote-as 200
  neighbor 10.40.1.2 route-reflector-client
  no auto-summary
R2#

R3#sh run | section bgp
router bgp 200
  no synchronization
  bgp cluster-id 200.200.200.200
  bgp log-neighbor-changes
  network 10.30.1.0 mask 255.255.255.0
  network 10.250.1.0 mask 255.255.255.0
  neighbor 10.30.1.1 remote-as 200
  neighbor 10.30.1.1 next-hop-self
  neighbor 10.41.1.2 remote-as 200
  neighbor 10.41.1.2 route-reflector-client
  no auto-summary
R3#


R4#sh run | section bgp
router bgp 200
  no synchronization
  bgp log-neighbor-changes
  network 10.252.1.0 mask 255.255.255.0
  neighbor 10.40.1.1 remote-as 200
  neighbor 10.41.1.1 remote-as 200
  no auto-summary
R4#
```

For the most part our BGP table looks healthy:

```
R1#sh ip bgp | beg Network
   Network          Next Hop         Metric LocPrf Weight Path
r>i10.20.10.0/24    10.20.10.2            0    100      0 i
*>i10.30.1.0/24     10.20.10.2            0    100      0 i
*>i10.40.1.0/24     10.20.10.2            0    100      0 i
*>i10.250.1.0/24    10.30.1.2             0    100      0 i
*>i10.251.1.0/24    10.20.10.2            0    100      0 i
*>i10.252.1.0/24    10.40.1.2             0    100      0 i
*>  172.20.1.0/24   0.0.0.0               0         32768 i
```

```
 *> 172.20.2.0/24       0.0.0.0                  0             32768 i
R1#

R2#sh ip bgp | beg Network
   Network             Next Hop            Metric LocPrf Weight Path
 *> 10.20.10.0/24       0.0.0.0                  0             32768 i
 *  i10.30.1.0/24       10.30.1.2                0    100      0 i
 *>                     0.0.0.0                  0             32768 i
 *> 10.40.1.0/24        0.0.0.0                  0             32768 i
 *>i10.250.1.0/24       10.30.1.2                0    100      0 i
 *> 10.251.1.0/24       0.0.0.0                  0             32768 i
 *>i10.252.1.0/24       10.40.1.2                0    100      0 i
 *>i172.20.1.0/24       10.20.10.1               0    100      0 i
 *>i172.20.2.0/24       10.20.10.1               0    100      0 i
R2#

R3#sh ip bgp | beg Network
   Network             Next Hop            Metric LocPrf Weight Path
 *>i10.20.10.0/24       10.30.1.1                0    100      0 i
 *> 10.30.1.0/24        0.0.0.0                  0             32768 i
 *  i                   10.30.1.1                0    100      0 i
 *>i10.40.1.0/24        10.30.1.1                0    100      0 i
 *> 10.250.1.0/24       0.0.0.0                  0             32768 i
 *>i10.251.1.0/24       10.30.1.1                0    100      0 i
 *>i10.252.1.0/24       10.41.1.2                0    100      0 i
R3#

R4#sh ip bgp | beg Network
   Network             Next Hop            Metric LocPrf Weight Path
 *  i10.20.10.0/24      10.30.1.1                0    100      0 i
 *>i                    10.40.1.1                0    100      0 i
 *>i10.30.1.0/24        10.41.1.1                0    100      0 i
 *  i                   10.40.1.1                0    100      0 i
 r  i10.40.1.0/24       10.30.1.1                0    100      0 i
 r>i                    10.40.1.1                0    100      0 i
 *  i10.250.1.0/24      10.30.1.2                0    100      0 i
 *>i                    10.41.1.1                0    100      0 i
 *  i10.251.1.0/24      10.30.1.1                0    100      0 i
 *>i                    10.40.1.1                0    100      0 i
 *> 10.252.1.0/24       0.0.0.0                  0             32768 i
 *>i172.20.1.0/24       10.20.10.1               0    100      0 i
 *>i172.20.2.0/24       10.20.10.1               0    100      0 i
R4#
```

We can see though, that R3 is missing the networks for R1's loopback interfaces. This is because the cluster-id acts as a loop-prevention mechanism. A router will not accept a route that contains its own cluster-id, in much the same way that a router will not accept a network with a path that contains its own AS number.

If we change the bgp cluster-id on R3 we can give it a fully populated BGP table, and confirm reachability:

```
R3#conf t
R3(config)#router bgp 200
R3(config-router)#bgp cluster-id 201.201.201.201
R3(config-router)#exit
R3(config)#exit
R3#sh ip bgp
R3#sh ip bgp | beg Network
   Network          Next Hop           Metric LocPrf Weight Path
*>i10.20.10.0/24    10.30.1.1               0    100      0 i
*>  10.30.1.0/24    0.0.0.0                 0         32768 i
*  i                10.30.1.1               0    100      0 i
*>i10.40.1.0/24     10.30.1.1               0    100      0 i
*>  10.250.1.0/24   0.0.0.0                 0         32768 i
*>i10.251.1.0/24    10.30.1.1               0    100      0 i
*  i10.252.1.0/24   10.40.1.2               0    100      0 i
*>i                 10.41.1.2               0    100      0 i
r>i172.20.1.0/24    10.20.10.1              0    100      0 i
*>i172.20.2.0/24    10.20.10.1              0    100      0 i
R3#ping 172.20.1.1

Type escape sequence to abort.
Sending 5, 100-byte ICMP Echos to 172.20.1.1:
!!!!!
Success rate is 100 percent (5/5)
R3#
```

If we look at one of R1's loopback routes, as it is seen by R4, we can see the route as advertised by both R2 and R3. As it passed through R3 the cluster list incremented with the newly changed cluster-id on R3:

```
R4#sh ip bgp 172.20.1.0
BGP routing table entry for 172.20.1.0/24, version 81
Paths: (2 available, best #2, table Default-IP-Routing-Table)
  Not advertised to any peer
  Local
    10.20.10.1 from 10.41.1.1 (200.200.200.200)
      Origin IGP, metric 0, localpref 100, valid, internal
      Originator: 172.20.2.1, Cluster list: 201.201.201.201,
200.200.200.200
  Local
```

```
        10.20.10.1 from 10.40.1.1 (10.251.1.1)
          Origin IGP, metric 0, localpref 100, valid, internal, best
          Originator: 172.20.2.1, Cluster list: 200.200.200.200
    R4#
```

We will return to cluster-ids when we look at the BGP decision process later on in this book.

6.8 local-as

Local AS allows us to be in one AS, but to appear as another AS. Using R12 for this example, we can see that we have an AS in brackets (65500). Until now we have set this router up as AS 300 and everything has worked fine. We will now remove the existing BGP configuration using the command "no router bgp 300" and configure it as AS 65500, but our peers will still connect to the same router, using AS 300:

```
    R12(config)#no router bgp 300
    %BGP-5-ADJCHANGE: neighbor 10.3.1.1 Down BGP protocol initialization
    %BGP-5-ADJCHANGE: neighbor 10.4.1.2 Down BGP protocol initialization
```

With no BGP process we can start again from scratch:

```
    R12(config)#router bgp 65500
    R12(config-router)#no synchronization
    R12(config-router)#bgp router-id 12.12.12.12
    R12(config-router)#bgp log-neighbor-changes
    R12(config-router)#network 10.3.1.0 mask 255.255.255.0
    R12(config-router)#network 10.4.1.0 mask 255.255.255.0
    R12(config-router)#network 172.18.1.0 mask 255.255.255.0
    R12(config-router)#network 172.18.2.0 mask 255.255.255.0
    R12(config-router)#neighbor 10.3.1.1 remote-as 200
    R12(config-router)#neighbor 10.4.1.2 remote-as 500
    R12(config-router)#no auto-summary
```

With our peer connections to R5 and R10 set up exactly as before, we can see errors pretty quickly:

```
    R12(config-router)#
    %BGP-3-NOTIFICATION: received from neighbor 10.4.1.2 2/2 (peer in
    wrong AS) 2 bytes FFDC
    R12(config-router)#
    %BGP-3-NOTIFICATION: received from neighbor 10.3.1.1 2/2 (peer in
    wrong AS) 2 bytes FFDC
    R12(config-router)#
```

We have started to get error notifications passed to us from the neighbor. What is useful here is that the message tells us what is wrong (peer in wrong AS), and if we convert FFDC from hex to decimal, we see that the ASN we have passed to our neighbor is 65500. We should be advertising ourselves as 300, and we do this using the command:

```
R12(config-router)#neighbor 10.3.1.1 local-as 300
R12(config-router)#neighbor 10.4.1.2 local-as 300
R12(config-router)#
%BGP-5-ADJCHANGE: neighbor 10.3.1.1 Up
R12(config-router)#
%BGP-5-ADJCHANGE: neighbor 10.4.1.2 Up
R12(config-router)#
```

The local-as command is most often used during migrations between ASNs (such as if a company is taken over by another company with an existing ASN, and the new owners want to keep their usual ASN).

If we have a look at the routing table of R10, we can see that this has had a somewhat strange effect:

```
R10#sh ip bgp
BGP table version is 65, local router ID is 10.10.10.10
Status codes: s suppressed, d damped, h history, * valid, > best, i -
internal,
              r RIB-failure, S Stale
Origin codes: i - IGP, e - EGP, ? - incomplete

   Network          Next Hop   Metric LocPrf Weight Path
*> 1.1.1.0/24       10.6.1.1                      0 400 200 105 i
*                   10.4.1.1                      0 300 65500 300 200 105 i
*> 1.2.1.0/24       10.6.1.1                      0 400 200 105 i
*                   10.4.1.1                      0 300 65500 300 200 105 i
*> 10.1.0.0/24      10.6.1.1                      0 400 200 105 i
*                   10.4.1.1                      0 300 65500 300 200 105 i
*> 10.1.1.0/24      10.6.1.1                      0 400 200 105 i
*                   10.4.1.1                      0 300 65500 300 200 105 i
```

Some of the routes are now much longer than before, as they appear to go into AS 300, then into AS 65500, and back into AS 300, before traversing the rest of the network. Taking 1.2.1.0/24 as an example we can actually take the longer route to this IP if we want to:

```
R10#ping 10.2.1.2 so s0/0
```

```
Type escape sequence to abort.
Sending 5, 100-byte ICMP Echos to 10.2.1.2:
Packet sent with a source address of 10.4.1.2
!!!!!
Success rate is 100 percent (5/5)
R10#
```

Therefore, we know that the route (despite looking a little odd) is actually very valid. Another way we can have routes that look like they shouldn't be in any valid routing table, would be to allow routes into our BGP table that actually contain our own AS number, which we will cover during the next chapter.

7. Communities and AS numbers

In this chapter we will look at BGP Communities, and how they will help us, as we get deeper into the mechanics of BGP and how we tune our topology to make the data flow in the ways we want it to. We will also look at how we can get our own AS number into our BGP table, or remove a private AS number from a BGP table.

7.1 Communities

BGP Community values are a BGP attribute, used mainly in the BGP decision process (see chapter 11). They do not directly influence the behavior of BGP, but are used to tag routes for later on.

We will head back to R4 for this first example, setting a community value of 200:300 on the 172.16.2.0/24 network. We already have a route-map to start off with, which we set up in the previous chapter:

```
R4(config)#route-map SET-NEXT-HOP
R4(config-route-map)#set ip next-hop peer-address
R4(config-route-map)#exit
```

This route-map has a single clause, and will match all traffic. We need to modify this to match our route, set the community value, and then for all routes, set the next-hop, in the same way as we have done already.

We start by matching our network with an access-list, and then set the community values. We also need a second clause to catch all traffic not matched by the first clause. The easiest way is to remove our route-map and start afresh:

```
R4(config)#access-list 101 permit ip 172.16.2.0 0.255.255.255 any
R4(config)#no route-map SET-NEXT-HOP
R4(config)#route-map SET-NEXT-HOP permit 10
R4(config-route-map)#match ip address 101
R4(config-route-map)#set community 200:300
R4(config-route-map)#set ip next-hop peer-address
R4(config-route-map)#exit
R4(config)#route-map SET-NEXT-HOP permit 20
R4(config-route-map)#set ip next-hop peer-address
R4(config-route-map)#exit
R4(config)#exit
R4#
```

So why does our route-map look like this? Well, with just the one clause, any traffic that did not match access-list 101 would be unchanged. So we need sequence 20 to catch the rest of the routes, and to set the next-hop address. If we omitted the setting of the next hop in sequence 10, then the route we wish to set the community on would be passed with the next hop unchanged - usually (and in this example) that's absolutely fine when tagging routes, but if this were a route that did not originate on R4 and we still wished to tag it using a community, then if we left this out the route would be passed with the incorrect next hop address.

In order for R2 and R5 to see the community value we have passed along with the route, we need to ensure that we are actually sending out this information. To do this we need to specify that we are going to send our community values to a neighbor (as we can be selective as to which neighbors we send our community values to), and this is done using the command "neighbor <neighbor ip address> send-community". On R4 we can do this as part of the peer group template:

```
R4(config-router)#neighbor AS200-PEERGROUP send-community
```

Finally, we attach our route-map in the appropriate direction to our neighbor (which we have already done in 6.4). Once we have these four things in place (the access-list, route-map, the send-community neighbor command, and the route-map attached to a neighbor), we can clear our bgp connection using the command "clear ip bgp <neighbor ip address> ", and then check out the route on one of our neighbors:

```
R5#sh ip bgp 172.16.1.0
BGP routing table entry for 172.16.1.0/24, version 123
Paths: (1 available, best #1, table Default-IP-Routing-Table, RIB-
failure(17))
Flag: 0x820
  Not advertised to any peer
  Local
    172.16.1.1 from 172.16.1.1 (4.4.4.4)
      Origin IGP, metric 0, localpref 100, valid, internal, best
R5#sh ip bgp 172.16.2.0
BGP routing table entry for 172.16.2.0/24, version 118
Paths: (1 available, best #1, table Default-IP-Routing-Table)
Flag: 0x820
  Not advertised to any peer
  Local
    172.16.1.1 from 172.16.1.1 (4.4.4.4)
      Origin IGP, metric 0, localpref 100, valid, internal, best
      Community: 13107500
R5#
```

So we can see that our access-list has worked as expected; only tagging the 172.16.2.0/24 route and not the 172.16.1.0 route. We can also see that the community value has been changed to the 32-bit version of 13107500, which is the default from IOS 12.0 onwards. We can switch the view, to show us the community value setting of 200:300, which is referred to as the AA:NN or new-format version, using the command:

```
R4(config)#ip bgp-community new-format
```

The first part of AA:NN represents the AS number (the convention is to use your own AS number), and the second part represents a 2-byte number (again the convention is to use the AS of the AS you are passing the route to). They both mean the same thing, so we can pass the decimal version, and then using a community-list acl on the AA:NN version. Communities can be in the range 1:0 to 65534:65535.

Let's walk through another example, this time setting a community on R1, and get R5 to make a decision based on that value.

```
R1#conf t
R1(config)#route-map SET-COMMUNITY permit 10
R1(config-route-map)#match ip address 101
R1(config-route-map)#set community 100:300
R1(config-route-map)#exit
R1(config)#route-map SET-COMMUNITY permit 20
R1(config-route-map)#exit
R1(config)#access-list 101 permit ip 10.1.0.0 0.0.0.255 any
R1(config)#router bgp 100
R1(config-router)#neighbor 10.1.1.2 send-community
R1(config-router)#neighbor 10.1.1.2 route-map SET-COMMUNITY out
R1(config-router)#
```

We can, after clearing the bgp peering, now see that this value is passed to R2:

```
R2#sh ip bgp 10.1.0.0/24
BGP routing table entry for 10.1.0.0/24, version 31
Paths: (1 available, best #1, table Default-IP-Routing-Table)
  Advertised to update-groups:
     1
  105, (received & used)
    10.1.1.1 from 10.1.1.1 (1.1.1.1)
      Origin IGP, metric 0, localpref 100, valid, external, best
R2#clear ip bgp 10.1.1.1
R2#
%BGP-5-ADJCHANGE: neighbor 10.1.1.1 Down User reset
R2#
```

```
%BGP-5-ADJCHANGE: neighbor 10.1.1.1 Up
R2#sh ip bgp 10.1.0.0/24
BGP routing table entry for 10.1.0.0/24, version 164
Paths: (1 available, best #1, table Default-IP-Routing-Table)
Flag: 0x820
  Advertised to update-groups:
    1
  105, (received & used)
    10.1.1.1 from 10.1.1.1 (1.1.1.1)
      Origin IGP, metric 0, localpref 100, valid, external, best
      Community: 6553900
R2#
```

On R2 and R3, we must instruct them to send the community values across to their neighbors as well:

```
R2(config)#router bgp 200
R2(config-router)#neighbor 172.17.1.1 send-community

R3(config)#router bgp 200
R3(config-router)#neighbor AS200-PEERGROUP send-community
```

We need to clear the peering and let it reestablish for the community value to be passed:

```
R3#sh ip bgp 10.1.0.0/24
BGP routing table entry for 10.1.0.0/24, version 57
Paths: (1 available, best #1, table Default-IP-Routing-Table)
Flag: 0x820
  Advertised to update-groups:
    1
  105, (Received from a RR-client), (received & used)
    172.17.0.1 from 172.17.0.1 (2.2.2.2)
      Origin IGP, metric 0, localpref 100, valid, internal, best
R3#clear ip bgp 172.17.0.1
R3#
%BGP-5-ADJCHANGE: neighbor 172.17.0.1 Down User reset
R3#
%BGP-5-ADJCHANGE: neighbor 172.17.0.1 Up
R3#sh ip bgp 10.1.0.0/24
BGP routing table entry for 10.1.0.0/24, version 83
Paths: (1 available, best #1, table Default-IP-Routing-Table)
Flag: 0x820
  Advertised to update-groups:
    1
  105, (Received from a RR-client), (received & used)
    172.17.0.1 from 172.17.0.1 (2.2.2.2)
      Origin IGP, metric 0, localpref 100, valid, internal, best
```

```
            Community: 6553900
    R3#clear ip bgp 172.17.5.1

    R5#sh ip bgp 10.1.0.0/24
    BGP routing table entry for 10.1.0.0/24, version 170
    Paths: (2 available, best #2, table Default-IP-Routing-Table)
      Advertised to update-groups:
          2
      105
        172.17.1.1 from 172.17.1.1 (3.3.3.3)
          Origin IGP, metric 0, localpref 100, valid, internal
          Community: 6553900
          Originator: 2.2.2.2, Cluster list: 3.3.3.3
      105
        172.16.1.1 from 172.16.1.1 (4.4.4.4)
          Origin IGP, metric 0, localpref 100, valid, internal, best
          Originator: 2.2.2.2, Cluster list: 4.4.4.4
    R5#
```

We can see that R5 is receiving the route twice, because it is dual homed, from R3 and from R4. R4's route is chosen, most likely due to the higher router ID. Now, on R5, we will change the local preference for the tagged route to be 150 (therefore preferred). In order to do this we need to first match the community value that we receive from R3, and then set our local preference accordingly. We match the community with a community-list, which works similarly to an ip access-list:

```
    R5#conf t
    R5(config)#ip community-list 1 permit 100:300
    R5(config)#route-map R3-PEER permit 10
    R5(config-route-map)#match community 1
    R5(config-route-map)#set local-preference 150
    R5(config-route-map)#exit
    R5(config)#route-map R3-PEER permit 20
    R5(config-route-map)#exit
    R5(config)#router bgp 200
    R5(config-router)#neighbor 172.17.1.1 route-map R3-PEER in
    R5(config-router)#exit
    R5(config)#exit
    R5#
```

With our community tweaking in place we get the following:

```
    R5#sh ip bgp 10.1.0.0/24
    BGP routing table entry for 10.1.0.0/24, version 2
    Paths: (2 available, best #2, table Default-IP-Routing-Table)
    Flag: 0x820
```

```
      Advertised to update-groups:
         2
      105
        172.16.1.1 from 172.16.1.1 (4.4.4.4)
          Origin IGP, metric 0, localpref 100, valid, internal
          Originator: 2.2.2.2, Cluster list: 4.4.4.4
      105
        172.17.1.1 from 172.17.1.1 (3.3.3.3)
          Origin IGP, metric 0, localpref 150, valid, internal, best
          Community: 6553900
          Originator: 2.2.2.2, Cluster list: 3.3.3.3
    R5#
```

R5 now prefers the route with the lower router-id source, but with the higher local preference, due to the way we handled the incoming community tag value.

We can do so much more with communities, such as using the "no-export" option to prevent a route being propagated outside of our own AS, or even to ensure that it is not advertised as all using the "no advertise" option.

We shall try both variations of this using R13, which is a good example, as this will also show the interaction of a confederation on these commands. R13 is advertising all of its loopback interfaces, and these can be seen by R5 (for example)

```
R5#sh ip bgp | beg 172.21
*  i172.21.1.0/24     172.17.1.1           0    100      0 105 i
*>i                   172.16.1.1           0    100      0 105 i
*  i172.21.2.0/24     172.17.1.1           0    100      0 105 i
*>i                   172.16.1.1           0    100      0 105 i
*  i172.21.3.0/24     172.17.1.1           0    100      0 105 i
*>i                   172.16.1.1           0    100      0 105 i
*  i172.21.4.0/24     172.17.1.1           0    100      0 105 i
*>i                   172.16.1.1           0    100      0 105 i
```

We will set the 172.21.2.0/24 to not be exported; we start with a prefix-list and incorporate this into a route-map, then apply it to the neighbor 1.1.1.1:

```
R13#conf t
R13(config)#ip prefix-list 172-21-2-Network seq 5 permit 172.21.2.0/24
R13(config)#route-map 172-21-2-NoExport permit 10
R13(config-route-map)#match ip address prefix-list 172-21-2-Network
R13(config-route-map)#set community no-export
R13(config-route-map)#exit
R13(config)#route-map 172-21-2-NoExport permit 20
```

```
R13(config-route-map)#exit
R13(config)#router bgp 101
R13(config-router)#neighbor 1.1.1.1 send-community
R13(config-router)#neighbor 1.1.1.1 route-map 172-21-2-NoExport out
R13(config-router)#do clear ip bgp *
R13(config-router)#
%BGP-5-ADJCHANGE: neighbor 1.1.1.1 Down User reset
%BGP-5-ADJCHANGE: neighbor 1.1.1.1 Up
R13(config-router)#
```

We can see that R1 still sees the route in its table, and that the community is set to no-export:

```
R1#sh ip bgp | i 172.21
*> 172.21.1.0/24    1.1.1.2              0    100       0 (101) i
*> 172.21.2.0/24    1.1.1.2              0    100       0 (101) i
*> 172.21.3.0/24    1.1.1.2              0    100       0 (101) i
*> 172.21.4.0/24    1.1.1.2              0    100       0 (101) i
R1#sh ip bgp 172.21.2.0
BGP routing table entry for 172.21.2.0/24, version 337
Paths: (1 available, best #1, table Default-IP-Routing-Table, not
advertised to EBGP peer)
Flag: 0x820
  Not advertised to any peer
  (101)
    1.1.1.2 from 1.1.1.2 (13.13.13.13)
      Origin IGP, metric 0, localpref 100, valid, confed-external,
best
      Community: no-export
R1#
```

But R5 cannot:

```
R5#sh ip bgp | beg 172.21
*  i172.21.1.0/24   172.17.1.1           0    100       0 105 i
*>i                 172.16.1.1           0    100       0 105 i
*  i172.21.3.0/24   172.17.1.1           0    100       0 105 i
*>i                 172.16.1.1           0    100       0 105 i
*  i172.21.4.0/24   172.17.1.1           0    100       0 105 i
*>i                 172.16.1.1           0    100       0 105 i
```

Therefore, R1 understands not to export the prefix to an eBGP peer, and just to be sure that it's definitely R1 that's not exporting it, let's look at R2, which should not be able to see the 172.21.2.0/24 network:

```
R2#sh ip bgp | beg 172.21
```

```
*> 172.21.1.0/24      10.1.1.1                        0 105 i
*> 172.21.3.0/24      10.1.1.1                        0 105 i
*> 172.21.4.0/24      10.1.1.1                        0 105 i
*> 172.22.1.0/24      10.1.1.1                        0 105 i
*> 172.22.2.0/24      10.1.1.1                        0 105 i
```

The no-advertise keyword works in a similar fashion, but is broader in scope. We need to amend our route-map now, and we will use the next loopback network on R13 as the example, starting with a new prefix-list:

```
R13#conf t
R13(config)#ip prefix-list 172-21-3-Network seq 5 permit 172.21.3.0/24
R13(config)#route-map 172-21-2-NoExport permit 20
R13(config-route-map)#match ip address prefix-list 172-21-3-Network
R13(config-route-map)#set community no-advertise
R13(config-route-map)#exit
R13(config)#route-map 172-21-2-NoExport permit 30
R13(config-route-map)#exit
R13(config)#exit
R13#
```

After an "ip bgp clear" R1 can still see the network, as we would expect.

```
R1#sh ip bgp | beg 172.21
*> 172.21.1.0/24      1.1.1.2          0     100       0 (101) i
*> 172.21.2.0/24      1.1.1.2          0     100       0 (101) i
*> 172.21.3.0/24      1.1.1.2          0     100       0 (101) i
*> 172.21.4.0/24      1.1.1.2          0     100       0 (101) i
*> 172.22.1.0/24      1.2.1.2          0     100       0 (102) i
*> 172.22.2.0/24      1.2.1.2          0     100       0 (102) i
*> 172.22.3.0/24      1.2.1.2          0     100       0 (102) i
*> 172.22.4.0/24      1.2.1.2          0     100       0 (102) i
*> 172.26.1.0/24      10.1.1.2                         0 200 400 i
*> 172.26.2.0/24      10.1.1.2                         0 200 400 i
*> 172.26.3.0/24      10.1.1.2                         0 200 400 i
R1#sh ip bgp 172.21.3.0
BGP routing table entry for 172.21.3.0/24, version 31
Paths: (1 available, best #1, table Default-IP-Routing-Table, not advertised to any peer)
Flag: 0x820
  Not advertised to any peer
  (101)
    1.1.1.2 from 1.1.1.2 (13.13.13.13)
      Origin IGP, metric 0, localpref 100, valid, confed-external, best
```

          Community: no-advertise
    R1#

Again R5 is now unaware of the network (as is R2 by the way)

```
R5#sh ip bgp | beg 172.21
*  i172.21.1.0/24    172.17.1.1       0    100      0 105 i
*>i                  172.16.1.1       0    100      0 105 i
*  i172.21.4.0/24    172.17.1.1       0    100      0 105 i
*>i                  172.16.1.1       0    100      0 105 i
*  i172.22.1.0/24    172.17.1.1       0    100      0 105 i
*>i                  172.16.1.1       0    100      0 105 i
```

So, from this standpoint, there would not appear to be any difference between no-export and no-advertise. To fully understand the difference between the two we must turn our attention to R14:

```
R14#sh ip bgp | beg 172.21
*> 172.21.1.0/24     1.2.1.1          0    100      0 (100 101) i
*> 172.21.2.0/24     1.2.1.1          0    100      0 (100 101) i
*> 172.21.4.0/24     1.2.1.1          0    100      0 (100 101) i
```

We can see that R1 has advertised the 172.21.2.0/24 network to R14, even though it is outside of its own AS, therefore technically an eBGP peer. Because both are within the same community it is advertised (exported), but R1 has not advertised the 172.21.3.0/24 network.

The complete prefix-list and route-map config on R13 looks like this:

```
ip prefix-list 172-21-2-Network seq 5 permit 172.21.2.0/24
!
ip prefix-list 172-21-3-Network seq 5 permit 172.21.3.0/24
!
route-map 172-21-2-NoExport permit 10
 match ip address prefix-list 172-21-2-Network
 set community no-export
!
route-map 172-21-2-NoExport permit 20
 match ip address prefix-list 172-21-3-Network
 set community no-advertise
!
route-map 172-21-2-NoExport permit 30
```

Hopefully, you should start being able to see how powerful communities are, but we are not finished with them yet. We can also change the community, by adding our own values as the route passes through us, using the additive command. At the moment the community setting on R1 is retained as it gets to R3:

```
R3#sh ip bgp 10.1.0.0/24
BGP routing table entry for 10.1.0.0/24, version 697
Paths: (1 available, best #1, table Default-IP-Routing-Table)
  Advertised to update-groups:
     1
  105, (Received from a RR-client), (received & used)
    172.17.0.1 from 172.17.0.1 (2.2.2.2)
      Origin IGP, metric 0, localpref 100, valid, internal, best
      Community: 6553900
```

We can change this on R2 using a route-map to match a community list:

```
R2#conf t
R2(config)#ip community-list 1 permit 6553900
R2(config)#route-map 10-1-0-0CommunityAdd100 permit 10
R2(config-route-map)#match community 1
R2(config-route-map)#set community 100:100 additive
R2(config-route-map)#exit
R2(config)#route-map 10-1-0-0CommunityAdd100 permit 20
R2(config-route-map)#exit
R2(config)#router bgp 200
R2(config-router)#neigh 172.17.1.1 route-map 10-1-0-0CommunityAdd100 out
R2(config-router)#
```

Interestingly, if we look at the output of the show run, we can see that the IOS has converted our number into the other format:

```
route-map 10-1-0-0CommunityAdd100 permit 10
 match community 1
 set community 6553700 additive
!
route-map 10-1-0-0CommunityAdd100 permit 20
```

So, how does R3 now see this route?

```
R3#sh ip bgp 10.1.0.0/24
BGP routing table entry for 10.1.0.0/24, version 698
Paths: (1 available, best #1, table Default-IP-Routing-Table)
Flag: 0x880
  Advertised to update-groups:
     1
  105, (Received from a RR-client), (received & used)
```

```
        172.17.0.1 from 172.17.0.1 (2.2.2.2)
          Origin IGP, metric 0, localpref 100, valid, internal, best
          Community: 6553700 6553900
    R3#
```

R3 sees it with both the original and the new community values. We can also see that this is still passed to R5:

```
    R5#sh ip bgp 10.1.0.0/24
    BGP routing table entry for 10.1.0.0/24, version 427
    Paths: (2 available, best #1, table Default-IP-Routing-Table)
    Flag: 0x880
      Advertised to update-groups:
          2
      105
        172.17.1.1 from 172.17.1.1 (3.3.3.3)
          Origin IGP, metric 0, localpref 150, valid, internal, best
          Community: 6553700 6553900
          Originator: 2.2.2.2, Cluster list: 3.3.3.3
      105
        172.16.1.1 from 172.16.1.1 (4.4.4.4)
          Origin IGP, metric 0, localpref 100, valid, internal
          Originator: 2.2.2.2, Cluster list: 4.4.4.4
    R5#
```

Our setting of the local-preference to 150 is retained, despite the change in the community list. If we omitted the "additive" keyword on R2, then it would overwrite any existing community value, so if the route-map looked like this:

```
    route-map 10-1-0-0CommunityAdd100 permit 10
     match community 1
     set community 6553700
    !
    route-map 10-1-0-0CommunityAdd100 permit 20
```

The route would look like this:

```
    R3#sh ip bgp 10.1.0.0/24
    BGP routing table entry for 10.1.0.0/24, version 741
    Paths: (1 available, best #1, table Default-IP-Routing-Table)
    Flag: 0x820
      Advertised to update-groups:
          1
      105, (Received from a RR-client), (received & used)
        172.17.0.1 from 172.17.0.1 (2.2.2.2)
          Origin IGP, metric 0, localpref 100, valid, internal, best
```

```
        Community: 6553700
R3#
```

R5 also, no longer applies the higher preference to the route coming into it:

```
R5#sh ip bgp 10.1.0.0/24
BGP routing table entry for 10.1.0.0/24, version 474
Paths: (2 available, best #2, table Default-IP-Routing-Table)
Flag: 0x820
  Not advertised to any peer
  105
    172.17.1.1 from 172.17.1.1 (3.3.3.3)
      Origin IGP, metric 0, localpref 100, valid, internal
      Community: 6553700
      Originator: 2.2.2.2, Cluster list: 3.3.3.3
  105
    172.16.1.1 from 172.16.1.1 (4.4.4.4)
      Origin IGP, metric 0, localpref 100, valid, internal, best
      Originator: 2.2.2.2, Cluster list: 4.4.4.4
R5#
```

For now, though, we will add back the additive keyword, and move on to extended communities.

7.2 Extended Communities

In 2006, the 8-octet Extended Community attribute was added under RFC 4360. It brought with it a type field (either one or two octets), and the remaining octets are used for the content. The remaining octets are used by MPLS (the Route Target Community and Route Origin Community) and in QoS. Extended communities will be covered in greater depth in the MPLS volume in this series.

7.3 allowas-in

The nature of BGP is to drop any route advertised to us that includes our own AS. There may, however, be times when we want to see routes with our own AS path included in them, and to do this we use the "allowas-in" command.

If we apply this to R10's connection to R6, we can see some changes in the RIB (the sh ip bgp output has been truncated to show just the affected routes):

```
R10#sh ip bgp | beg 172.19
*> 172.19.1.0/24   0.0.0.0      0     32768 i
```

```
*> 172.19.2.0/24    0.0.0.0         0           32768 i
*> 172.19.3.0/24    0.0.0.0         0           32768 i
*> 172.19.4.0/24    0.0.0.0         0           32768 i
*  172.20.1.0/24    10.4.1.1                    0 300 65500 300 200 400 11000 i
*>                  10.6.1.1                    0 400 11000 i
*  172.20.2.0/24    10.4.1.1                    0 300 65500 300 200 400 11000 i
*>                  10.6.1.1                    0 400 11000 i
```

We then change the neighbor to allow routes containing our own AS number to be installed into out BGP table:

```
R10#conf t
R10(config)#router bgp 500
R10(config-router)#neighbor 10.6.1.1 allowas-in
R10(config-router)#exit
R10(config)#exit
```

And now, we can see the effect that this has:

```
R10#sh ip bgp | beg 172.19
*  172.19.1.0/24    10.6.1.1                    0 400 500 i
*>                  0.0.0.0         0           32768 i
*  172.19.2.0/24    10.6.1.1                    0 400 500 i
*>                  0.0.0.0         0           32768 i
*  172.19.3.0/24    10.6.1.1                    0 400 500 i
*>                  0.0.0.0         0           32768 i
*  172.19.4.0/24    10.6.1.1                    0 400 500 i
*>                  0.0.0.0         0           32768 i
*  172.20.1.0/24    10.4.1.1                    0 300 65500 300 200 400 11000 i
*>                  10.6.1.1                    0 400 11000 i
*  172.20.2.0/24    10.4.1.1                    0 300 65500 300 200 400 11000 i
*>                  10.6.1.1                    0 400 11000 i
```

It is rare that we will want to accept routes with our own AS in it. There are times, however, that we will want to remove AS numbers from an AS Path.

7.4 remove-private-as

When we configured R12 in section 6.8, we set it up to use a private-as number, these are not routable over the Internet, and so have little bearing to us. Private AS numbers can be removed using the remove-private-as command, however until IOS XE 3.1S there were some pretty big restrictions on how this worked:

- If the AS path included both private and public AS numbers, using the neighbor remove-private-as command would not remove the private AS numbers.
- If the AS path contained confederation segments, using the neighbor remove-private-as command would remove private AS numbers only if the private AS numbers followed the confederation portion of the autonomous path.
- If the AS path contained the AS number of the eBGP neighbor, the private AS numbers would not be removed.

As R12 includes both private and public AS numbers we can see that adding the remove-private-as command actually has no effect. Therefore we will step away from the topology to set up a quick example of this in action:

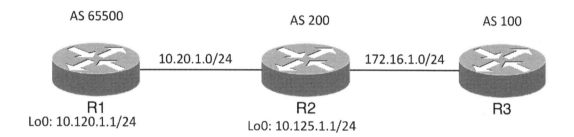

The configurations are as follows:

R1:

```
interface Loopback0
 ip address 10.120.1.1 255.255.255.0
!
interface FastEthernet0/0
 ip address 10.20.1.1 255.255.255.0
 duplex auto
 speed auto
!
router bgp 65500
 bgp router-id 1.1.1.1
 bgp log-neighbor-changes
 network 10.120.1.0 mask 255.255.255.0
 neighbor 10.20.1.2 remote-as 200
```

R2:

```
interface Loopback0
 ip address 10.125.1.1 255.255.255.0
```

```
!
interface FastEthernet0/0
 ip address 10.20.1.2 255.255.255.0
 duplex auto
 speed auto
!
interface FastEthernet0/1
 ip address 172.16.1.1 255.255.255.0
 duplex auto
 speed auto
!
router bgp 200
 bgp log-neighbor-changes
 network 10.125.1.0 mask 255.255.255.0
 neighbor 10.20.1.1 remote-as 65500
 neighbor 172.16.1.2 remote-as 100
```

R3:

```
interface FastEthernet0/1
 ip address 172.16.1.2 255.255.255.0
 duplex auto
 speed auto
!
router bgp 100
 bgp log-neighbor-changes
 network 172.16.1.0 mask 255.255.255.0
 neighbor 172.16.1.1 remote-as 200
```

R3's BGP table looks like this:

```
R3#sh ip bgp | beg Network
   Network          Next Hop         Metric LocPrf Weight Path
*> 10.120.1.0/24    172.16.1.1                         0 200 65500 i
*> 10.125.1.0/24    172.16.1.1            0            0 200 i
R3#
```

As you can see within this small topology, the private AS of R1 is being passed within the AS_PATH attribute. Now let's see what happens when we instruct R2 not to advertise the private AS of R1 to R3:

```
R2(config)#router bgp 200
R2(config-router)#neighbor 172.16.1.2 remove-private-as

R3#sh ip bgp | beg Network
   Network          Next Hop         Metric LocPrf Weight Path
```

```
*> 10.120.1.0/24      172.16.1.1                          0 200 i
*> 10.125.1.0/24      172.16.1.1              0           0 200 i
```

We can see that R2 has passed the route through to R3, but not the private ASN, but is it still reachable?

```
R3#ping 10.120.1.1
Type escape sequence to abort.
Sending 5, 100-byte ICMP Echos to 10.120.1.1:
!!!!!
Success rate is 100 percent (5/5)
R3#
```

Yes, it is still reachable. This method is implemented by a number of ISPs, especially where a customer cannot get a public AS from their local RIR, or may not want to pay for one. The customer can still get a BGP presence on the internet, they just need to peer to the ISP as per normal, and point their routers to the ISP for internet access, generally as a static route, setting the ISP as the next-hop. This brings us to move on to the next chapter; Advanced BGP Routing, where we will look at, amongst other topics, default and static routes, and we will look at the summarization and filtering of routes. Before we move on, though, we will have a quick look at the 4-byte AS numbers.

7.5 4-Byte AS numbers

I am using the older version AS numbers, but to use the new version is just as simple. Stepping away from our main topology for a moment we will connect two routers and use the new format AS numbering system.

We can set an AS of 250.300 using the commands:

```
R1(config)#router bgp 250.300
R1(config-router)#bgp router-id 1.1.1.1
```

When we look at the configuration we will see that this has been changed to the following:

```
R1(config-router)#do sh run | section bgp
router bgp 16384300
 bgp router-id 1.1.1.1
 bgp log-neighbor-changes
R1(config-router)#
```

We can connect to neighbors using the new format:

```
R1(config-router)#neigh 1.1.1.1 remote-as 250.350
```

But they are also changed in the configuration:

```
R1(config-router)#do sh run | section bgp
router bgp 16384300
 bgp router-id 1.1.1.1
 bgp log-neighbor-changes
 neighbor 1.1.1.1 remote-as 16384350
R1(config-router)#

R2(config-if)#router bgp 250.350
R2(config-router)#bgp router-id 2.2.2.2
R2(config-router)#neigh 1.1.1.2 remote-as 250.300
R2(config-router)#
%BGP-5-ADJCHANGE: neighbor 1.1.1.2 Up
R2(config-router)#
```

The default is for IOS to use ASPLAIN notation. We can change how IOS handles the newer version AS numbers, and instruct it to show us in the format we entered it (ASDOT):

```
R1(config-router)#bgp asnotation dot
R1(config-router)#do sh run | section bgp
router bgp 250.300
 bgp router-id 1.1.1.1
 bgp asnotation dot
 bgp log-neighbor-changes
 neighbor 1.1.1.1 remote-as 250.350
R1(config-router)#
```

8. Advanced BGP Routing

We are going to start addressing some more complex routing issues in this chapter; looking at how we can advertised a static, or default route into the network, how we can summarize, or even "unsummarize" network prefixes depending on requirements, how we can advertise some networks depending on who we receive other prefixes from, how to inject routes into the BGP table of other routers, and lastly how to filter out the routes that we don't want.

8.1 Default routes and static routes

So far, we have a very self-contained topology, with no routes out to the wider Internet. In order to simulate this default route, and the same can apply for static routes in general, we will create a static default route on R12 pointing to Null0. We don't actually need it to go anywhere, just prove that it is propagated to the other routers in our topology.

```
R12#conf t
R12(config)#ip route 0.0.0.0 0.0.0.0 null0
R12(config)#exit
R12#sh ip route | i 0.0.0.0
Gateway of last resort is 0.0.0.0 to network 0.0.0.0
     10.0.0.0/24 is subnetted, 10 subnets
S*   0.0.0.0/0 is directly connected, Null0
```

With our default route in place, we have a couple of options available as to how to advertise default and static routes to our peers, and have them propagate through the rest of our topology, some are better than others, and some are only partially suitable.

Our options are the redistribution of static routes, using the network command, and the "default-originate" command.

Static Redistribution

We can use the BGP command "redistribute static" to inject all of our static routes into the BGP table.

```
R12(config)#router bgp 65500
R12(config-router)#redistribute static
R12(config-router)#
```

But, if we look at R5's BGP table we can see that "redistribute static" does not work for default routes:

```
R5#sh ip bgp 0.0.0.0
% Network not in table
R5#
```

And, to prove that this is the case, let's set up another static route on R12, and check that it is redistributed to R5:

```
R12#conf t
R12(config)#ip route 172.18.3.0 255.255.255.0 Null0
R12(config)#exit

R5#sh ip bgp 172.18.3.0
BGP routing table entry for 172.18.3.0/24, version 51
Paths: (2 available, best #2, table Default-IP-Routing-Table)
Flag: 0x820
  Advertised to update-groups:
     1          2
  400 500 300 65500
    10.5.1.2 from 10.5.1.2 (6.6.6.6)
      Origin incomplete, localpref 100, valid, external
  300 65500
    10.3.1.2 from 10.3.1.2 (12.12.12.12)
      Origin incomplete, metric 0, localpref 100, valid, external, best
R5#
```

So that works for non-default static routes, but what about the default route?

The network command

We can advertise the default route as a network using the usual commands:

```
R12(config)#router bgp 65500
R12(config-router)#network 0.0.0.0
R12(config-router)#
```

Now, we can see that R5 has this new route:

```
R5#sh ip bgp 0.0.0.0
BGP routing table entry for 0.0.0.0/0, version 52
Paths: (1 available, best #1, table Default-IP-Routing-Table)
Flag: 0x820
```

```
    Advertised to update-groups:
       1          2
    300 65500
       10.3.1.2 from 10.3.1.2 (12.12.12.12)
         Origin IGP, metric 0, localpref 100, valid, external, best
R5#sh ip route | i 0.0.0.0
Gateway of last resort is 10.3.1.2 to network 0.0.0.0
     10.0.0.0/24 is subnetted, 11 subnets
B*   0.0.0.0/0 [20/0] via 10.3.1.2, 00:01:02
R5#
```

This works perfectly well, following all the rules and benefits of BGP. However, that is the same reason that we should not use this approach. Advertising 0.0.0.0 works fine in our topology but should not be done outside of a lab environment, for the obvious reason being, that you might end up advertising a default route back to your ISP. Instead we should be more selective than blindly advertising a default route out onto the Internet. We can do this by removing the network statement and instead use the neighbor command "default-originate".

Default Originate

The default-originate command advertises the default route on our router to the neighbors that we explicitly configure, in this example we will configure R12 to send the default route to R5:

```
R12(config)#router bgp 65500
R12(config-router)#no network 0.0.0.0
R12(config-router)#neigh 10.3.1.1 default-originate
R12(config-router)#
```

We can check R5 again, and confirm that it still has the route:

```
R5#sh ip bgp 0.0.0.0
BGP routing table entry for 0.0.0.0/0, version 55
Paths: (1 available, best #1, table Default-IP-Routing-Table)
Flag: 0x820
  Advertised to update-groups:
     1          2
  300 65500
     10.3.1.2 from 10.3.1.2 (12.12.12.12)
       Origin IGP, metric 0, localpref 100, valid, external, best
R5#sh ip route | i 0.0.0.0
Gateway of last resort is 10.3.1.2 to network 0.0.0.0
     10.0.0.0/24 is subnetted, 11 subnets
B*   0.0.0.0/0 [20/0] via 10.3.1.2, 00:00:42
```

R5#

Here we can see that unlike before, where R5 had two valid routes in its BGP table (one from R12 and one from R6), it now just has the one. This is because R12 has not advertised the network down to R10; therefore although both R10 and R6 will still learn of the default route (R6 learning from R5 and R10 in turn learning from R6), due to the loop-free nature of BGP this second route will not be advertised back to R5.

```
R6#sh ip bgp 0.0.0.0
BGP routing table entry for 0.0.0.0/0, version 44
Paths: (1 available, best #1, table default)
  Advertised to update-groups:
     1
  200 300 65500
    10.5.1.1 from 10.5.1.1 (5.5.5.5)
      Origin IGP, localpref 100, valid, external, best
R6#

R10#sh ip bgp 0.0.0.0
BGP routing table entry for 0.0.0.0/0, version 67
Paths: (1 available, best #1, table Default-IP-Routing-Table)
  Advertised to update-groups:
     1
  400 200 300 65500
    10.6.1.1 from 10.6.1.1 (6.6.6.6)
      Origin IGP, localpref 100, valid, external, best
R10#
```

We can, should we wish to, advertise the default route to R10, which makes sense; otherwise the "internet" traffic from R6 and R10 takes the less direct route via R5 to each R12:

```
R12(config-router)#neighbor 10.4.1.2 default-originate
```

Now, R6 should receive the route from both directions, and pick the best route:

```
R6#sh ip bgp 0.0.0.0
BGP routing table entry for 0.0.0.0/0, version 44
Paths: (2 available, best #2, table default)
  Advertised to update-groups:
     1
  500 300 65500
    10.6.1.2 from 10.6.1.2 (10.10.10.10)
      Origin IGP, localpref 100, valid, external
  200 300 65500
    10.5.1.1 from 10.5.1.1 (5.5.5.5)
```

```
                Origin IGP, localpref 100, valid, external, best
R6#
```

8.2 Route summarization and aggregation

Route summarization is used for a number of reasons, primarily though to reduce the size of BGP and routing tables. Summarization also allows us to be selective over what summarized routes are advertised to different peers. We will look at a couple of different summarization examples, to show where location can be an important factor in how we summarize.

We will start on the left hand-side of our topology, with the R14 router. We can see that it has had a few loopback interfaces added:

```
R14#sh ip int bri | i Loopback
Loopback0                  172.22.1.1      YES NVRAM  up        up
Loopback1                  172.22.2.1      YES manual up        up
Loopback2                  172.22.3.1      YES manual up        up
Loopback3                  172.22.4.1      YES manual up        up
R14#
```

These have been advertised into BGP:

```
R14#sh run | section bgp
router bgp 102
 no synchronization
 bgp router-id 14.14.14.14
 bgp log-neighbor-changes
 bgp confederation identifier 105
 bgp confederation peers 100
 network 1.2.1.0 mask 255.255.255.0
 network 172.22.1.0 mask 255.255.255.0
 network 172.22.2.0 mask 255.255.255.0
 network 172.22.3.0 mask 255.255.255.0
 network 172.22.4.0 mask 255.255.255.0
 neighbor 1.2.1.1 remote-as 100
 no auto-summary
R14#
```

R2 can see these routes in the manner that we would expect:

```
R2#sh ip bgp | i 172.22
*> 172.22.1.0/24     10.1.1.1                              0 105 i
*> 172.22.2.0/24     10.1.1.1                              0 105 i
```

```
*> 172.22.3.0/24    10.1.1.1                          0 105 i
*> 172.22.4.0/24    10.1.1.1                          0 105 i
R2#sh ip route | i 172.22
     172.22.0.0/24 is subnetted, 4 subnets
B       172.22.2.0 [20/0] via 10.1.1.1, 00:16:22
B       172.22.3.0 [20/0] via 10.1.1.1, 00:16:22
B       172.22.1.0 [20/0] via 10.1.1.1, 00:16:22
B       172.22.4.0 [20/0] via 10.1.1.1, 00:16:22
R2#
```

Now let's aggregate them. The closest subnet we can use is a /21, which gives us the range 172.22.0.1 through to 172.22.7.254. We can choose to send all the existing routes, along with a summary route, or just the summary route:

```
R14(config)#router bgp 102
R14(config-router)#aggregate-address 172.22.1.0 255.255.248.0
R14(config-router)#
```

```
R2#sh ip bgp | i 172.22
*> 172.22.0.0/21    10.1.1.1                          0 105 i
*> 172.22.1.0/24    10.1.1.1                          0 105 i
*> 172.22.2.0/24    10.1.1.1                          0 105 i
*> 172.22.3.0/24    10.1.1.1                          0 105 i
*> 172.22.4.0/24    10.1.1.1                          0 105 i
R2#
```

Without any additional keywords, the default nature will be to send all the component routes, and the summary routes to its peers, as we can see from R2's BGP table above. We can send just the summary route by adding the keyword "summary-only" to the command:

```
R14(config-router)#aggregate-address 172.22.1.0 255.255.248.0 summary-only
```

Now, if we look at R2's BGP table, we can see that we have been passed one route instead of the original four and the aggregate route:

```
R2#sh ip bgp | i 172.22
*> 172.22.0.0/21    10.1.1.1                          0 105 i
R2#sh ip route | i 172.22
     172.22.0.0/21 is subnetted, 1 subnets
B       172.22.0.0 [20/0] via 10.1.1.1, 00:04:09
R2#
```

Because of how the confederation of AS 105 works, we can see that nothing has changed. If, however, we apply the same logic to AS 500, and summarize the networks on their entry point into AS 200 (which is R5) then we can see the potential issues.

We have created the same number of loopback interfaces on R10, and again these are advertised into BGP:

```
R10#sh run | section bgp
router bgp 500
 no synchronization
 bgp router-id 10.10.10.10
 bgp log-neighbor-changes
 network 172.19.1.0 mask 255.255.255.0
 network 172.19.2.0 mask 255.255.255.0
 network 172.19.3.0 mask 255.255.255.0
 network 172.19.4.0 mask 255.255.255.0
 neighbor 10.4.1.1 remote-as 300
 neighbor 10.6.1.1 remote-as 400
 neighbor 10.6.1.1 allowas-in
 no auto-summary
R10#
```

R5 can see the loopback addresses:

```
R5#sh ip bgp | beg 172.19
*> 172.19.1.0/24    10.5.1.2                0 400 500 i
*                   10.3.1.2                0 300 65500 300 500 i
*> 172.19.2.0/24    10.5.1.2                0 400 500 i
*                   10.3.1.2                0 300 65500 300 500 i
*> 172.19.3.0/24    10.5.1.2                0 400 500 i
*                   10.3.1.2                0 300 65500 300 500 i
*> 172.19.4.0/24    10.5.1.2                0 400 500 i
*                   10.3.1.2                0 300 65500 300 500 i
```

As can R2:

```
R2#sh ip bgp | beg 172.19
*  i172.19.1.0/24   172.17.1.1      0   100   0 400 500 i
*>i                 172.16.1.1      0   100   0 400 500 i
*  i172.19.2.0/24   172.17.1.1      0   100   0 400 500 i
*>i                 172.16.1.1      0   100   0 400 500 i
*  i172.19.3.0/24   172.17.1.1      0   100   0 400 500 i
*>i                 172.16.1.1      0   100   0 400 500 i
*  i172.19.4.0/24   172.17.1.1      0   100   0 400 500 i
*>i                 172.16.1.1      0   100   0 400 500 i
```

Now let's summarize these routes on R5, using the same /21 subnet mask, and the same "summary-only" keyword.

```
R5(config-router)#aggregate-address 172.19.1.0 255.255.248.0 summary-only
```

Now if we look at R2 we can start to see an issue:

```
R2#sh ip bgp | beg 172.19
*>i172.19.0.0/21    172.16.1.1         0    100    0 i
* i                 172.17.1.1         0    100    0 i
```

The routes are showing as valid but we have lost the AS PATH. We can ensure that the summarizing router does not remove the AS_PATH, by adding the keyword "as-set".

8.3 as-set

We can make sure that when we aggregate a network during advertisement to other peers, that we retain the as-path information through the use of the "as-set" keyword:

```
R5(config-router)#aggregate-address 172.19.1.0 255.255.248.0 summary-only as-set
```

And now the AS PATH information is retained, and passed through the peer routers:

```
R2#sh ip bgp | beg 172.19
*>i172.19.0.0/21    172.16.1.1         0    100    0 400 500 i
* i                 172.17.1.1         0    100    0 400 500 i
```

Using the aggregate-address and the as-set keyword opens up more avenues in which we can fine-tune how, and what, we advertise to our peers. We can even aggregate a number of addresses, and then only advertise a subset of these using a suppress-map.

8.4 Suppress maps

As we have seen above, we can aggregate addresses and send a summary network in their place. We may find that there may be a requirement to send an aggregate route as well as a subset of the routes. We can advertise a subset of aggregated routes using a suppress map.

Once we have set up a very basic peering between R7 and R11 (which we will replace with something a bit more exciting later on), we can see that R7 is advertising all of its loopback addresses:

```
R7#sh ip bgp neigh 10.8.1.2 advertised-routes | i 0.0.0.0
*> 0.0.0.0          172.26.1.1                0 400 200 300 65500 i
*> 10.7.1.0/24      0.0.0.0         0         32768 i
*> 172.20.1.0/24    0.0.0.0         0         32768 i
*> 172.20.2.0/24    0.0.0.0         0         32768 i
*> 172.20.3.0/24    0.0.0.0         0         32768 i
*> 172.20.4.0/24    0.0.0.0         0         32768 i
```

Unsurprisingly, these are received as separate entries by R11:

```
R11#sh ip bgp | i 172.20
*> 172.20.1.0/24    10.8.1.1        0         0 11000 i
*> 172.20.2.0/24    10.8.1.1        0         0 11000 i
*> 172.20.3.0/24    10.8.1.1        0         0 11000 i
*> 172.20.4.0/24    10.8.1.1        0         0 11000 i
```

If we now summarize these routes:

```
R7#conf t
R7(config)#router bgp 11000
R7(config-router)#aggregate-address 172.20.0.0 255.255.248.0
```

Then R11 gets the individual routes as well as the summary:

```
R11#sh ip bgp | i 172.20
*> 172.20.0.0/21    10.8.1.1        0         0 11000 i
*> 172.20.1.0/24    10.8.1.1        0         0 11000 i
*> 172.20.2.0/24    10.8.1.1        0         0 11000 i
*> 172.20.3.0/24    10.8.1.1        0         0 11000 i
*> 172.20.4.0/24    10.8.1.1        0         0 11000 i
R11#
```

Now say, for instance, that we only wanted to send the summary and a subset of the component routes from R7, such as just the 172.20.2.0/24 and 172.20.3.0/24 networks. To do this we would use a suppress-map to suppress the 172.20.1.0/24 and 172.20.3.0/24 networks:

```
R7(config)#ip access-list standard Suppress-1-4
R7(config-std-nacl)#permit 172.20.1.0 0.0.0.255
R7(config-std-nacl)#permit 172.20.4.0 0.0.0.255
R7(config-std-nacl)#exit
```

```
R7(config)#route-map Suppress-Map
R7(config-route-map)#match ip address Suppress-1-4
R7(config-route-map)#exit
R7(config)#router bgp 11000
R7(config-router)#aggregate-address 172.20.0.0 255.255.248.0
suppress-map Suppress-Map
```

We can now see the effect on R11

```
R11#sh ip bgp | i 172.20
*> 172.20.0.0/21    10.8.1.1         0              0 11000 i
*> 172.20.2.0/24    10.8.1.1         0              0 11000 i
*> 172.20.3.0/24    10.8.1.1         0              0 11000 i
R11#
```

Now, we can see the routes that have not matched our ACL as well as the summary route are advertised to R11. This is not to say that the routes that have been suppressed are unavailable; they can be reached through the summary address:

```
R11#ping 172.20.1.1

Type escape sequence to abort.
Sending 5, 100-byte ICMP Echos to 172.20.1.1:
!!!!!
Success rate is 100 percent (5/5)
R11#
```

There may be a time when we want to be selective about our suppression, and allow some of our neighbors to see the suppressed routes, we can do this using an unsuppress map.

8.5 Unsuppress maps

If we look at R6, we can see that it has also inherited the suppress map from R7. Now we must assume that R6 requires the full routing table, and must therefore see the suppressed routes.

At the moment our BGP table looks like this:

```
R6#sh ip bgp | i 172.20
r> 10.7.1.0/24      172.20.1.1       0              0 11000 i
*> 172.20.0.0/21    172.20.1.1       0              0 11000 i
*> 172.20.2.0/24    172.20.1.1       0              0 11000 i
*> 172.20.3.0/24    172.20.1.1       0              0 11000 i
```

```
R6#
```

Now let's get those routes back into R6.

```
R7(config)#ip prefix-list ALLOW-ALL-TO-R6 seq 5 permit 0.0.0.0/0 le 32
R7(config)#route-map ALLOW-ALL-TO-R6 permit 10
R7(config-route-map)#match ip address prefix-list ALLOW-ALL-TO-R6
R7(config-route-map)#exit
R7(config)#router bgp 11000
R7(config-router)#neigh 172.26.1.1 unsuppress-map ALLOW-ALL-TO-R6
R7(config-router)#
```

Here, we are allowing every route. If we omitted the "le 32" we would just match the default route (if one were actually being sent from R7 to R6, which it is not in our topology), and now R6 has all the routes:

```
R6#sh ip bgp | i 172.20
 r> 10.7.1.0/24       172.20.1.1      0     0 11000 i
 *> 172.20.0.0/21     172.20.1.1      0     0 11000 i
 r> 172.20.1.0/24     172.20.1.1      0     0 11000 i
 *> 172.20.2.0/24     172.20.1.1      0     0 11000 i
 *> 172.20.3.0/24     172.20.1.1      0     0 11000 i
 *> 172.20.4.0/24     172.20.1.1      0     0 11000 i
R6#
```

If we look further up in the topology, then we can see that R6 is advertising both the summary and all the component routes:

```
R5#sh ip bgp | beg 172.20
 *> 172.20.0.0/21     10.5.1.2           0 400 11000 i
 *  172.20.1.0/24     10.3.1.2           0 300 65500 300 500 400 11000 i
 *>                   10.5.1.2           0 400 11000 i
 *  172.20.2.0/24     10.3.1.2           0 300 65500 300 500 400 11000 i
 *>                   10.5.1.2           0 400 11000 i
 *  172.20.3.0/24     10.3.1.2           0 300 65500 300 500 400 11000 i
 *>                   10.5.1.2           0 400 11000 i
 *  172.20.4.0/24     10.3.1.2           0 300 65500 300 500 400 11000 i
 *>                   10.5.1.2           0 400 11000 i
```

8.6 conditional advertisement

Conditional advertisement, as the name suggests, will advertise routes based on certain conditions. We can test this out on R6, and make the condition for the advertisement to be the advertisement of the 172.18.2.0/24 network, which will come from R10 and R5 (as R6 is multi-homed). If it is advertised by R10, then we will, in turn, advertise our loopback interface networks to R10 only, if not then we will advertise them to R5 instead.

The logic of conditional advertisement is to specify an advertise-map, which is the routes that we wish to advertise, and to specify a clause, which is either an exist-map or a non-exist-map, that we are dependent on. When we specify an exist-map, if the condition is met, and the advertise-map and the exist-map match, then the route will be advertised. If we use a non-exist-map then if no match is found then the route will be advertised.

```
neighbor 10.5.1.1 advertise-map 172-26-to-AS200 non-exist-map AS300-prefix
```

With the above command, we will advertise the routes matched in the route-map 172-26-to-AS200 only if the routes matched in route-map AS300-prefix are not in the BGP table. We start by confirming that we are actually getting the 172.18.2.0/24 network as expected:

```
R6#sh ip bgp 172.18.2.0
BGP routing table entry for 172.18.2.0/24, version 21
Paths: (2 available, best #2, table default)
  Advertised to update-groups:
     1
  500 300 65500
    10.6.1.2 from 10.6.1.2 (10.10.10.10)
      Origin IGP, localpref 100, valid, external
  200 300 65500
    10.5.1.1 from 10.5.1.1 (5.5.5.5)
      Origin IGP, localpref 100, valid, external, best
R6#
```

Next, we create an ip prefix-list to match the networks that we will be conditionally advertising, followed by a prefix-list to match the network that our conditional advertisement is reliant upon.

```
R6(config)#ip prefix-list lo-prefix seq 5 permit 172.26.1.0/24
R6(config)#ip prefix-list lo-prefix seq 10 permit 172.26.2.0/24
R6(config)#ip prefix-list lo-prefix seq 15 permit 172.26.3.0/24
R6(config)#ip prefix-list 172-18-2-prefix seq 5 permit 172.18.2.0/24
```

Then we will set up a community list in order to track where the route is coming from:

```
R6(config)#ip community-list 1 permit 300:500
```

Now, we can start building our route-maps, first matching the community and the required network

```
R6(config)#route-map AS300-prefix permit 10
R6(config-route-map)#match community 1
R6(config-route-map)#match ip address prefix-list 172-18-2-prefix
R6(config-route-map)#exit
```

Then we create another route-map to match the prefixes that we want to advertise out:

```
R6(config)#route-map 172-26-to-AS200 permit 10
R6(config-route-map)#match ip address prefix-list lo-prefix
R6(config-route-map)#exit
```

Next we set up a community tag:

```
R6(config)#route-map set_community permit 10
R6(config-route-map)#set community 300:500
R6(config-route-map)#exit
R6(config)#exit
```

Before we assign our route-maps, let's just check that R5 and R10 have the best information available:

```
R5#sh ip bgp | beg 172.26
*    172.26.1.0/24    10.3.1.2                   0 300 65500 300 500 400 i
*>                    10.5.1.2         0         0 400 i
*    172.26.2.0/24    10.3.1.2                   0 300 65500 300 500 400 i
*>                    10.5.1.2         0         0 400 i
*    172.26.3.0/24    10.3.1.2                   0 300 65500 300 500 400 i
*>                    10.5.1.2         0         0 400 i
R5#

R10#sh ip bgp | beg 172.26
*> 172.26.1.0/24      10.6.1.1         0         0 400 i
*> 172.26.2.0/24      10.6.1.1         0         0 400 i
*> 172.26.3.0/24      10.6.1.1         0         0 400 i
R10#
```

Looks good, so let's apply our route-maps:

```
R6(config)#router bgp 400
R6(config-router)#neighbor 10.6.1.2 route-map set_community in
R6(config-router)#neighbor 10.5.1.1 advertise-map 172-26-to-AS200 non-exist-map AS300-prefix
```

```
R6(config-router)#
```

So, here we are going to advertise our networks (within the 172-26-to-AS200 route-map) only if the routes within the non-exist-map (AS300-prefix) are not in our BGP table. As the route-map will not have the routes coming in from R5 tagged (therefore does not fulfil the requirements of the non-exist-map), then we will not advertise our networks to it.

Given a little time for peers to re-establish after doing a "clear ip bgp *", and for BGP to calculate the new best paths, we can see that our prefix tagging is working:

```
R6#sh ip bgp 172.18.2.0
BGP routing table entry for 172.18.2.0/24, version 23
Paths: (2 available, best #2, table default)
  Advertised to update-groups:
     4
  500 300 65500
    10.6.1.2 from 10.6.1.2 (10.10.10.10)
      Origin IGP, localpref 100, valid, external
      Community: 19661300
  200 300 65500
    10.5.1.1 from 10.5.1.1 (5.5.5.5)
      Origin IGP, localpref 100, valid, external, best
R6#
```

Now R10 should get the prefixes directly from R6

```
R10#sh ip bgp | beg 172.26
 *   172.26.1.0/24    10.4.1.1              0 300 65500 300 200 400 i
 *>                   10.6.1.1         0    0 400 i
 *   172.26.2.0/24    10.4.1.1              0 300 65500 300 200 400 i
 *>                   10.6.1.1         0    0 400 i
 *   172.26.3.0/24    10.4.1.1              0 300 65500 300 200 400 i
 *>                   10.6.1.1         0    0 400 i
R10#
```

And it does. R5 however should not be able to get the 172.26 networks from R6

```
R5#sh ip bgp | beg 172.26
 *> 172.26.1.0/24    10.3.1.2              0 300 65500 300 500 400 i
 *> 172.26.2.0/24    10.3.1.2              0 300 65500 300 500 400 i
 *> 172.26.3.0/24    10.3.1.2              0 300 65500 300 500 400 i
R5#
```

We can see that it doesn't, but it actually gets them via R12 and R10, and we can confirm what R6 is advertising to which router:

```
R6#sh ip bgp neigh 10.6.1.2 advertised-routes | i 172.26
*> 172.26.1.0/24     0.0.0.0                  0         32768 i
*> 172.26.2.0/24     0.0.0.0                  0         32768 i
*> 172.26.3.0/24     0.0.0.0                  0         32768 i
R6#sh ip bgp neigh 10.5.1.1 advertised-routes | i 172.26
R6#
```

This proves that as R6 is getting the 172.18.2.0/24 network from R10, then we are only advertising back to R10. To further prove this conditional advertisement in action we must now block R10 from advertising the 172.18.2.0/24 network to R6. This will therefore ensure that the non-exist-map conditions are not met in our BGP table, which should cause R6 to advertise the networks to R5. To do this we can use the "community no-export" concept that we visited earlier:

```
R12(config)#ip prefix-list 172-18-2-Network seq 5 permit 172.18.2.0/24
R12(config)#route-map 172-18-2-NoExport permit 10
R12(config-route-map)#match ip address prefix-list 172-18-2-Network
R12(config-route-map)#set community no-export
R12(config-route-map)#exit
R12(config)#route-map 172-18-2-NoExport permit 20
R12(config-route-map)#exit
R12(config)#router bgp 65500
R12(config-router)#neigh 10.4.1.2 route-map 172-18-2-NoExport out
R12(config-router)#neigh 10.4.1.2 send-community
R12(config-router)#exit
R12(config)#exit
R12#
R12#clear ip bgp 10.4.1.2
R12#
%BGP-5-ADJCHANGE: neighbor 10.4.1.2 Down User reset
R12#
%BGP-5-ADJCHANGE: neighbor 10.4.1.2 Up
R12#
```

We can now see the effect of this on R10:

```
R10#sh ip bgp 172.18.2.0
BGP routing table entry for 172.18.2.0/24, version 213
Paths: (2 available, best #1, table Default-IP-Routing-Table, not advertised to EBGP peer)
Flag: 0x820
  Advertised to update-groups:
     1
  300 65500
```

```
        10.4.1.1 from 10.4.1.1 (12.12.12.12)
          Origin IGP, metric 0, localpref 100, valid, external, best
          Community: no-export
    400 200 300 65500
        10.6.1.1 from 10.6.1.1 (6.6.6.6)
          Origin IGP, localpref 100, valid, external
R10#
```

On R6 we can check where we are getting the 172.18.2.0/24 network:

```
R6#sh ip bgp 172.18.2.0
BGP routing table entry for 172.18.2.0/24, version 23
Paths: (1 available, best #1, table default)
  Advertised to update-groups:
     4
  200 300 65500
    10.5.1.1 from 10.5.1.1 (5.5.5.5)
      Origin IGP, localpref 100, valid, external, best
R6#
```

Because we are only getting the route from R5, we should see what routes we are advertising to R5:

```
R6#sh ip bgp neigh 10.5.1.1 advertised-routes | i 172.26
*> 172.26.1.0/24    0.0.0.0              0         32768 i
*> 172.26.2.0/24    0.0.0.0              0         32768 i
*> 172.26.3.0/24    0.0.0.0              0         32768 i
R6#
```

Lastly, we can confirm on R5 that we can see the routes from both peers:

```
R5#sh ip bgp | beg 172.26
*> 172.26.1.0/24    10.5.1.2         0         0 400 i
*                   10.3.1.2                   0 300 65500 300 500 400 i
*> 172.26.2.0/24    10.5.1.2         0         0 400 i
*                   10.3.1.2                   0 300 65500 300 500 400 i
*> 172.26.3.0/24    10.5.1.2         0         0 400 i
*                   10.3.1.2                   0 300 65500 300 500 400 i
R5#
```

8.7 Route Injection

Earlier, on R5, we aggregated the loopback addresses of R10 into one summary address, so that instead of advertising the four separate /24 networks, we aggregated the addresses into one /21 network.

Route injection works in the opposite way, with slightly more commands required. It takes an aggregated address, and splits it into the underlying subnets according to a route-map and prefix-list, similar to an unsuppress-map and conditional advertisement.

For this example, we will take the aggregated address of R10's loopbacks, and configure our network so that when the routes get into AS 105, they have returned to their individual subnets. At the moment R1 is receiving the aggregate route from R2:

```
R2#sh ip bgp neigh 10.1.1.1 advertised-routes | i 172.19
*>i172.19.0.0/21    172.16.1.1    0    10    0 300 65500 300 500 i
R2#

R1#sh ip bgp | i 172.19
*>  172.19.0.0/21    10.1.1.2                 0 200 300 65500 300 500 i
R1#
```

There are a number of components to route injection. First we will create a prefix-list that will contain all of the routes we want to create (inject), we are using the original /24 routes, but we could as easily create two /25 networks, depending on the requirements:

```
R2(config)#ip prefix-list Advertise-19-2 seq 10 permit 172.19.1.0/24
R2(config)#ip prefix-list Advertise-19-2 seq 20 permit 172.19.2.0/24
R2(config)#ip prefix-list Advertise-19-2 seq 30 permit 172.19.3.0/24
R2(config)#ip prefix-list Advertise-19-2 seq 40 permit 172.19.4.0/24
```

We then create another prefix list with the aggregate route we want to "capture":

```
R2(config)#ip prefix-list Aggregate-19-2 seq 10 permit 172.19.0.0/21
```

Next, we can specify the source of the aggregate routes; in our case it is the R3 and R4 routers:

```
R2(config)#ip prefix-list Adv-Source-1 seq 10 permit 172.17.1.1/32
R2(config)#ip prefix-list Adv-Source-1 seq 20 permit 172.16.1.1/32
```

Now we can start creating our route-maps. The first one will be to create the networks for injection, based upon our first prefix-list:

```
R2(config)#route-map ADVERTISE-MAP-1
R2(config-route-map)#set ip address prefix-list Advertise-19-2
R2(config-route-map)#exit
```

The second route-map will match our aggregate address, and the sources we gained it from:

```
R2(config)#route-map EXIST-MAP-1
R2(config-route-map)#match ip address prefix-list Aggregate-19-2
R2(config-route-map)#match ip route-source prefix-list Adv-Source-1
```

Lastly, we create our inject-map, which says to inject the routes if the conditions of the exist-map are true:

```
R2(config-route-map)#router bgp 200
R2(config-router)#bgp inject-map ADVERTISE-MAP-1 exist-map EXIST-MAP-1
R2(config-router)#
```

Now R2 is passing the aggregate and the component routes, as specified in our IP prefix-list Advertise-19-2:

```
R2#sh ip bgp neigh 10.1.1.1 advertised-routes | i 172.19
*>i172.19.0.0/21    172.16.1.1            0    100       0 400 500 i
*>i172.19.1.0/24    172.17.1.1                           0 ?
*>i172.19.2.0/24    172.17.1.1                           0 ?
*>i172.19.3.0/24    172.17.1.1                           0 ?
*>i172.19.4.0/24    172.17.1.1                           0 ?
R2#
```

R1 is adding them to its BGP table.

```
R1#sh ip bgp | beg 172.19
*> 172.19.0.0/21    10.1.1.2                             0 200 400 500 i
*> 172.19.1.0/24    10.1.1.2                             0 200 ?
*> 172.19.2.0/24    10.1.1.2                             0 200 ?
*> 172.19.3.0/24    10.1.1.2                             0 200 ?
*> 172.19.4.0/24    10.1.1.2                             0 200 ?
*> 172.20.0.0/21    10.1.1.2                             0 200 400 11000 i
*> 172.20.1.0/24    10.1.1.2                             0 200 400 11000 i
*> 172.20.2.0/24    10.1.1.2                             0 200 400 11000 i
*> 172.20.3.0/24    10.1.1.2                             0 200 400 11000 i
*> 172.20.4.0/24    10.1.1.2                             0 200 400 11000 i
*> 172.21.1.0/24    1.1.1.2            0    100          0 (101) i
*> 172.21.2.0/24    1.1.1.2            0    100          0 (101) i
*> 172.21.3.0/24    1.1.1.2            0    100          0 (101) i
*> 172.21.4.0/24    1.1.1.2            0    100          0 (101) i
*> 172.22.0.0/21    1.2.1.2            0    100          0 (102) i
*> 172.26.1.0/24    10.1.1.2                             0 200 400 i
*> 172.26.2.0/24    10.1.1.2                             0 200 400 i
```

```
*> 172.26.3.0/24      10.1.1.2                         0 200 400 i
```

However, R1 is missing the full AS-Path though, which is visible on the aggregate. Nevertheless, the loopback IP addresses on R10 are still reachable:

```
R1#ping 172.19.1.1

Type escape sequence to abort.
Sending 5, 100-byte ICMP Echos to 172.19.1.1:
!!!!!
Success rate is 100 percent (5/5)
R1#
```

We can make our BGP table look better, and include complete the AS-Path by copying it from the aggregate route, using the copy-attributes keyword:

```
R2(config-router)#bgp inject-map ADVERTISE-MAP-1 exist-map EXIST-MAP-1 copy-attributes
```

Now R1 has the component routes, with their full AS-Path information:

```
R1#clear ip bgp 10.1.1.2
R1#
%BGP-5-ADJCHANGE: neighbor 10.1.1.2 Down User reset
%BGP-5-ADJCHANGE: neighbor 10.1.1.2 Up
R1#sh ip bgp | beg 172.19
*> 172.19.0.0/21     10.1.1.2                       0 200 400 500 i
*> 172.19.1.0/24     10.1.1.2                       0 200 400 500 i
*> 172.19.2.0/24     10.1.1.2                       0 200 400 500 i
*> 172.19.3.0/24     10.1.1.2                       0 200 400 500 i
*> 172.19.4.0/24     10.1.1.2                       0 200 400 500 i
```

We have now seen a number of ways to reduce, and expand, the BGP table according to our requirements. Sometimes, we will only need a couple of routes in the routing table from a neighbor, especially if we are multi-homed and want to only use one as a backup route. We cannot however change the networks a router is advertising, but we can tell it what networks we want it to send to us using outbound route filtering.

8.8 Outbound route filtering

Because of the layout of the routers at the bottom of the topology, it makes sense for R8 to try and simplify its BGP table. There is no real need (under optimal conditions and network stability), to be receiving routes for ASs that come into R7 from R6 through R9 when the more direct route straight to R7 exists. In the event that the link to R7 goes down then we would expect to still be able to reach everything though. At this stage a very basic eBGP connection has been created between R7, R11, R9 and R8. R9 is advertising its loopback interface and the networks of its serial interfaces.

We can implement Outbound Route Filtering (orf) to accomplish this, R8 can instruct R9 to send as many, or as few, routes as it dictates.

At the moment R8's BGP table looks a bit like this:

```
R8#sh ip bgp | beg Network
     Network        Next Hop    Wght Path
 *   0.0.0.0        10.10.1.2      0 13500 12000 11000 400 200 300 65500 i
 *>                 10.9.1.1       0 11000 400 200 300 65500 i
 *   1.1.1.0/24     10.10.1.2      0 13500 12000 11000 400 200 105 i
 *>                 10.9.1.1       0 11000 400 200 105 i
 *   1.2.1.0/24     10.10.1.2      0 13500 12000 11000 400 200 105 i
 *>                 10.9.1.1       0 11000 400 200 105 i
 *   10.1.0.0/24    10.10.1.2      0 13500 12000 11000 400 200 105 i
 *>                 10.9.1.1       0 11000 400 200 105 i
```

I have truncated the output, but I am sure that you get the picture. For a quick overview you can jump straight to the total number of advertised routes:

```
R9#sh ip bgp neigh 10.10.1.1 advertised-routes | i Total
Total number of prefixes 36
R9#
```

We start by instructing our routers to either send, or receive, an orf prefix-list. R8 will send, and R9 will receive, this list, using the neighbor command "capability orf prefix-list <action>", where action is either to send a prefix-list of the routes that you want, or to be able to receive a list of routes that you are being sent. There is a third option, which is "capability orf prefix-list both", which, as it might suggest, allows the sending and receiving of prefix-lists. Whichever option you choose, will trigger the dropping and reestablishment of a neighbor relationship.

```
R8#conf t
R8(config)#router bgp 11100
R8(config-router)#neighbor 10.10.1.2 capability orf prefix-list send
R8(config-router)#
%BGP-5-ADJCHANGE: neighbor 10.10.1.2 Down Capability changed
%BGP-5-ADJCHANGE: neighbor 10.10.1.2 Up
R8(config-router)#

R9#conf t
R9(config)#router bgp 13500
```

```
R9(config-router)#neigh 10.10.1.1 capability orf prefix-list receive
R9(config-router)#
%BGP-5-ADJCHANGE: neighbor 10.10.1.1 Down Capability changed
R9(config-router)#
%BGP-5-ADJCHANGE: neighbor 10.10.1.1 Up
R9(config-router)#
```

We now create our prefix-list to allow just the default route:

```
R8(config)#ip prefix-list ONLY-DEFAULT-IN permit 0.0.0.0/0
```

We assign it to our neighbor:

```
R8(config)#router bgp 11100
R8(config-router)#neigh 10.10.1.2 prefix-list ONLY-DEFAULT-IN in
```

We can see the before and after effects, once we clear our neighbor relationship:

```
R9#sh ip bgp neigh 10.10.1.1 advertised-routes | i Total
Total number of prefixes 36
```

Then after we clear the peering from R8:

```
R9#sh ip bgp neigh 10.10.1.1 advertised-routes | i Total
Total number of prefixes 1
R9#
```

We can also check what prefix-list request R9 is seeing from R8:

```
R9#sh ip bgp neigh 10.10.1.1 received prefix-filter
Address family: IPv4 Unicast
ip prefix-list 10.10.1.1: 1 entries
   seq 5 permit 0.0.0.0/0
R9#
```

Now R8 has a much simpler view of the world:

```
R8#sh ip bgp | beg Network
   Network         Next Hop Weight Path
*  0.0.0.0         10.10.1.2    0 13500 12000 11000 400 200 300 65500 i
*>                 10.9.1.1     0 11000 400 200 300 65500 i
*> 1.1.1.0/24      10.9.1.1     0 11000 400 200 105 i
*> 1.2.1.0/24      10.9.1.1     0 11000 400 200 105 i
*> 10.1.0.0/24     10.9.1.1     0 11000 400 200 105 i
*> 10.1.1.0/24     10.9.1.1     0 11000 400 200 105 i
```

The downside to what we have implemented, is that R8 won't take the most direct route to R9's loopback interface:

```
R8#sh ip bgp 192.168.3.0/24
BGP routing table entry for 192.168.3.0/24, version 38
Paths: (1 available, best #1, table Default-IP-Routing-Table)
Flag: 0x820
  Advertised to update-groups:
     1
  11000 12000 13500
    10.9.1.1 from 10.9.1.1 (7.7.7.7)
      Origin IGP, localpref 100, valid, external, best
R8#
```

So, let's fix this by adding another sequence to our prefix-list, and seeing what filter list R9 is receiving after we clear the peering:

```
R8(config)#ip prefix-list ONLY-DEFAULT-IN seq 10 permit 192.168.3.0/24
%BGP-5-ADJCHANGE: neighbor 10.10.1.1 Down Peer closed the session
%BGP-5-ADJCHANGE: neighbor 10.10.1.1 Up
R9#sh ip bgp neigh 10.10.1.1 received prefix-filter
Address family: IPv4 Unicast
ip prefix-list 10.10.1.1: 2 entries
   seq 5 permit 0.0.0.0/0
   seq 10 permit 192.168.3.0/24
R9#
```

Now R8's access to the 192.168.3.0/24 network takes a much more direct route:

```
R8#sh ip bgp 192.168.3.0/24
BGP routing table entry for 192.168.3.0/24, version 38
Paths: (2 available, best #1, table Default-IP-Routing-Table)
  Advertised to update-groups:
     1
  13500
    10.10.1.2 from 10.10.1.2 (9.9.9.9)
      Origin IGP, metric 0, localpref 100, valid, external, best
  11000 12000 13500
    10.9.1.1 from 10.9.1.1 (7.7.7.7)
      Origin IGP, localpref 100, valid, external
R8#
```

We can confirm that we still have reachability in the event that our direct route to R7 goes down:

```
R8#conf t
R8(config)#int s0/0
R8(config-if)#shut
%BGP-5-ADJCHANGE: neighbor 10.9.1.1 Down Interface flap
R8(config-if)#exit
R8(config)#
%LINK-5-CHANGED: Interface Serial0/0, changed state to
administratively down
%LINEPROTO-5-UPDOWN: Line protocol on Interface Serial0/0, changed
state to down
R8(config)#exit
R8#sh ip route | beg Gateway
Gateway of last resort is 10.10.1.2 to network 0.0.0.0

     10.0.0.0/24 is subnetted, 1 subnets
C       10.10.1.0 is directly connected, Serial0/1
C    192.168.2.0/24 is directly connected, Loopback0
B    192.168.3.0/24 [20/0] via 10.10.1.2, 00:03:33
B*   0.0.0.0/0 [20/0] via 10.10.1.2, 00:00:58
R8#ping 1.2.1.1

Type escape sequence to abort.
Sending 5, 100-byte ICMP Echos to 1.2.1.1:
!!!!!
Success rate is 100 percent (5/5)
R8#
```

So, not only have we tidied up our BGP table, we have also given us a secondary route to anywhere in the network. Before we move on to the next chapter, we'll need to switch our interface on again:

```
R8#conf t
R8(config)#int s0/0
R8(config-if)#no shut
```

We'll need it for the next chapter, in which we'll remove our neighbor statements for R11 and R8 on R7 and look at a nice way to connect our peers dynamically.

8.9 Distribute Lists

An alternative to using outbound route filtering would be to use a distribute list.

Using a simple access-list we can block routes being advertised out, or received in. In this example we will not advertise the 172.18.1.0/24 network on R12 to R5. It is being received by R5 from two sources:

```
R5#sh ip bgp | beg 172.18
*   172.18.1.0/24   10.5.1.2              0 400 500 300 65500 i
*>                  10.3.1.2       0      0 300 65500 i
*>  172.18.2.0/24   10.3.1.2       0      0 300 65500 i
*>  172.18.3.0/24   10.3.1.2       0      0 300 65500 ?
```

We start with a simple access-list to block the 172.18.1.0/24 network and permit anything else. Then we enter our BGP process and attach it to our neighbor statement for R5:

```
R12(config)#access-list 1 deny 172.18.1.0 0.0.0.255
R12(config)#access-list 1 permit any
R12(config)#router bgp 65500
R12(config-router)#neigh 10.3.1.1 distribute-list 1 out
```

We can see the result on R5:

```
R5#clear ip bgp 10.3.1.2 soft in
R5#sh ip bgp | beg 172.18
*>  172.18.1.0/24   10.5.1.2              0 400 500 300 65500 i
*>  172.18.2.0/24   10.3.1.2       0      0 300 65500 i
*>  172.18.3.0/24   10.3.1.2       0      0 300 65500 ?
*                   10.5.1.2              0 400 500 300 65500 ?
```

As mentioned earlier, we will now move on to the next section, in which we will make BGP more dynamic.

9. Making BGP easier

In this chapter, we will look at how to form neighbor relationships by listening to an entire subnet, and having the peers form dynamically, rather than explicitly specifying each neighbor. We will then put some peers into templates, looking at template inheritance, and what we can do with peer and session templates.

9.1 Dynamic peers

So far all our neighbors have been set up in pretty much the same manner, either through a directly connected serial connection, or through a loopback interface, which necessitates the need for an IGP, or static routes pointing in the right direction. We have also seen that, using peer groups, we can simplify a number of neighbors with similar configurational requirements, but they still need to have their IP addresses specified.

There is a way to have peer relationships form dynamically. This was first introduced in IOS 12.2(33)SXH, and then disappeared again until IOS 15.0 emerged. According to Cisco's web page on dynamic BGP peers, the only IOS releases to support it (as of November 2012[5]) are the following:

12.2(33)SXH
15.1(2)T
15.0(1)S
15.1(1)SG
Cisco IOS XE Release 3.1S
Cisco IOS XE Release 3.3SG

It is unusual to see this on eBGP facing routers, as it goes against the secure nature of BGP. It is more commonly used with iBGP peers, and it does allow a more rapid deployment.

The way in which we set up a router for dynamic peering is one we have already looked at, and that is using a peer-group. We instruct the router to "listen" to a range of IP addresses, and then, if we want to, we can limit down the number of peers we allow our router to create dynamically.

At the moment R7 has three neighbor peerings, to R11, R8 and R6:

---

[5] http://www.cisco.com/en/US/docs/ios-xml/ios/iproute_bgp/configuration/xe-3sg/irg-dynamic-neighbor.html

```
R7#sh ip bgp neigh | i external
BGP neighbor is 10.8.1.2,   remote AS 12000, external link
BGP neighbor is 10.9.1.2,   remote AS 11100, external link
BGP neighbor is 172.26.1.1,  remote AS 400, external link
R7#
```

We need to remove the peerings to R8 and R11:

```
R7(config)#router bgp 11000
R7(config-router)#no neigh 10.8.1.2
R7(config-router)#
%BGP_SESSION-5-ADJCHANGE: neighbor 10.8.1.2 IPv4 Unicast topology
base removed from session  Neighbor deleted
%BGP-5-ADJCHANGE: neighbor 10.8.1.2 Down Neighbor deleted
R7(config-router)#no neigh 10.9.1.2
R7(config-router)#exit
R7(config)#exit
R7#sh ip bgp neigh | i external
BGP neighbor is 172.26.1.1,  remote AS 400, external link
R7#
```

And now we can start by creating the bgp listen ranges, and specifying the peer-group(s):

```
R7(config)#router bgp 11000
R7(config-router)#bgp listen range 10.8.1.0/24 peer-group AS12000
R7(config-router)#bgp listen range 10.9.1.0/24 peer-group AS11100
```

If we want to allow both R11 and R8 to dynamically peer with R7, we actually need to have two peer-groups, to accommodate the different AS numbers that they are in (again this is why it's predominantly used in iBGP rather than eBGP).

We then (if we want to) limit down how many dynamic peers we are going to allow to connect, and set up the peer-group information:

```
R7(config-router)#bgp listen limit 2
R7(config-router)#neighbor AS12000 peer-group
R7(config-router)#neighbor AS12000 remote-as 12000
%BGP-5-ADJCHANGE: neighbor *10.8.1.2 Up
R7(config-router)#neighbor AS11100 peer-group
R7(config-router)#neighbor AS11100 remote-as 11100
%BGP-5-ADJCHANGE: neighbor *10.9.1.2 Up
```

If we look at R7, we can see, in the BGP summary, that R11 and R8 are dynamically created peers:

```
R7#sh ip bgp summ | beg Neighb
Neighbor      V     AS MsgRcd MsgSnt TblVer  InQ OutQ Up/Down  Stat/PfxRcd
*10.8.1.2     4  12000     27     28     47    0    0 00:10:38           4
*10.9.1.2     4  11100     29     28     47    0    0 00:11:01           2
172.26.1.1    4    400     30     21     47    0    0 00:10:37          33
* Dynamically created based on a listen range command
Dynamically created neighbors: 2, Subnet ranges: 2

BGP peergroup AS12000 listen range group members:
   10.8.1.0/24
BGP peergroup AS11100 listen range group members:
   10.9.1.0/24

Total dynamically created neighbors: 2/(2 max), Subnet ranges: 2

R7#
```

We can only have one side set up to be dynamic. A router configured to use dynamic peering does not actively probe for peers, but will, instead, listen to the entire subnet range for connection requests. The other side must be set up in the standard way, in order that the connection is established (in much the same way we set up one side to be passive in section 6.2). If both sides are listening, no one is talking. It may not be the most secure way of forming BGP peers, but there are ways to improve the security, which we will cover later on.

9.2 Peer templates

Peer templates are quite similar to peer groups, but allow for greater flexibility. We covered peer groups back in section 6.5, and although we can achieve much of the same with peer templates, peer templates also offer inheritance of other templates, allowing for a nested approach to configuration. There are two types of template; session templates (used in the creation of peer relationships), and policy templates (used to set attributes).

Peer Session templates

We will set up some templates on R9, for our connections to R8 and R11. We will have three templates in all. One for R8 and one for R11, these will be specific for their AS number. Both of these templates will inherit a more generic template.

First we create our templates, starting with a global template, which will be very generalized, and just set the timers:

```
R9(config)#router bgp 13500
R9(config-router)#template peer-session GLOBAL
R9(config-router-stmp)#description "For all Peers"
R9(config-router-stmp)#timers 30 300
R9(config-router-stmp)#exit-peer-session
```

Next we can create AS specific templates:

```
R9(config-router)#template peer-session R8
R9(config-router-stmp)#description "R8 template"
R9(config-router-stmp)#remote-as 11100
R9(config-router-stmp)#inherit peer-session GLOBAL
R9(config-router-stmp)#exit
R9(config-router)#template peer-session R11
R9(config-router-stmp)#description "R11 template"
R9(config-router-stmp)#inherit peer-session GLOBAL
R9(config-router-stmp)#remote-as 12000
R9(config-router-stmp)#exit-peer-session
```

Finally, we link these templates to our neighbors:

```
R9(config-router)#neighbor 10.11.1.1 inherit peer-session R11
R9(config-router)#neighbor 10.10.1.1 inherit peer-session R8
```

Once completed, our configuration on R9 looks like this:

```
R9#sh run | section bgp
router bgp 13500
 template peer-session GLOBAL
  description "For all Peers"
  timers 30 300
 exit-peer-session
 !
 template peer-session R8
  remote-as 11100
  description "R8 template"
  inherit peer-session GLOBAL
 exit-peer-session
 !
 template peer-session R11
  remote-as 12000
  description "R11 template"
  inherit peer-session GLOBAL
```

```
  exit-peer-session
 !
 no synchronization
 bgp router-id 9.9.9.9
 bgp log-neighbor-changes
 network 10.10.1.0 mask 255.255.255.0
 network 10.11.1.0 mask 255.255.255.0
 network 192.168.3.0
 neighbor 10.10.1.1 remote-as 11100
 neighbor 10.10.1.1 inherit peer-session R8
 neighbor 10.10.1.1 capability orf prefix-list receive
 neighbor 10.11.1.1 remote-as 12000
 neighbor 10.11.1.1 inherit peer-session R11
 no auto-summary
R9#
```

We can look at individual templates to confirm which AS they are connected to, and which (if any) templates they inherit:

```
R9#sh ip bgp template peer-session R8
Template:R8, index:2
Local policies:0x101, Inherited polices:0x20
This template inherits:
  GLOBAL index:1 flags:0x0
Locally configured session commands:
 remote-as 11100
 description "R8 template"
Inherited session commands:
 timers 30 300

R9#
```

There is a great deal we can do with session templates, such as changing the ebgp-multihop, or ttl-security, setting allowas-in, changing the timers, and specify a local AS number. Generally, anything that controls how a session is established can be configured using a peer-session template, and for anything after that, such as influencing metrics, we have peer policies.

Peer Policy templates

Peer policy templates are set up in the same was as peer session templates. We can start with the most general one:

```
R9(config-router)#template peer-policy GLOBAL
R9(config-router-ptmp)#send-community both
```

```
R9(config-router-ptmp)#soft-reconfiguration inbound
R9(config-router-ptmp)#allowas-in
R9(config-router-ptmp)#exit-peer-policy
```

We then inherit that into a template that is more peer specific:

```
R9(config-router)#template peer-policy R8
R9(config-router-ptmp)#weight 200
R9(config-router-ptmp)#capability orf prefix-list both
R9(config-router-ptmp)#inherit peer-policy GLOBAL 10
R9(config-router-ptmp)#exit-peer-policy
```

We can have a template call a route-map, for instance:

```
R9(config-router)#exit
R9(config)#route-map AS12000-Community permit 10
R9(config-route-map)#set community 13500:12000
R9(config-route-map)#exit
R9(config)#router bgp 13500
R9(config-router)#template peer-policy R11
R9(config-router-ptmp)#inherit peer-policy GLOBAL 10
R9(config-router-ptmp)#route-map AS12000-Community in
R9(config-router-ptmp)#exit-peer-policy
R9(config-router)#
```

Before we apply these, let's have a look at R9s routing table (for the sake of brevity I have only included a few of the routes):

```
R9#sh ip bgp | beg 172.20
*   172.20.0.0/21    10.10.1.1             0 11100 11000 i
*>                   10.11.1.1             0 12000 11000 i
*   172.20.2.0/24    10.10.1.1             0 11100 11000 i
*>                   10.11.1.1             0 12000 11000 i
*   172.20.3.0/24    10.10.1.1             0 11100 11000 i
*>                   10.11.1.1             0 12000 11000 i
*   172.21.1.0/24    10.10.1.1             0 11100 11000 400 200 105 i
*>                   10.11.1.1             0 12000 11000 400 200 105 i
*   172.21.4.0/24    10.10.1.1             0 11100 11000 400 200 105 i
*>                   10.11.1.1             0 12000 11000 400 200 105 i
*   172.22.0.0/21    10.10.1.1             0 11100 11000 400 200 105 i
*>                   10.11.1.1             0 12000 11000 400 200 105 i
```

Then we apply the new templates to the neighbors:

```
R9(config-router)#neighbor 10.11.1.1 inherit peer-policy R11
R9(config-router)#neighbor 10.10.1.1 inherit peer-policy R8
```

Then we can see if our bgp table has changed:

```
R9#sh ip bgp | beg 172.20
*> 172.20.0.0/21    10.10.1.1           200 11100 11000 i
*                   10.11.1.1             0 12000 11000 i
*> 172.20.2.0/24    10.10.1.1           200 11100 11000 i
*                   10.11.1.1             0 12000 11000 i
*> 172.20.3.0/24    10.10.1.1           200 11100 11000 i
*                   10.11.1.1             0 12000 11000 i
*> 172.21.1.0/24    10.10.1.1           200 11100 11000 400 200 105 i
*                   10.11.1.1             0 12000 11000 400 200 105 i
*> 172.21.4.0/24    10.10.1.1           200 11100 11000 400 200 105 i
*                   10.11.1.1             0 12000 11000 400 200 105 i
*> 172.22.0.0/21    10.10.1.1           200 11100 11000 400 200 105 i
*                   10.11.1.1             0 12000 11000 400 200 105 i
```

Here we can see that the weight for routes advertised by R8 is now 200, making them the preferred routes. We also have routes in our BGP table that would ordinarily be filtered out as they contain our own AS number (13500) because we used the "allowas-in" command, and, if we look closer at a route, we can see that the community has also been changed:

```
R9#sh ip bgp | beg 192.168
*   192.168.2.0     10.11.1.1                 0 12000 13500 11100 i
*>                  10.10.1.1           0   200 11100 i
*   192.168.3.0     10.10.1                   200 11100 13500 i
*                   10.11.1.1                   0 12000 13500 i
*>                  0.0.0.0             32768 i
R9#sh ip bgp 192.168.2.0/24
BGP routing table entry for 192.168.2.0/24, version 221
Paths: (4 available, best #3, table Default-IP-Routing-Table)
Flag: 0x820
  Advertised to update-groups:
     1
  12000 13500 11100
    10.11.1.1 from 10.11.1.1 (11.11.11.11)
      Origin IGP, localpref 100, valid, external
      Community: 884748000
  12000 13500 11100, (received-only)
    10.11.1.1 from 10.11.1.1 (11.11.11.11)
      Origin IGP, localpref 100, valid, external
  11100
    10.10.1.1 from 10.10.1.1 (8.8.8.8)
      Origin IGP, metric 0, localpref 100, weight 200, valid, external, best
```

```
    11100, (received-only)
      10.10.1.1 from 10.10.1.1 (8.8.8.8)
        Origin IGP, metric 0, localpref 100, valid, external
R9#
```

We can confirm the settings applied directly, and inherited by, our peer policy templates using the command "sh ip bgp template peer-policy <policy name>":

```
R9#sh ip bgp template peer-policy R8
Template:R8, index:2.
Local policies:0x2000800, Inherited polices:0x218000
This template inherits:
  GLOBAL, index:1, seq_no:10, flags:0x2000800
Locally configured policies:
  weight 200
  capability orf prefix-list both
Inherited policies:
  send-community both
  soft-reconfiguration inbound
  allowas-in 3

R9#
```

So with the use of session templates and policies, we have a large level of control over how our network is formed. We will revisit many of these in chapter 11 when we look at the BGP Path Selection algorithm in greater detail.

10. Multiprotocol BGP and Address Families

So far we have just concentrated on IPv4, but BGP can handle so much more than that. So let's look at how we can run IPv4 and IPv6 at the same time.

Multiprotocol BGP (MPBGP, or MBGP) was defined in RFC 2283, and is an extension to BGP allowing it to carry more than just IPv4 routes, such as IPv4 unicast and multicast, IPv6 unicast and MPLS VPN.

MBGP brings with it separate RIBs, for each type of routing information that is being exchanged. Though, it is also important to note that, unlike the IGPs such as RIP, OSPF and EIGRP with their IPv6 equivalent (RIPng, OSPFv3 and EIGRPv6), there is no separate IPv6 for BGP, and there are no IPv6 specific commands for BGP.

I think that setting up MPLS within our topology is a little beyond the scope of this book, and will be better saved until the MPLS volume in this series "MPLS for Cisco Networks" where along with setting up an MPLS topology we will also delve deeper into MBGP and MPLS VPNs.

For the moment though we will use MBGP to move some IPv6 data around, and again, we will step away from our current topology and start with a blank canvas.

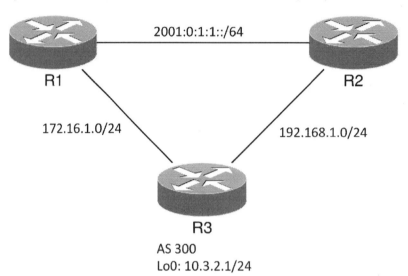

It would be easy to have an even simpler topology, using just two routers (such as R1 and R2), both running purely IPv6, however this would not demonstrate multiprotocol BGP fully, the same steps would be followed for R1 and R2, but we would not be including IPv4, hence the addition of R3.

Let's start with just the basic configuration, concentrating on the IPv4 side of things:

R1:

```
interface Loopback0
  ip address 10.3.0.1 255.255.255.0
  no shut
interface FastEthernet0/1
  ip address 172.16.1.1 255.255.255.0
  no shut
router bgp 100
  network 10.3.0.0 mask 255.255.255.0
  neighbor 172.16.1.2 remote-as 300
```

R2:

```
interface Loopback0
  ip address 10.3.1.1 255.255.255.0
```

```
    no shut
  interface FastEthernet0/1
    ip address 192.168.1.1 255.255.255.0
    no shut
  router bgp 200
    network 10.3.1.0 mask 255.255.255.0
    neighbor 192.168.1.2 remote-as 300
```

R3:

```
  interface Loopback0
    ip address 10.3.2.1 255.255.255.0
  interface FastEthernet0/0
    ip address 192.168.1.2 255.255.255.0
    no shut
  interface FastEthernet0/1
    ip address 172.16.1.2 255.255.255.0
    no shut
  router bgp 300
    network 10.3.2.0 mask 255.255.255.0
    neighbor 172.16.1.1 remote-as 100
    neighbor 192.168.1.1 remote-as 200
```

With the above, we should have bgp peers form between R1 and R3, and also between R2 and R3.

```
  R3(config-router)#do sh ip bgp | beg Network
     Network          Next Hop          Metric LocPrf Weight Path
  *> 10.3.0.0/24      172.16.1.1             0             0 100 i
  *> 10.3.1.0/24      192.168.1.1            0             0 200 i
  *> 10.3.2.0/24      0.0.0.0                0         32768 i
  R3(config-router)#
```

To start implementing IPv6 we need, first, to enable the routers to support it:

```
  R1(config)#ipv6 unicast-routing

  R2(config)#ipv6 unicast-routing
```

We can now add our IPv6 addresses:

```
  R1(config)#int lo0
  R1(config-if)#ipv6 address 2001:0:0:10::1/64
  R1(config-if)#exit
  R1(config)#int fa0/0
  R1(config-if)#ipv6 address 2001:0:1:1::1/64
```

```
R1(config-if)#no shut
R1(config-if)#exit
R1(config)#exit

R2(config)#int lo0
R2(config-if)#ipv6 address 2001:0:0:20::1/64
R2(config-if)#exit
R2(config)#int fa0/0
R2(config-if)#ipv6 address 2001:0:1:1::2/64
R2(config-if)#no shut
R2(config-if)#exit
R2(config)#exit
```

We should be able to confirm reachability with an ipv6 ping:

```
R2#ping ipv6 2001:0:1:1::1

Type escape sequence to abort.
Sending 5, 100-byte ICMP Echos to 2001:0:1:1::1:
!!!!!
Success rate is 100 percent (5/5)
R2#
```

Now we can start configuring our MBGP. To do this we must first disable the default behavior of only supporting IPv4:

```
R1(config)#router bgp 100
R1(config-router)#no bgp default ipv4-unicast

R2(config)#router bgp 200
R2(config-router)#no bgp default ipv4-unicast
```

As stated before, with MBGP comes a separate RIB for each protocol, similarly the BGP configuration is also separated, somewhat, into address families (AF).

10.1 Address families

So far all our IPv4 neighbors have exchanged all the routes we have defined. For example, if we have two neighbors and four network statements, the four network prefixes will be advertised to both neighbors. Once we start adding different protocols, such as IPv6, or MPLS VPNv4, then, if we followed the same configurational design as we have seen so far, the IPV6 neighbors would have the IPv6 routes and the VPNv4 routes, and similarly the VPNv4 neighbors would have their designated routes as well as the IPv6 routes advertised to it, which is less than ideal.

Address families overcome this. Neighbors are defined under the address family with which we want to exchange routes with from. It enables BGP to be more modular and much more scalable through the use of the address family identifier (AFI) and the subsequent address family identifier (SAFI). Policies can be assigned per-address family, with SAFI being a child of the parent AFI allowing for even more refinement of the BGP configuration

We start by creating our IPv6 address family using the commands:

```
R1(config-router)#address-family ipv6

R2(config-router)#address-family ipv6
```

Now, we can create our peers using the IPv6 addresses:

```
R1(config-router-af)#neighbor 2001:0:1:1::2 remote-as 200

R2(config-router-af)#neighbor 2001:0:1:1::1 remote-as 100
```

Unlike our IPv4 configurations, because we have implemented address families, we need to activate our neighbors:

```
R1(config-router-af)#neighbor 2001:0:1:1::2 activate

R2(config-router-af)#neighbor 2001:0:1:1::1 activate
```

Now, we can advertise our loopback interfaces:

```
R1(config-router-af)#network 2001:0:0:10::/64

R2(config-router-af)#network 2001:0:0:20::/64
```

The full configuration will look as follows:

```
R1(config)#router bgp 100
R1(config-router)#no bgp default ipv4-unicast
R1(config-router)#address-family ipv6
R1(config-router-af)#neighbor 2001:0:1:1::2 remote-as 200
R1(config-router-af)#neighbor 2001:0:1:1::2 activate
R1(config-router-af)#network 2001:0:0:10::/64

R2(config)#router bgp 200
R2(config-router)#no bgp default ipv4-unicast
```

```
R2(config-router)#address-family ipv6
R2(config-router-af)#neighbor 2001:0:1:1::1 remote-as 100
R2(config-router-af)#neighbor 2001:0:1:1::1 activate
R2(config-router-af)#network 2001:0:0:20::/64
```

Our peers should become established in the normal manner. Depending how quick you are, they might come up before the network statements are added. We will not be able to see our IPv6 routes in the normal "sh ip bgp" fashion, and there is not a helpful "sh ipv6 bgp", instead we need to use "sh ipv6 routes", thankfully the code of "B", again, denotes that the route was learned through BGP:

```
R1#sh ip bgp | beg Network
   Network          Next Hop         Metric LocPrf Weight Path
*> 10.3.0.0/24      0.0.0.0               0         32768 i
*> 10.3.1.0/24      172.16.1.2                          0 300 200 i
*> 10.3.2.0/24      172.16.1.2            0             0 300 i
R1#sh ipv6 route
IPv6 Routing Table - 7 entries
Codes: C - Connected, L - Local, S - Static, R - RIP, B - BGP
       U - Per-user Static route
       I1 - ISIS L1, I2 - ISIS L2, IA - ISIS interarea, IS - ISIS
summary
       O - OSPF intra, OI - OSPF inter, OE1 - OSPF ext 1, OE2 - OSPF
ext 2
       ON1 - OSPF NSSA ext 1, ON2 - OSPF NSSA ext 2
C   2001:0:0:10::/64 [0/0]
     via ::, Loopback0
L   2001:0:0:10::1/128 [0/0]
     via ::, Loopback0
B   2001:0:0:20::/64 [20/0]
     via FE80::CE01:30FF:FE76:0, FastEthernet0/0
C   2001:0:1:1::/64 [0/0]
     via ::, FastEthernet0/0
L   2001:0:1:1::1/128 [0/0]
     via ::, FastEthernet0/0
L   FE80::/10 [0/0]
     via ::, Null0
L   FF00::/8 [0/0]
     via ::, Null0
R1#

R2#sh ip bgp | beg Network
   Network          Next Hop         Metric LocPrf Weight Path
*> 10.3.0.0/24      192.168.1.2                         0 300 100 i
*> 10.3.1.0/24      0.0.0.0               0         32768 i
*> 10.3.2.0/24      192.168.1.2           0             0 300 i
```

```
R2#sh ipv6 route
IPv6 Routing Table - 7 entries
Codes: C - Connected, L - Local, S - Static, R - RIP, B - BGP
       U - Per-user Static route
       I1 - ISIS L1, I2 - ISIS L2, IA - ISIS interarea, IS - ISIS
summary
       O - OSPF intra, OI - OSPF inter, OE1 - OSPF ext 1, OE2 - OSPF
ext 2
       ON1 - OSPF NSSA ext 1, ON2 - OSPF NSSA ext 2
B   2001:0:0:10::/64 [20/0]
     via FE80::CE00:30FF:FE76:0, FastEthernet0/0
C   2001:0:0:20::/64 [0/0]
     via ::, Loopback0
L   2001:0:0:20::1/128 [0/0]
     via ::, Loopback0
C   2001:0:1:1::/64 [0/0]
     via ::, FastEthernet0/0
L   2001:0:1:1::2/128 [0/0]
     via ::, FastEthernet0/0
L   FE80::/10 [0/0]
     via ::, Null0
L   FF00::/8 [0/0]
     via ::, Null0
R2#
```

If we look at our BGP configurations, we can see that the IOS has formatted things nicely for us, including the addition of an IPv4 address family:

```
R1#sh run | section bgp
router bgp 100
 no bgp default ipv4-unicast
 bgp log-neighbor-changes
 neighbor 2001:0:1:1::2 remote-as 200
 neighbor 172.16.1.2 remote-as 300
 !
 address-family ipv4
  neighbor 172.16.1.2 activate
  no auto-summary
  no synchronization
  network 10.3.0.0 mask 255.255.255.0
 exit-address-family
 !
 address-family ipv6
  neighbor 2001:0:1:1::2 activate
  network 2001:0:0:10::/64
 exit-address-family
R1#
```

```
R2#sh run | section bgp
router bgp 200
 no bgp default ipv4-unicast
 bgp log-neighbor-changes
 neighbor 2001:0:1:1::1 remote-as 100
 neighbor 192.168.1.2 remote-as 300
 !
 address-family ipv4
  neighbor 192.168.1.2 activate
  no auto-summary
  no synchronization
  network 10.3.1.0 mask 255.255.255.0
 exit-address-family
 !
 address-family ipv6
  neighbor 2001:0:1:1::1 activate
  network 2001:0:0:20::/64
 exit-address-family
R2#
```

And there we have Multiprotocol BGP. Again, there will more on this in a later volume in this series.

11. Attributes and Decisions

I am sure that many of you have probably wondered why I have left this chapter until now. It is certainly one of the most important chapters, in both understanding how BGP networks are formed, and from the CCIE certification perspective where it will (probably) be heavily tested on. The reason I have left it until now is so that we can watch our topology evolve, and gain a better understand how the paths through the network are created and selected. Certainly, we have seen this so far with how the AS_PATH has changed as our network grows, and now we have a fairly decent network with which to manipulate the different BGP attributes that determine our paths. Before we start looking at how the attributes influence our topology let's have a look at the attributes themselves

11.1 BGP Attributes

BGP attributes are used to determine the best route to a destination, when more than one route exists. Our topology has a number of multi-homed systems; in fact it is easier to list the routers that are not multi-homed (R13 and R14) than it is to list the multi-homed ones. We have already seen, or even manipulated, some of the attributes in previous chapters such as weight, local preference and, of course, the as_path attribute, and it has been these that we have looked at in terms of how our BGP table is formed. There are a number of BGP attributes that make up the path decision process, which we will look at as we go through the best path algorithm. Attributes also fall into different categories, and these controls how an attribute is handled when being passed from one router, or one AS, to the next. These categories are:

- Well-Known, Mandatory
- Well-Known, Discretionary
- Optional, Transitive
- Optional, Non-Transitive

Well-Known, Mandatory attributes must appear in every UPDATE message, and <u>must be</u> supported by all BGP implementations. If such an attribute is missing from an UPDATE message, then a NOTIFICATION message is sent to the peer, and the message is discarded as being invalid. Attributes included in this category are AS_PATH, ORIGIN and NEXT_HOP.

Well-Known, Discretionary attributes must still be supported by all BGP implementations, but do not have to be included in an UPDATE message. This category includes LOCAL_PREF and ATOMIC_AGGREGATE.

Optional attributes may, or may not, be supported in all BGP implementations. Transitive attributes, such as AGGREGATOR and COMMUNITY, will be passed on to the next AS, whereas Non-Transitive (such as MED, ORIGINATOR_ID and Cluster List) will not be passed on.

We'll start looking at these in greater depth in a moment, and see how changing the values can influence the routing decisions made by a router. Before we do, we need to talk about what methods we can implement to change the values.

We have used route-maps quite a bit, as well as peer-policy templates. Both have worked well for us, but we have a couple of other methods in our arsenal. Take weight for instance. We have used a peer-policy template on R9 to set the weight for routes coming in from R8, we could have, instead, used the weight command along with the neighbor command to set the weight to 200:

```
R9(config-router)#neighbor 10.10.1.1 weight 200
```

We have also seen how we can use route-maps to set information on routes, such as the next hop. We can also use them to set, or change, our metrics, such as community, metric, origin and weight. This is known as an Attribute-Map when applied to a summary route. Recall on R5, we are summarizing the loopback interfaces on R10 (aggregate-address 172.19.0.0 255.255.248.0 as-set summary-only); we can also create a route-map and attach it to this aggregate address.

At the moment R2 sees the aggregate address as follows:

```
R2#sh ip bgp 172.19.0.0/21
BGP routing table entry for 172.19.0.0/21, version 50
Paths: (2 available, best #1, table Default-IP-Routing-Table)
  Advertised to update-groups:
     3
  400 500, (aggregated by 200 5.5.5.5)
    172.16.1.1 from 172.16.1.1 (4.4.4.4)
      Origin IGP, metric 0, localpref 100, valid, internal, best
      Originator: 5.5.5.5, Cluster list: 4.4.4.4
  400 500, (aggregated by 200 5.5.5.5)
    172.17.1.1 from 172.17.1.1 (3.3.3.3)
      Origin IGP, metric 0, localpref 100, valid, internal
      Originator: 5.5.5.5, Cluster list: 3.3.3.3
R2#sh ip bgp | beg 172.19.0.0/21
*>i172.19.0.0/21    172.16.1.1           0    100      0 400 500 i
* i                 172.17.1.1           0    100      0 400 500 i
* i172.19.1.0/24    172.17.1.1           0    100      0 400 500 i
*>i                 172.16.1.1           0    100      0 400 500 i
```

```
*  i172.19.2.0/24    172.17.1.1         0    100      0 400 500 i
*>i                  172.16.1.1         0    100      0 400 500 i
*  i172.19.3.0/24    172.17.1.1         0    100      0 400 500 i
*>i                  172.16.1.1         0    100      0 400 500 i
*  i172.19.4.0/24    172.17.1.1         0    100      0 400 500 i
*>i                  172.16.1.1         0    100      0 400 500 i
```

We create the following route-map on R5:

```
R5(config)#route-map MyAttributes permit 10
R5(config-route-map)#set metric 10
R5(config-route-map)#exit
```

This route-map is then attached to the aggregate address:

```
R5(config)#router bgp 200
R5(config-router)#aggregate-address 172.19.0.0 255.255.248.0 as-set
summary-only attribute-map MyAttributes
```

Then, once we clear the BGP peering on R5 and allow it to reestablish, R2 sees the modified metric, which is now set to 10:

```
R2#sh ip bgp | beg 172.19.0.0/21
*>i172.19.0.0/21    172.16.1.1        10    100      0 400 500 i
*  i                172.17.1.1        10    100      0 400 500 i
*  i172.19.1.0/24   172.17.1.1        10    100      0 400 500 i
*>i                 172.16.1.1        10    100      0 400 500 i
*  i172.19.2.0/24   172.17.1.1        10    100      0 400 500 i
*>i                 172.16.1.1        10    100      0 400 500 i
*  i172.19.3.0/24   172.17.1.1        10    100      0 400 500 i
*>i                 172.16.1.1        10    100      0 400 500 i
*  i172.19.4.0/24   172.17.1.1        10    100      0 400 500 i
*>i                 172.16.1.1        10    100      0 400 500 i
R2#sh ip bgp 172.19.0.0/21
BGP routing table entry for 172.19.0.0/21, version 62
Paths: (2 available, best #1, table Default-IP-Routing-Table)
  Advertised to update-groups:
     3
  400 500, (aggregated by 200 5.5.5.5)
    172.16.1.1 from 172.16.1.1 (4.4.4.4)
      Origin IGP, metric 10, localpref 100, valid, internal, best
      Originator: 5.5.5.5, Cluster list: 4.4.4.4
  400 500, (aggregated by 200 5.5.5.5)
    172.17.1.1 from 172.17.1.1 (3.3.3.3)
      Origin IGP, metric 10, localpref 100, valid, internal
      Originator: 5.5.5.5, Cluster list: 3.3.3.3
```

R2#

The other alternative is to use as-path access-lists. These work like any other access-list, but use regular expressions to match as-paths.

11.2 BGP Regular expressions

We can use regular expressions (regexp) to do a number of activities with BGP. We can use it in show commands to limit the output, or in as-path access-lists to control path selection based on the as-path contained within the update. Using R9 to test these with we'll go through them one by one. Because R9 is multi-homed, to R11 in AS 12000 and R8 in AS 11100, as well as its placement at the end of our topology, it makes for a good router to test with. The basic command we will be using is "sh ip bgp regexp <regex command>". Without the regexp the first few lines of R9's BGP table look like this:

```
R9#sh ip bgp | beg Network
   Network          Next Hop        Weight Path
*  0.0.0.0          10.11.1.1            0 12000 11000 400 200 300 65500 i
*>                  10.10.1.1          200 11100 11000 400 200 300 65500 i
*  1.1.1.0/24       10.11.1.1            0 12000 11000 400 200 105 i
*>                  10.10.1.1          200 11100 11000 400 200 105 i
*  1.2.1.0/24       10.11.1.1            0 12000 11000 400 200 105 i
*>                  10.10.1.1          200 11100 11000 400 200 105 i
*  10.1.0.0/24      10.11.1.1            0 12000 11000 400 200 105 i
*>                  10.10.1.1          200 11100 11000 400 200 105 i
*  10.1.1.0/24      10.11.1.1            0 12000 11000 400 200 105 i
*>                  10.10.1.1          200 11100 11000 400 200 105 i
```

Because we know that R9's paths will either be through AS 12000, or AS 11100, it's well suited to testing the regular expressions. So what are the regular expressions?

The simplest regexp would be (without the quote marks) ".*". The dot signifies any single character ,and the star represents one of more instances - this would match anything, as the below truncated output shows:

```
R9#sh ip bgp regexp .*
BGP table version is 39, local router ID is 9.9.9.9
Status codes: s suppressed, d damped, h history, * valid, > best, i -
internal,
              r RIB-failure, S Stale
Origin codes: i - IGP, e - EGP, ? - incomplete

   Network          Next Hop    Metric LocPrf Weight Path
```

```
<truncated>
*> 10.2.1.0/24    10.10.1.1              200 11100 11000 400 200 i
*> 10.2.2.0/24    10.10.1.1              200 11100 11000 400 200 i
*> 10.2.3.0/24    10.10.1.1              200 11100 11000 400 200 i
*> 10.2.4.0/24    10.10.1.1              200 11100 11000 400 200 i
<truncated>
```

^

The ^ denotes the start of a string. Because R9 is connected to AS 12000 and AS 11100, we can find all the routes that have come to us from AS 12000 using the following command:

```
R9#sh ip bgp regexp ^12
BGP table version is 45, local router ID is 9.9.9.9
Status codes: s suppressed, d damped, h history, * valid, > best, i -
internal,
              r RIB-failure, S Stale
Origin codes: i - IGP, e - EGP, ? - incomplete

    Network         Next Hop         Weight Path
*   0.0.0.0         10.11.1.1             0 12000 11000 400 200 300 65500 i
*   1.1.1.0/24      10.11.1.1             0 12000 11000 400 200 105 i
*   1.2.1.0/24      10.11.1.1             0 12000 11000 400 200 105 i
*   10.1.0.0/24     10.11.1.1             0 12000 11000 400 200 105 i
*   10.1.1.0/24     10.11.1.1             0 12000 11000 400 200 105 i
```

$

The dollar sign signifies the end of a string. This is usually combined with the previous example. Using just the two together we can see the routes that originated from us:

```
R9#sh ip bgp regexp ^$
BGP table version is 45, local router ID is 9.9.9.9
Status codes: s suppressed, d damped, h history, * valid, > best, i -
internal,
              r RIB-failure, S Stale
Origin codes: i - IGP, e - EGP, ? - incomplete

    Network            Next Hop         Metric LocPrf Weight Path
*>  10.10.1.0/24       0.0.0.0               0              32768 i
*>  10.11.1.0/24       0.0.0.0               0              32768 i
*>  192.168.3.0        0.0.0.0               0              32768 i
```

Or routes that originated from AS 11100:

```
R9#sh ip bgp regexp ^11100$
BGP table version is 45, local router ID is 9.9.9.9
Status codes: s suppressed, d damped, h history, * valid, > best, i -
internal,
              r RIB-failure, S Stale
Origin codes: i - IGP, e - EGP, ? - incomplete

   Network          Next Hop            Metric LocPrf Weight Path
*> 192.168.2.0      10.10.1.1                0              200 11100 i
R9#
```

We can add AS numbers into the above example. To find routes that were advertised to us from AS 12000, but originated in AS 11000, we could do the following:

```
R9#sh ip bgp regexp ^12000 11000$
BGP table version is 45, local router ID is 9.9.9.9
Status codes: s suppressed, d damped, h history, * valid, > best, i -
internal,
              r RIB-failure, S Stale
Origin codes: i - IGP, e - EGP, ? - incomplete

   Network          Next Hop            Metric LocPrf Weight Path
*  10.7.1.0/24      10.11.1.1                              0 12000 11000 i
*  172.20.0.0/21    10.11.1.1                              0 12000 11000 i
*  172.20.2.0/24    10.11.1.1                              0 12000 11000 i
*  172.20.3.0/24    10.11.1.1                              0 12000 11000 i
R9#
```

[]

There is another way to find all the networks that have originated from a directly connected neighbor, and that involves using brackets to specify a range of characters, and the + sign to denote one or more instance:

```
R9#sh ip bgp regexp ^[0-9]+$
BGP table version is 47, local router ID is 9.9.9.9
Status codes: s suppressed, d damped, h history, * valid, > best, i -
internal,
              r RIB-failure, S Stale
Origin codes: i - IGP, e - EGP, ? - incomplete

   Network          Next Hop            Metric LocPrf Weight Path
*  192.168.1.0      10.11.1.1                0              0 12000 i
*> 192.168.2.0      10.10.1.1                0            200 11100 i
R9#
```

The brackets will read any number, and the + sign means that these number can occur more than once, i.e., to capture all five instances of the numbers 0-9 in our neighbors AS number. It will match one AS because we are not matching any spaces within the regexp.

If we omitted the + sign we get 0 results:

```
R9#sh ip bgp regexp ^[0-9]$

R9#
```

However, if we were directly connected to an AS with a singular number for their AS (such as AS 2), we would get some data returned.

_

The underscore is very powerful. It will match a comma (,), left brace ({), right brace (}), left parenthesis ((), right parenthesis ()), the beginning of the string, the end of the string, or a space. In an example above, we saw that we could see what routes started in AS 11000, and came through AS 12000 to get to us (^12000 11000$). This, however, didn't show the best routes. If we know the originating AS we can find this by using:

```
R9#sh ip bgp regexp _11000$
BGP table version is 45, local router ID is 9.9.9.9
Status codes: s suppressed, d damped, h history, * valid, > best, i -
internal,
              r RIB-failure, S Stale
Origin codes: i - IGP, e - EGP, ? - incomplete

    Network          Next Hop        Metric LocPrf Weight Path
*   10.7.1.0/24      10.11.1.1                         0 12000 11000 i
*>                   10.10.1.1              200          11100 11000 i
*   172.20.0.0/21    10.11.1.1                         0 12000 11000 i
*>                   10.10.1.1              200          11100 11000 i
*   172.20.2.0/24    10.11.1.1                         0 12000 11000 i
*>                   10.10.1.1              200          11100 11000 i
*   172.20.3.0/24    10.11.1.1                         0 12000 11000 i
*>                   10.10.1.1              200          11100 11000 i
R9#
```

Here the underscore is matching the space between 12000 and 11000 and the dollar matches the 11000 at the end of the string, it also shows us that the route through AS 11100 is preferred.

Alternatively, if we wanted to find just the routes learned from AS 12000, we could match the start of the string and a space after the AS number:

```
R9#sh ip bgp regexp ^12000_
BGP table version is 45, local router ID is 9.9.9.9
Status codes: s suppressed, d damped, h history, * valid, > best, i -
internal,
              r RIB-failure, S Stale
Origin codes: i - IGP, e - EGP, ? - incomplete

   Network          Next Hop         Weight Path
*  0.0.0.0          10.11.1.1             0 12000 11000 400 200 300 65500 i
*  1.1.1.0/24       10.11.1.1             0 12000 11000 400 200 105 i
*  1.2.1.0/24       10.11.1.1             0 12000 11000 400 200 105 i
*  10.1.0.0/24      10.11.1.1             0 12000 11000 400 200 105 i
*  10.1.1.0/24      10.11.1.1             0 12000 11000 400 200 105 i
*  10.2.1.0/24      10.11.1.1             0 12000 11000 400 200 i
*  10.2.2.0/24      10.11.1.1             0 12000 11000 400 200 i
*  10.2.3.0/24      10.11.1.1             0 12000 11000 400 200 i
*  10.2.4.0/24      10.11.1.1             0 12000 11000 400 200 i
```

If we use the underscore at either side of an AS number, we can see what routes came through that AS:

```
R9#sh ip bgp regexp _200_
BGP table version is 45, local router ID is 9.9.9.9
Status codes: s suppressed, d damped, h history, * valid, > best, i -
internal,
              r RIB-failure, S Stale
Origin codes: i - IGP, e - EGP, ? - incomplete

   Network          Next Hop         Weight Path
*  0.0.0.0          10.11.1.1             0 12000 11000 400 200 300 65500 i
*>                  10.10.1.1           200 11100 11000 400 200 300 65500 i
*  1.1.1.0/24       10.11.1.1             0 12000 11000 400 200 105 i
*>                  10.10.1.1           200 11100 11000 400 200 105 i
*  1.2.1.0/24       10.11.1.1             0 12000 11000 400 200 105 i
*>                  10.10.1.1           200 11100 11000 400 200 105 i
*  10.1.0.0/24      10.11.1.1             0 12000 11000 400 200 105 i
*>                  10.10.1.1           200 11100 11000 400 200 105 i
```

So far, all the examples have included the router ID, status codes and origin codes, these I have normally hidden away using the modifier "I beg Network". However, when we use the regexp command, the pipe (I) is taken as part of the regexp and prevents the results being returned:

```
R9#sh ip bgp regexp ^12000_ | i 10.2

R9#
```

We can, instead, use the command "quote-regexp" if we want to use output modifiers:

```
R9#sh ip bgp quote-regexp ^12000_ | i 10.2
*   10.2.1.0/24      10.11.1.1         0 12000 11000 400 200 i
*   10.2.2.0/24      10.11.1.1         0 12000 11000 400 200 i
*   10.2.3.0/24      10.11.1.1         0 12000 11000 400 200 i
*   10.2.4.0/24      10.11.1.1         0 12000 11000 400 200 i
R9#sh ip bgp quote-regexp ^12000_ | beg Network
    Network          Next Hop          Weight Path
*   0.0.0.0          10.11.1.1         0 12000 11000 400 200 300 65500 i
*   1.1.1.0/24       10.11.1.1         0 12000 11000 400 200 105 i
*   1.2.1.0/24       10.11.1.1         0 12000 11000 400 200 105 i
*   10.1.0.0/24      10.11.1.1         0 12000 11000 400 200 105 i
*   10.1.1.0/24      10.11.1.1         0 12000 11000 400 200 105 i
```

()

We can look for routes that came to us from a confederation peer, by placing that peers AS number in parentheses:

```
R1#sh ip bgp quote-regexp (102) | beg Network
    Network          Next Hop          Metric LocPrf Weight Path
r>  1.2.1.0/24       1.2.1.2              0    100      0 (102) i
*>  172.22.0.0/21    1.2.1.2              0    100      0 (102) i
R1#sh ip bgp quote-regexp (101) | beg Network
    Network          Next Hop          Metric LocPrf Weight Path
r>  1.1.1.0/24       1.1.1.2              0    100      0 (101) i
*>  172.21.1.0/24    1.1.1.2              0    100      0 (101) i
*>  172.21.2.0/24    1.1.1.2              0    100      0 (101) i
*>  172.21.3.0/24    1.1.1.2              0    100      0 (101) i
*>  172.21.4.0/24    1.1.1.2              0    100      0 (101) i
R1#
```

Lastly, before we move on, if we know that routes have originated from an AS that begins with a certain sequence of number, but we can't remember the complete AS number, we can put most of what we have used so far into one regexp. So, if we know that the AS begins with 655, but are not sure of the next numbers, or even how many numbers, we can use the following:

```
R9#sh ip bgp quote-regexp _655+[0-9]*$ | beg Network
```

```
        Network          Next Hop         Weight Path
 *      0.0.0.0          10.11.1.1            0 12000 11000 400 200 300 65500 i
 *>                      10.10.1.1          200 11100 11000 400 200 300 65500 i
 *      10.3.1.0/24      10.11.1.1            0 12000 11000 400 200 300 65500 i
 *>                      10.10.1.1          200 11100 11000 400 200 300 65500 i
 *      10.4.1.0/24      10.11.1.1            0 12000 11000 400 200 300 65500 i
 *>                      10.10.1.1          200 11100 11000 400 200 300 65500 i
 *      172.18.1.0/24    10.11.1.1            0 12000 11000 400 200 300 65500 i
 *>                      10.10.1.1          200 11100 11000 400 200 300 65500 i
 *      172.18.2.0/24    10.11.1.1            0 12000 11000 400 200 300 65500 i
 *>                      10.10.1.1          200 11100 11000 400 200 300 65500 i
 *      172.18.3.0/24    10.11.1.1            0 12000 11000 400 200 300 65500 ?
 *>                      10.10.1.1          200 11100 11000 400 200 300 65500 ?
R9#
```

This will match the space before 65500, the first three numbers (655), the next number, because of the [0-9], and any subsequent numbers (the * denoting one or more instances). We could also have matched 65501, 65502, and so on.

Regexp can also be used to limit down the routes we want to receive or advertise in conjunction with a filter list. Although this can potentially cause problems with alternate routes (if we filter incoming routes), a filter list is very useful in the event that we want to prevent another router using us as a transit AS.

If we wanted to prevent R11 from using R9 as a transit AS (therefore preferring R7 as its gateway to the rest of the network), we would implement the following:

```
R9(config)#router bgp 13500
R9(config-router)#template peer-policy R11
R9(config-router-ptmp)#filter-list 1 out
R9(config-router-ptmp)#exit
R9(config-router)#
R9(config-router)#exit
R9(config)#ip as-path access-list 1 permit ^$
R9(config)#exit
```

This would still advertise anything originated by R9 to R11, but nothing else.

Before we implement the filter list we can see the (slightly truncated) BGP table on R11:

```
R11#sh ip bgp | beg 192.168
*> 192.168.1.0       0.0.0.0           0      32768 i
 * 192.168.2.0       10.11.1.2                0 13500 11100 i
*>                   10.8.1.1                 0 11000 11100 i
*> 192.168.3.0       10.11.1.2         0      0 13500 i
```

```
*                       10.8.1.1                              0 11000 11100 13500 i
R11#
```

After we perform a soft refresh on R9:

```
R9#clear ip bgp 10.11.1.1 out
R9#
```

We can see that R11 has far fewer routes:

```
R11#sh ip bgp | beg 172.21
*> 172.21.1.0/24      10.8.1.1                              0 11000 400 200 105 i
*> 172.21.4.0/24      10.8.1.1                              0 11000 400 200 105 i
*> 172.22.0.0/21      10.8.1.1                              0 11000 400 200 105 i
*> 172.26.1.0/24      10.8.1.1                              0 11000 400 i
*> 172.26.2.0/24      10.8.1.1                              0 11000 400 i
*> 172.26.3.0/24      10.8.1.1                              0 11000 400 i
*> 192.168.1.0        0.0.0.0              0        32768 i
*> 192.168.2.0        10.8.1.1                              0 11000 11100 i
*> 192.168.3.0        10.11.1.2            0                0 13500 i
*                     10.8.1.1                              0 11000 11100 13500 i
R11#
```

If we were being generous, and allowed R11 access to AS 11100 through us we could also use this as-path access-list:

```
R9(config)#ip as-path access-list 1 permit ^[11100]+$
R9(config)#ip as-path access-list 1 permit ^$
```

Which will (again after a refresh) make R11's BGP table look like this:

```
R11#sh ip bgp | beg 172.21
*> 172.21.1.0/24      10.8.1.1                              0 11000 400 200 105 i
*> 172.21.4.0/24      10.8.1.1                              0 11000 400 200 105 i
*> 172.22.0.0/21      10.8.1.1                              0 11000 400 200 105 i
*> 172.26.1.0/24      10.8.1.1                              0 11000 400 i
*> 172.26.2.0/24      10.8.1.1                              0 11000 400 i
*> 172.26.3.0/24      10.8.1.1                              0 11000 400 i
*> 192.168.1.0        0.0.0.0              0        32768 i
*  192.168.2.0        10.11.1.2                             0 13500 11100 i
*>                    10.8.1.1                              0 11000 11100 i
*> 192.168.3.0        10.11.1.2            0                0 13500 i
*                     10.8.1.1                              0 11000 11100 13500 i
R11#
```

Now we have see how we can match routes based on the AS path sequence, and, using as-path access lists, how we can use regexp to deny or permit prefixes.

Let us now have a look at how BGP makes its decisions, and how we can influence them.

11.3 BGP Best Path Selection Algorithm

There are a large number of factors that BGP will take into account when choosing the best path (the one that is inserted into the routing table). Below is the list in order, as published by Cisco[6], and we will go through each of these in order.

1. Verify that the next hop is reachable
2. Prefer the path with the highest weight
3. Prefer the path with the highest LOCAL_PREF (100 by default)
4. Prefer the path that was originated locally or through redistribution from an IGP
5. Prefer the path with the shortest AS_PATH
6. Prefer the path with the lowest origin type
7. Prefer the path with the lowest MED
8. Prefer eBGP over iBGP paths
9. Prefer the path with the lowest IGP metric to the BGP next hop
10. Determine if multiple paths require installation in routing table
11. Prefer the path that was received first (oldest)
12. Prefer the route that comes from the BGP router with the lowest router ID
13. Prefer the path with the minimum cluster list length
14. Prefer the path that comes from the lowest neighbor address

Valid next hop

This is probably stating the obvious, but if an update is received, and the next hop is not reachable, the update will be dropped. If it is valid the router will then look at the weight.

Highest weight

Weight is specific to Cisco implementations of BGP, and is only relevant to the local router. It is not passed in BGP UPDATE messages. Weight is a number between 0 and

---

[6] http://www.cisco.com/en/US/tech/tk365/technologies_tech_note09186a0080094431.shtml

65,535, with 0 being the default weight applied to routes advertised to the local router, and 32,768 being set on routes originating from the local router.

In the path selection algorithm highest weight wins.

Take this example, from when we set up peer policy templates earlier:

```
R9#sh ip bgp | beg 192.168.2
*   192.168.2.0       10.11.1.1                0 12000 13500 11100 i
*>                    10.10.1.1         0    200 11100 i
*   192.168.3.0       10.10.1.1              200 11100 13500 i
*                     10.11.1.1                0 12000 13500 i
*>                    0.0.0.0           0  32768 i
```

We set a policy to assign a weight of 200 for routes originating from R8, we can also see that, due to the allow-as command being set, the 192.168.3.0/24 network is passed back to R9. Even with the weight from R8 being set to 200, because the route is generated locally, its weight is set to 32768, and therefore it is the preferred route.

There are number of ways we can influence weight. We can use the neighbor command, as we saw earlier, and set the weight for the neighbor at the level we want. This, however, will set the weight for all the routes coming advertised to us by that neighbor. So let's see how we could influence the weight of one route, based on an AS Path.

In its simplest form, an as-path access list looks like this:

```
router(config)#ip as-path access-list 5 permit ^100$
```

We can then combine it with a route-map:

```
router(config)#route-map SETWEIGHT200 permit 10
router(config-route-map)#match as-path 5
router(config-route-map)#set weight 200
```

Or a filter-list:

```
router(config-router)#neighbor 1.1.1.1 filter-list 5 weight 200
```

To see this in action we will look at the 172.18.1.0/24 route, which originates on R12 (AS 65500), and how we can choose which route R6 will take to get to it.

Currently, R6 has two entries for this network, and we can see that it favors R5:

```
R6#sh ip bgp 172.18.1.0/24
BGP routing table entry for 172.18.1.0/24, version 20
Paths: (2 available, best #2, table default)
  Advertised to update-groups:
     1
  500 300 65500
    10.6.1.2 from 10.6.1.2 (10.10.10.10)
      Origin IGP, localpref 100, valid, external
      Community: 19661300
  200 300 65500
    10.5.1.1 from 10.5.1.1 (5.5.5.5)
      Origin IGP, localpref 100, valid, external, best
R6#sh ip bgp | beg 172.18.1.0
*   172.18.1.0/24    10.6.1.2                        0 500 300 65500 i
*>                   10.5.1.1                        0 200 300 65500 i
```

Let's make the route go through R10 instead. R6 already has a route-map associated with R10, as part of our foray into conditional advertisement, so we will append to that.

Currently the route-map for R10 looks like this:

```
route-map set_community permit 10
  set community 19661300
```

We will start with an IP prefix-list to match our network, and then also make the route-map check the as-path as well. We could just set the weight based on the prefix-list, as this would achieve the objective, but it's useful to add the additional match command, so we can see how to use as-path access-lists:

```
R6#conf t
R6(config)#ip prefix-list 172-18 permit 172.18.1.0/24
R6(config)#ip as-path access-list 5 permit _300_
R6(config)#route-map set_community permit 10
R6(config-route-map)#match ip address prefix-list 172-18
R6(config-route-map)#match as-path 5
R6(config-route-map)#set weight 100
R6(config-route-map)#set community 19661300
R6(config-route-map)#exit
R6(config)#route-map set_community permit 20
R6(config-route-map)#set community 19661300
R6(config-route-map)#exit
R6(config)#
```

I have chosen to match AS 300 in the as-path access-list, as matching AS 500 (our directly connected peer) would be too obvious.

The end result is that R6 now prefers the path through AS 500 to reach R12:

```
R6#sh ip bgp | beg 172.18.1.0
*> 172.18.1.0/24    10.6.1.2                100 500 300 65500 i
*                   10.5.1.1                  0 200 300 65500 i
```

Another alternative would have been to apply a similar route-map to both R10 and R5, both matching the same prefix list. However, the as-path access list would be looking for AS 500 (ip as-path access-list 5 permit _500_). The route via R5 would fail the second check, and therefore the path through R10 would be preferred.

```
R6(config)#no ip as-path access-list 5 permit _300_
R6(config)#ip as-path access-list 5 permit _500_
R6(config)#route-map set-R5-172-18-weight permit 10
R6(config-route-map)#match ip address prefix-list 172-18
R6(config-route-map)#match as-path 5
R6(config-route-map)#set weight 100
R6(config-route-map)#exit
R6(config)#route-map set-R5-172-18-weight permit 20
R6(config-route-map)#exit
R6(config)#router bgp 400
R6(config-router)#neighbor 10.5.1.1 route-map set-R5-172-18-weight in
```

R6 will still prefer the route via R10, because the route-map attached to R5 is unable to match all the conditions.

```
R6#sh ip bgp 172.18.1.0/24
BGP routing table entry for 172.18.1.0/24, version 75
Paths: (2 available, best #1, table default)
  Advertised to update-groups:
      1          2
  500 300 65500
    10.6.1.2 from 10.6.1.2 (10.10.10.10)
      Origin IGP, localpref 100, weight 100, valid, external, best
      Community: 19661300
  200 300 65500
    10.5.1.1 from 10.5.1.1 (5.5.5.5)
      Origin IGP, localpref 100, valid, external
R6#
```

In the event that one neighbor will be preferred for all routes, instead of a subnet, then we can use the neighbor weight command:

```
R6#conf t
```

```
R6(config)#router bgp 400
R6(config-router)#neighbor 10.6.1.2 weight 200
```

If the weight is equal for the same route, the router will then try and use the highest local preference.

Highest LOCAL_PREF

We have set the local pref previously, and seen the effect that is has had. Local preference is about how an AS considers a route in order to exit an AS. The higher local preference the better, and the default is 100. Local preference is exchanged within an AS.

At the moment R3, R4 and R12 receive the 172.26.3.0/24 prefix from R5:

```
R4#sh ip bgp | i 172.26.3
*>i172.26.3.0/24    172.17.5.1       0    100      0 400 i
R4#

R3#sh ip bgp | i 172.26.3
*>i172.26.3.0/24    172.17.5.1       0    100      0 400 i
R3#

R12#sh ip bgp 172.26.3.0
BGP routing table entry for 172.26.3.0/24, version 121
Paths: (2 available, best #2, table Default-IP-Routing-Table)
  Advertised to update-groups:
     2
  300 200 400
    10.3.1.1 from 10.3.1.1 (5.5.5.5)
      Origin IGP, localpref 100, valid, external
  300 500 400
    10.4.1.2 from 10.4.1.2 (10.10.10.10)
      Origin IGP, localpref 100, valid, external, best
R12#
```

R5, in turn, gets it from R6 directly, which of course will be the preferred route, and also through R12:

```
R5#sh ip bgp 172.26.3.0
BGP routing table entry for 172.26.3.0/24, version 155
Paths: (2 available, best #2, table Default-IP-Routing-Table)
  Advertised to update-groups:
     1          2
  300 65500 300 500 400
```

```
      10.3.1.2 from 10.3.1.2 (12.12.12.12)
        Origin IGP, localpref 100, valid, external
  400
     10.5.1.2 from 10.5.1.2 (6.6.6.6)
        Origin IGP, metric 0, localpref 100, valid, external, best
R5#
```

We will see now what happens to the local preference once it is set, and how this is carried over AS boundaries. First, we will create a prefix list to match the prefix and a route-map to match that prefix-list.

```
R5(config)#ip prefix-list R12-172-26-3 permit 172.26.3.0/24
R5(config)#route-map set-R12-localpref permit 10
R5(config-route-map)#match ip address prefix-list R12-172-26-3
R5(config-route-map)#set local-preference 150
R5(config-route-map)#exit
R5(config)#route-map set-R12-localpref permit 20
R5(config-route-map)#exit
R5(config)#router bgp 200
R5(config-router)#neighbor 10.3.1.2 route-map set-R12-localpref in
R5(config-router)#exit
R5(config)#exit
R5#clear ip bgp 10.3.1.2
R5#
%BGP-5-ADJCHANGE: neighbor 10.3.1.2 Down User reset
R5#
%BGP-5-ADJCHANGE: neighbor 10.3.1.2 Up
R5#sh ip bgp 172.26.3.0
BGP routing table entry for 172.26.3.0/24, version 176
Paths: (2 available, best #1, table Default-IP-Routing-Table)
Flag: 0x820
  Advertised to update-groups:
     1        2
  300 65500 300 500 400
     10.3.1.2 from 10.3.1.2 (12.12.12.12)
        Origin IGP, localpref 150, valid, external, best
  400
     10.5.1.2 from 10.5.1.2 (6.6.6.6)
        Origin IGP, metric 0, localpref 100, valid, external
R5#
```

We can see on R4 and R3 the before and after effects of this change:

```
R4#sh ip bgp | i 172.26.3
*>i172.26.3.0/24    172.17.5.1      0    100    0 400 i
R4#sh ip bgp | i 172.26.3
```

```
*>i172.26.3.0/24    172.17.5.1    0    150    0 300 65500 300 500 400 i
R4#

R3#sh ip bgp | i 172.26.3
*>i172.26.3.0/24    172.17.5.1    0    100    0 400 i
R3#sh ip bgp | i 172.26.3
*>i172.26.3.0/24    172.17.5.1    0    150    0 300 65500 300 500 400 i
R3#
```

This is carried over to R2:

```
R2#sh ip bgp | beg 172.26.
*  i172.26.1.0/24    172.17.1.1    0    100    0 400 i
*>i                  172.16.1.1    0    100    0 400 i
*  i172.26.2.0/24    172.17.1.1    0    100    0 400 i
*>i                  172.16.1.1    0    100    0 400 i
*  i172.26.3.0/24    172.17.1.1    0    150    0 300 65500 300 500 400 i
*>i                  172.16.1.1    0    150    0 300 65500 300 500 400 i
```

The localpref is not carried over to R1 (as it cannot be passed between AS):

```
R1#sh ip bgp | beg 172.26
*> 172.26.1.0/24    10.1.1.2              0 200 400 i
*> 172.26.2.0/24    10.1.1.2              0 200 400 i
*> 172.26.3.0/24    10.1.1.2              0 200 300 65500 300 500 400 i
```

If the local preference is equal, then the router will then prefer locally originating routes:

Locally originated routes

The next step, when considering the best path to the same prefix that is advertised by two routers (where the weight and local preference are both equal), is to consider whether the route originated locally. The router will prefer the path that was locally originated, such as via a network or aggregate BGP subcommand or through redistribution from an IGP.

We already know that locally originated routes will by default have their weight set at 32768:

```
R9#sh ip bgp | beg 192.168.2
*  192.168.2.0    10.11.1.1                0 12000 13500 11100 i
*>                10.10.1.1       0        200 11100 i
*  192.168.3.0    10.10.1.1                200 11100 13500 i
*                 10.11.1.1                0 12000 13500 i
*>                0.0.0.0         0        32768 i
```

But what if the weight and local preference are the same? We will test this out on R5, which is currently advertising a summary of the loopback addresses on R10:

```
R5#sh ip bgp | beg 172.19
*> 172.19.0.0/21     0.0.0.0          10     100     150 400 500 i
```

We can see that, due to adding an attribute map in section 11.1, the metric has been set to 10 for the 172.19.0.0/21 aggregate, the local preference has been set to 100 and the weight to 150. So, according to the algorithm, if we summarized the same set of addresses on R6, with the same set of metrics, R5 should prefer its own aggregated route.

First of all we will create the summary on R6:

```
R6(config)#router bgp 400
R6(config-router)#aggregate-address 172.19.0.0 255.255.248.0 as-set
R6(config-router)#
```

Which will be advertised to R5 from R6, and also from R12:

```
R5#sh ip bgp | beg 172.19
*    172.19.0.0/21   10.3.1.2              0 300 65500 300 500 400 500 i
*                    10.5.1.2        0     0 400 500 i
*>                   0.0.0.0        10   100 150 400 500 i
```

At the moment R5 prefers its own route, the weight and local preference are both higher than the routes advertised to it, so this is hardly surprising. We need to add another prefix list for the aggregated prefix, along with another clause in the route-map attached to R12, which we created in 11.3, in order to make the weight and local preference match, as well as creating a matching route-map for R6:

```
R5(config)#ip prefix-list 172-19-0 permit 172.19.0.0/21
R5(config)#route-map set-R12-localpref permit 20
R5(config-route-map)#match ip address prefix-list 172-19-0
R5(config-route-map)#set local-pref 100
R5(config-route-map)#set metric 10
R5(config-route-map)#set weight 150
R5(config-route-map)#exit
R5(config)#route-map set-R12-localpref permit 30
R5(config-route-map)#exit
R5(config)#route-map set-R6-routes permit 10
R5(config-route-map)#match ip address prefix-list 172-19-0
R5(config-route-map)#set local-pref 100
R5(config-route-map)#set metric 10
R5(config-route-map)#set weight 150
```

```
R5(config-route-map)#exit
R5(config)#route-map set-R6-routes permit 20
R5(config-route-map)#exit
R5(config)#router bgp 200
R5(config-router)#neigh 10.5.1.2 route-map set-R6-routes in
```

The result is as expected. R5 prefers its own locally generated route rather than those from R6 or R12.

```
R5#sh ip bgp | beg 172.19.0.0
*   172.19.0.0/21   10.5.1.2   10   100   150 400 500 i
*>                  0.0.0.0    10   100   150 400 500 i
*                   10.3.1.2   10   100   150 300 65500 300 500 400 500 i
R5#sh ip bgp 172.19.0.0/21
BGP routing table entry for 172.19.0.0/21, version 139
Paths: (3 available, best #2, table Default-IP-Routing-Table)
  Advertised to update-groups:
      1          2
  400 500, (aggregated by 400 6.6.6.6)
    10.5.1.2 from 10.5.1.2 (6.6.6.6)
      Origin IGP, metric 10, localpref 100, weight 150, valid, external
  400 500, (aggregated by 200 5.5.5.5)
    0.0.0.0 from 0.0.0.0 (5.5.5.5)
      Origin IGP, metric 10, localpref 100, weight 150, valid, aggregated, local, best
  300 65500 300 500 400 500, (aggregated by 400 6.6.6.6)
    10.3.1.2 from 10.3.1.2 (12.12.12.12)
      Origin IGP, metric 10, localpref 100, weight 150, valid, external
R5#
```

The path from R12 was never much of a consideration for R5, due to having the longer AS Path length. The best path algorithm prefers the shortest AS Path, which, after preferring locally originated routes, comes next.

Shortest AS_PATH

Shortest AS Path is the most obvious decision maker. Weight is Cisco specific, and specific to a singular router, and local preference has no effect outside of its own AS. It is also not often that we are likely to encounter a route being advertised to us that is identical to one we ourselves have originated. So, for the majority of the path decisions that BGP makes, the shortest AS Path will win.

This is not to say that we cannot change this if we want to.

On R5 we set the local preference for the 172.26.3.0/24 network to 150. Now, we will do a similar example, using another of the networks advertised by R6:

```
R5#sh ip bgp 172.26.2.0
BGP routing table entry for 172.26.2.0/24, version 135
Paths: (2 available, best #2, table Default-IP-Routing-Table)
  Advertised to update-groups:
     1         2
  300 65500 300 500 400
    10.3.1.2 from 10.3.1.2 (12.12.12.12)
      Origin IGP, localpref 100, valid, external
  400
    10.5.1.2 from 10.5.1.2 (6.6.6.6)
      Origin IGP, metric 0, localpref 100, valid, external, best
R5#
```

So, we have no weight set on either of the routes, and the local preference matches on both. Neither originated locally, so the best path must have been selected due to the AS Path length.

We can change the AS path. Naturally, we cannot make it shorter, but we can make it longer; by using the as-path prepend command within a route-map:

```
R5(config)#ip prefix-list 172-26-2 seq 5 permit 172.26.2.0/24
R5(config)#route-map set-R6-routes permit 20
R5(config-route-map)#match ip address prefix-list 172-26-2
R5(config-route-map)#set as-path prepend 200 200 200 200 200
R5(config-route-map)#exit
R5(config)#route-map set-R6-routes permit 30
R5(config-route-map)#exit
R5(config)#
```

The above route-map adds five instances of our own AS number (and it is best practice to use your own AS number and not other people's AS number when using AS prepend), therefore making the route less desirable than it previously was. The AS path has six entries compared to the five entries in the route from R12. Subsequently, the other route is installed into the routing table:

```
R5#sh ip bgp 172.26.2.0
BGP routing table entry for 172.26.2.0/24, version 168
Paths: (2 available, best #2, table Default-IP-Routing-Table)
Flag: 0x820
  Advertised to update-groups:
     1         2
```

```
                  200 200 200 200 200 400
                    10.5.1.2 from 10.5.1.2 (6.6.6.6)
                      Origin IGP, metric 0, localpref 100, valid, external
                  300 65500 300 500 400
                    10.3.1.2 from 10.3.1.2 (12.12.12.12)
                      Origin IGP, localpref 100, valid, external, best
        R5#sh ip route 172.26.2.0
        Routing entry for 172.26.2.0/24
          Known via "bgp 200", distance 20, metric 0
          Tag 300, type external
          Last update from 10.3.1.2 00:19:42 ago
          Routing Descriptor Blocks:
          * 10.3.1.2, from 10.3.1.2, 00:19:42 ago
              Route metric is 0, traffic share count is 1
              AS Hops 5
              Route tag 300

        R5#
```

In the event that the AS path is of equal length, then the router will next look for the origin type.

Lowest origin type

The origin type is not to be confused with whether the route originated locally (as we have already covered that). The origin indicates how a route was learned. There are three different values, but generally only two are ever encountered.

IGP (value 0) - set when a route is injected into BGP through the network command
EGP (value 1) - the route was learned via the Exterior Border Gateway Protocol (EBGP), rarely encountered
INCOMPLETE (value 2) - this occurs when a route is redistributed into BGP, which we will see later on, or if the origin is unknown.

When evaluating identical routes, one with a value of IGP (0) will be preferred over EGP (1), as it is lower, and EGP is preferred, again as it is lower, than INCOMPLETE (2).

Let's switch the route on R5, which we used in the previous example, to have the same AS length as the other route, and see the effect that the origin type has on the path choice:

```
    R5(config)#route-map set-R6-routes permit 20
    R5(config-route-map)#no set as-path prepend 200 200 200 200 200
    R5(config-route-map)#set as-path prepend 200 200 200 200
```

Now, we can see that the AS paths are equal and R5 prefers the route through R12:

```
R5#sh ip bgp 172.26.2.0
BGP routing table entry for 172.26.2.0/24, version 260
Paths: (2 available, best #2, table Default-IP-Routing-Table)
  Advertised to update-groups:
     1          2
  200 200 200 200 400
    10.5.1.2 from 10.5.1.2 (6.6.6.6)
      Origin IGP, metric 0, localpref 100, valid, external
  300 65500 300 500 400
    10.3.1.2 from 10.3.1.2 (12.12.12.12)
      Origin IGP, localpref 100, valid, external, best
R5#
```

So, let us set the origin of the route coming from R12, to be lower than the one coming from R6:

```
R5(config)#route-map set-R12-localpref permit 30
R5(config-route-map)#match ip address prefix-list 172-26-2
R5(config-route-map)#set origin incomplete
R5(config-route-map)#exit
R5(config)#route-map set-R12-localpref permit 40
R5(config-route-map)#exit
R5(config)#
```

Previously, the route advertised by R12 was preferred, but with a setting of incomplete the route through R6 is now preferred:

```
R5#sh ip bgp 172.26.2.0
BGP routing table entry for 172.26.2.0/24, version 46
Paths: (2 available, best #2, table Default-IP-Routing-Table)
Flag: 0x820
  Advertised to update-groups:
     1          2
  300 65500 300 500 400
    10.3.1.2 from 10.3.1.2 (12.12.12.12)
      Origin incomplete, localpref 100, valid, external
  200 200 200 200 400
    10.5.1.2 from 10.5.1.2 (6.6.6.6)
      Origin IGP, metric 0, localpref 100, valid, external, best
R5#
```

For completeness let's check how changing the origin to EGP looks. When we use this option we must set an AS number for the remote AS:

```
R5(config)#route-map set-R12-localpref permit 30
R5(config-route-map)#no set origin incomplete
R5(config-route-map)#set origin egp 400
R5(config-route-map)#exit
R5(config)#exit
```

The result (after clearing the bgp peering and letting it reestablish) is:

```
R5#sh ip bgp 172.26.2.0
BGP routing table entry for 172.26.2.0/24, version 46
Paths: (2 available, best #2, table Default-IP-Routing-Table)
Flag: 0x820
  Advertised to update-groups:
      1          2
  300 65500 300 500 400
    10.3.1.2 from 10.3.1.2 (12.12.12.12)
      Origin EGP, localpref 100, valid, external
  200 200 200 200 400
    10.5.1.2 from 10.5.1.2 (6.6.6.6)
      Origin IGP, metric 0, localpref 100, valid, external, best
R5#
```

We again prefer R6 for this route.

If the origin type for this route had been equal, then the router would use the MED value as the next check.

Lowest MED

MED (or Multi-Exit Discriminator) is an optional, non-transitive attribute. It works as a hint to external neighbors about the preferred path into an AS which has multiple entry points. This is the Metric value that is seen in the output of a "sh ip bgp" command. During the path selection process, a lower MED is preferred.

We will return the 172.26.2.0/24 route to its default origin type and, instead, use MED to influence our path decision. This time we will send the traffic through R12, setting the MED to 100, and the MED for the route through R6 to be 200:

```
R5#conf t
R5(config)#route-map set-R12-localpref permit 30
R5(config-route-map)#no set origin egp 400
```

```
R5(config-route-map)#set metric 100
R5(config-route-map)#exit
R5(config)#route-map set-R6-routes permit 20
R5(config-route-map)#set metric 200
R5(config-route-map)#exit
R5(config)#exit
R5#
```

Once the peerings for R12 and R6 have been cleared and allowed to reestablish, we can see the origin is again equal (IGP), and that our metric settings have had the desired effect, making the route through R12 the preferred path:

```
R5#sh ip bgp 172.26.2.0
BGP routing table entry for 172.26.2.0/24, version 127
Paths: (2 available, best #2, table Default-IP-Routing-Table)
Flag: 0x820
  Advertised to update-groups:
        1          2
  200 200 200 200 400
    10.5.1.2 from 10.5.1.2 (6.6.6.6)
      Origin IGP, metric 200, localpref 100, valid, external
  300 65500 300 500 400
    10.3.1.2 from 10.3.1.2 (12.12.12.12)
      Origin IGP, metric 100, localpref 100, valid, external, best
R5#sh ip bgp quote-regexp _400$ | beg Network
   Network          Next Hop  Metric LocPrf Wght Path
r> 10.5.1.0/24      10.5.1.2       0             0 400 i
r                   10.3.1.2                     0 300 65500 300 500 400 i
*> 10.6.1.0/24      10.5.1.2       0             0 400 i
*                   10.3.1.2                     0 300 65500 300 500 400 i
*> 172.26.1.0/24    10.5.1.2       0             0 400 i
*                   10.3.1.2                     0 300 65500 300 500 400 i
*  172.26.2.0/24    10.5.1.2     200             0 200 200 200 200 400 i
*>                  10.3.1.2     100             0 300 65500 300 500 400 i
*  172.26.3.0/24    10.5.1.2       0             0 400 i
*>                  10.3.1.2            150      0 300 65500 300 500 400 i
R5#
```

There are a few other things we can do with the MED value before we move on.

If a route does not have a MED value, then the Cisco IOS assigns one to it, and that is a value of 0. Therefore, because there is not a number lower than a 0, it will be considered the best path (lowest MED wins). The alternative is to globally set the router to assign a route, which is missing the MED value, the highest possible MED value of infinity (4294967294). These routes will be the least desirable. This is accomplished using the bgp command "bgp bestpath med missing-as-worst":

```
R5(config)#router bgp 200
R5(config-router)#bgp bestpath med missing-as-worst
```

The default behavior of Cisco IOS is only to compare MED in AS_PATHS, which share the same first AS. We can make the IOS compare all the MED values coming in by using the command "bgp always-compare-med":

```
R5(config)#router bgp 200
R5(config-router)#bgp always-compare-med
```

Used with the always-compare-med command, is the command "bgp deterministic-med":

```
R5(config)#router bgp 200
R5(config-router)#bgp always-compare-med
R5(config-router)#bgp deterministic-med
```

Once the always-compare-med command has been configured, then all paths for the same prefix that have been received from different neighbors within the same AS, are grouped and then sorted by the MED value. All routers within the local AS should either have the deterministic-med command enabled, or all should have it disabled, in order for the routes to be in sync.

If the metrics are the same for the routes then the router will compare eBGP-learned routes to iBGP-learned routes.

eBGP vs. iBGP

Every route type has a default administrative distance (AD). The lower the AD the better it is considered to be. A connected route is the best of all routes with an AD of 0, static routes have an AD of 1, an eBGP route has an AD of 20, and an iBGP route has an AD of 200.

The full table of administrative distances is below:

Type	AD
Connected	0
Static	1

Type	AD
eBGP	20
EIGRP (internal)	90
IGRP	100
OSPF	110
IS-IS	115
RIP	120
EIGRP (external)	170
iBGP	200
EIGRP summary route	5

If there is a tie then the lowest IGP metric is preferred.

Lowest IGP metric

If identical routes are being learned from two different IGPs, then the IGP with the lower metric (see the table above) will be the preferred route. If the best path is selected at this point the process still continues, and will check to see if multiple paths are required. IGPs and BGP will be covered in more depth in chapter 12.

Multiple paths

BGP allows more than one path to be installed into the routing table for the same destination, enabling the router to load balance between the routes. For this to occur the following must match:

- Weight
- Local preference
- AS-Path length
- Origin
- MED
- IGP Metric

We can change the number of iBGP paths with the following:

```
R5(config)#router bgp 200
R5(config-router)#maximum-paths ibgp 2
R5(config-router)#exit
R5(config)#exit
```

And we can see the effect that this has on our routing table:

```
R5#sh ip route | beg Gateway
Gateway of last resort is 10.3.1.2 to network 0.0.0.0

         1.0.0.0/24 is subnetted, 2 subnets
B           1.1.1.0 [200/0] via 172.17.1.1, 00:00:21
                    [200/0] via 172.16.1.1, 00:00:21
B           1.2.1.0 [200/0] via 172.17.1.1, 00:00:21
                    [200/0] via 172.16.1.1, 00:00:21
         172.17.0.0/24 is subnetted, 4 subnets
C           172.17.5.0 is directly connected, Loopback0
S           172.17.1.0 [1/0] via 10.2.3.1
B            172.17.0.0 [200/0] via 172.17.1.1, 00:00:21
                        [200/0] via 172.16.1.1, 00:00:21
B           172.17.2.0 [200/0] via 172.17.1.1, 00:03:03
         172.16.0.0/24 is subnetted, 2 subnets
S           172.16.1.0 [1/0] via 10.2.4.2
B           172.16.2.0 [200/0] via 172.16.1.1, 00:03:03
         172.19.0.0/16 is variably subnetted, 5 subnets, 2 masks
B           172.19.4.0/24 [20/0] via 10.5.1.2, 00:03:03
B           172.19.3.0/24 [20/0] via 10.5.1.2, 00:03:03
B           172.19.2.0/24 [20/0] via 10.5.1.2, 00:03:03
B           172.19.1.0/24 [20/0] via 10.5.1.2, 00:03:03
B           172.19.0.0/21 [20/10] via 10.5.1.2, 00:03:05
         172.18.0.0/24 is subnetted, 3 subnets
B           172.18.2.0 [20/0] via 10.3.1.2, 00:03:12
B           172.18.3.0 [20/0] via 10.3.1.2, 00:03:12
B           172.18.1.0 [20/0] via 10.3.1.2, 00:03:12
         172.21.0.0/24 is subnetted, 2 subnets
B            172.21.1.0 [200/0] via 172.17.1.1, 00:00:30
                        [200/0] via 172.16.1.1, 00:00:30
B            172.21.4.0 [200/0] via 172.17.1.1, 00:00:30
                        [200/0] via 172.16.1.1, 00:00:30
```

Now, R5 will happily load-balance across both paths where it is learned from an iBGP source (therefore having an AD of 200). To enable eBGP multipath, or to enable this for both iBGP and eBGP in one command, we need to use address families.

If you recall from the Multiprotocol BGP chapter, we introduced the idea of address families (AFs). Address families also allow us to use eBGP multipath load sharing, and eibgp multipaths (external and internal bgp multipath). These require the setting of an address first, and then they can be set up using the commands "maximum paths eBGP <number of paths>" or "maximum paths eibgp <number of paths>" respectively[7].

Regardless of whether multipathing is required or not, if we reach this point in the process, the path selection continues and will next look at which route was received first.

Received first

If both the paths are external and equal in all settings and metrics up to now, then the path received first will be preferred. This is to minimize flapping of routes, so that a newly received route does not over-rule an existing route. However, if no current best-path has been chosen, then this step is skipped and the process still continues.

Lowest router ID

The router ID is checked next and lowest wins. If the router ID is the same, then we move on.

Minimum cluster list length

This is only applicable when dealing with route reflectors; the lowest cluster list length will win.

Lowest neighbor address

Finally, we get to the last in the list, when all else has been checked and calculated, it is the route that came from the lowest neighbor IP address that will win.

11.4 mnemonics

There we have the BGP path selection process in full. There are a lot of factors to take into consideration, but only when we start to tweak the defaults. For two identical paths being advertised to a router, without the tweaking of weight or local preference, then chances are that we will only be concerned with the shortest AS path, and if they are equal, then it is most likely that the decider will be the router ID or the lowest neighbor

---

[7] http://www.cisco.com/en/US/docs/ios-xml/ios/iproute_bgp/configuration/15-s/irg-eibgp-multipath-for-nonvrf-interfaces.html

address. It is not an easy list or process to memorize, but there are a couple of aide-memoir that can help.

There are mnemonics for everything, and the BGP path selection process is no exception to this.

Mnemonics take the first (or most pertinent letter), and replace them with something more memorable to remember the correct sequence, such as "Richard Of York Gave Battle In Vain" to remember the colors of the rainbow (Red, Orange, Yellow, Green, Blue, Indigo, Violet), or Every Good Boy Deserves Fudge (which, depending on your preference, is either an excellent Mudhoney album, or the musical notes on the treble clef).

One of the better mnemonics for the BGP path selection process is:

We **L**ove **O**ranges **A**s **O**ranges **M**ean **P**ure **R**efreshment:

W	Weight (Highest)
L	Local Preference (Highest)
O	Originated locally
AS	AS Path (Shortest)
O	Origin code (IGP vs. EGP vs. Incomplete)
M	MED (Lowest)
P	Path (ebgp vs. ibgp)
R	Router ID (lowest)

In the next chapter we will look a little closer at the IGP related decision process stages that we skipped earlier, as well as covering BGP and redistribution from IGPs.

12. BGP and IGPs

Redistribution into and from BGP is fairly straight forward, but not without its caveats. There are some good reasons why we would avoid redistributing an IGP into BGP, or from BGP into an IGP. The primary reason to avoid it is the sheer number of routes that we could be bringing into our IGP. IGPs are by their very definition designed to hold a much smaller number of networks, certainly much smaller than the close to 500,000 routes that are currently in the BGP table. Most non-service provider networks cannot hold this number of routes, and it will cause the average organizations' router to crash due to the sheer size of the table. Cisco recommends 1 GB of RAM to hold the full routing table from one ISP[8].

That said, there maybe times when redistribution is our only option, and this chapter is one of those times. Later in this chapter we will look at BGP backdoors.

Before we start, we should remind ourselves of the Administrative Distances we will be dealing with. The ones we will concentrate on are eBGP, EIGRP (internal), OSPF, EIGRP (external) and iBGP:

Type	AD
Connected	0
Static	1
eBGP	20
EIGRP (internal)	90
IGRP	100
OSPF	110
IS-IS	115
RIP	120
EIGRP (external)	170
iBGP	200

8

http://www.cisco.com/en/US/tech/tk365/technologies_configuration_example09186a008009456d.shtml

Type	AD
EIGRP summary route	5

12.1 BGP and IGP redistribution

The topology we will be using is below:

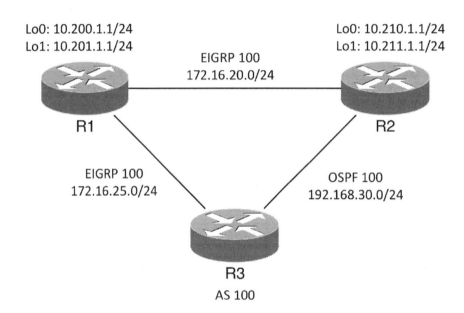

The basic configurations for R1 and R2 are below:

R1 configuration:

```
interface Loopback0
 ip address 10.200.1.1 255.255.255.0
!
interface Loopback1
 ip address 10.201.1.1 255.255.255.0
!
interface FastEthernet0/0
 ip address 172.16.20.1 255.255.255.0
 speed auto
 full-duplex
!
```

```
interface FastEthernet0/1
 ip address 172.16.25.1 255.255.255.0
 speed auto
 full-duplex
!
router eigrp 100
 network 10.200.1.0 0.0.0.255
 network 10.201.1.0 0.0.0.255
 network 172.16.20.0 0.0.0.255
 network 172.16.25.0 0.0.0.255
 no auto-summary
```

R2 configuration:

```
interface Loopback0
 ip address 10.210.1.1 255.255.255.0
 ip ospf network point-to-point
!
interface Loopback1
 ip address 10.211.1.1 255.255.255.0
 ip ospf network point-to-point
!
interface FastEthernet0/0
 ip address 172.16.20.2 255.255.255.0
 speed auto
 full-duplex
!
interface FastEthernet0/1
 ip address 192.168.30.1 255.255.255.0
 speed auto
 full-duplex
!
router eigrp 100
 redistribute ospf 100 metric 100 0 100 1 1500
 network 10.210.1.0 0.0.0.255
 network 10.211.1.0 0.0.0.255
 network 172.16.20.0 0.0.0.255
 no auto-summary
!
router ospf 100
 log-adjacency-changes
 redistribute eigrp 100 metric 1 subnets
 network 10.210.1.0 0.0.0.255 area 0
 network 10.211.1.0 0.0.0.255 area 0
 network 192.168.30.0 0.0.0.255 area 0
```

At the moment we can see the result of redistributing OSFP into EIGRP. On R1 we can see the 192.168.30.0/24 network appearing as an EIGRP external (D EX) route, with an AD of 170.

```
R1#sh ip route | beg Gateway
Gateway of last resort is not set

D EX 192.168.30.0/24 [170/25602560] via 172.16.20.2, 00:00:32, Fa0/0
     172.16.0.0/24 is subnetted, 2 subnets
C        172.16.25.0 is directly connected, FastEthernet0/1
C        172.16.20.0 is directly connected, FastEthernet0/0
     10.0.0.0/24 is subnetted, 4 subnets
C        10.201.1.0 is directly connected, Loopback1
C        10.200.1.0 is directly connected, Loopback0
D        10.211.1.0 [90/156160] via 172.16.20.2, 00:00:32, Fa0/0
D        10.210.1.0 [90/156160] via 172.16.20.2, 00:00:32, Fa0/0
R1#
```

Because EIGRP has the lower (and therefore better) AD than OSPF, R2 sees the EIGRP routes in its routing table (noted with a "D"):

```
R2#sh ip route | beg Gateway
Gateway of last resort is not set

C    192.168.30.0/24 is directly connected, FastEthernet0/1
     172.16.0.0/24 is subnetted, 2 subnets
D        172.16.25.0 [90/30720] via 172.16.20.1, 00:03:15, Fa0/0
C        172.16.20.0 is directly connected, FastEthernet0/0
     10.0.0.0/24 is subnetted, 4 subnets
D        10.201.1.0 [90/156160] via 172.16.20.1, 00:03:15, Fa0/0
D        10.200.1.0 [90/156160] via 172.16.20.1, 00:03:15, Fa0/0
C        10.211.1.0 is directly connected, Loopback1
C        10.210.1.0 is directly connected, Loopback0
R2#
```

Moving on to R3, first we will configure the basic interface and IGP functionality:

R3 configuration:

```
interface FastEthernet0/0
 ip address 172.16.25.2 255.255.255.0a
 speed auto
 full-duplex
!
interface FastEthernet0/1
 ip address 192.168.30.2 255.255.255.0
```

```
 speed auto
 full-duplex
!
router eigrp 100
 network 172.16.25.0 0.0.0.255
 no auto-summary
!
router ospf 100
 log-adjacency-changes
 network 192.168.30.0 0.0.0.255 area 0
```

Again, because of the lower AD, R3 prefers the EIGRP networks

```
R3#sh ip route | beg Gateway
Gateway of last resort is not set

C    192.168.30.0/24 is directly connected, FastEthernet0/1
     172.16.0.0/24 is subnetted, 2 subnets
C       172.16.25.0 is directly connected, FastEthernet0/0
D       172.16.20.0 [90/30720] via 172.16.25.1, 00:03:45, Fa0/0
     10.0.0.0/24 is subnetted, 4 subnets
D       10.201.1.0 [90/156160] via 172.16.25.1, 00:03:45, Fa0/0
D       10.200.1.0 [90/156160] via 172.16.25.1, 00:03:45, Fa0/0
D       10.211.1.0 [90/158720] via 172.16.25.1, 00:03:45, Fa0/0
D       10.210.1.0 [90/158720] via 172.16.25.1, 00:03:45, Fa0/0
R3#
```

As we mentioned in the previous chapter, the path selection process will prefer the IGP with the lowest type (AD value), so let's add BGP into the mix, and see how things look after we redistribute both of our IGPs into BGP:

```
R3#conf t
R3(config)#router bgp 100
R3(config-router)#bgp router-id 3.3.3.3
R3(config-router)#redistribute eigrp 100 metric 0
R3(config-router)#redistribute ospf 100 metric 0
R3(config-router)#exit
R3(config)#exit
R3#
```

We have set a metric of 0 to both the EIGRP and OSPF redistributed routes. We can actually omit this and still get the same metric value. Looking at the BGP table, we can see that the preferred path to all the networks is through R1. Note that the path is showing with an Origin code of incomplete (?), because it comes from redistribution (as we saw earlier when we looked at the origin type). The weight for all the routes is set at 32,768, because, due to redistribution, the router itself generates the routes.

```
R3#sh ip bgp | beg Network
   Network          Next Hop         Metric LocPrf Weight Path
*> 10.200.1.0/24    172.16.25.1           0              32768 ?
*> 10.201.1.0/24    172.16.25.1           0              32768 ?
*> 10.210.1.0/24    172.16.25.1           0              32768 ?
*> 10.211.1.0/24    172.16.25.1           0              32768 ?
*> 172.16.20.0/24   172.16.25.1           0              32768 ?
*> 172.16.25.0/24   0.0.0.0               0              32768 ?
*> 192.168.30.0     0.0.0.0               0              32768 ?
R3#
```

If we now shut down the link to R1, we should see the routes through R2 being installed into the BGP table:

```
R3(config)#int f0/0
R3(config-if)#shut
R3(config-if)#exit
R3(config)#exit
R3#sh ip bgp | beg Network
%LINK-5-CHANGED: Interface FastEthernet0/0, changed state to
administratively down
%LINEPROTO-5-UPDOWN: Line protocol on Interface FastEthernet0/0,
changed state to down
R3#sh ip bgp | beg Network
   Network          Next Hop         Metric LocPrf Weight Path
*> 10.210.1.0/24    192.168.30.1          0              32768 ?
*> 10.211.1.0/24    192.168.30.1          0              32768 ?
*> 192.168.30.0     0.0.0.0               0              32768 ?
R3#
```

Although R2 is presenting itself as a valid route, BGP is not seeing all of the routes, just the Intra-area routes (denoted with an O in the routing table). This is because, by default, only the routes advertised by R2 have been redistributed. We can see that the routing table shows the routes as OSPF External type 2 (E2):

```
R3#sh ip route | beg Gateway
Gateway of last resort is not set

C    192.168.30.0/24 is directly connected, Fa0/1
     172.16.0.0/24 is subnetted, 2 subnets
O E2    172.16.25.0 [110/1] via 192.168.30.1, 00:00:05, Fa0/1
O E2    172.16.20.0 [110/1] via 192.168.30.1, 00:00:05, Fa0/1
     10.0.0.0/24 is subnetted, 4 subnets
```

```
O E2      10.201.1.0 [110/1] via 192.168.30.1, 00:00:05, Fa0/1
O E2      10.200.1.0 [110/1] via 192.168.30.1, 00:00:05, Fa0/1
O         10.211.1.0 [110/2] via 192.168.30.1, 00:00:05, Fa0/1
O         10.210.1.0 [110/2] via 192.168.30.1, 00:00:05, Fa0/1
R3#
```

In order to install these routes into our BGP table, along with the existing Internal ones, we need to amend our redistribution command in BGP and use the "match" command to make sure that these routes are redistributed as well.

```
R3(config)#router bgp 100
R3(config-router)#redistribute ospf 100 metric 0 match internal external 2
```

We can also match nssa-external routes type 1 and 2 (or both), external type 1, and internal. If we wanted to match everything we could use the command:

```
R3(config-router)#redistribute ospf 100 metric 0 match internal external nssa-external
```

The above command would match nssa-external types 1 and 2, internal (Inter-area and Intra-area), and external types 1 and 2.

With our match in place, our BGP table now looks as follows:

```
R3#sh ip bgp | beg Network
   Network          Next Hop         Metric LocPrf Weight Path
*> 10.200.1.0/24    192.168.30.1          0          32768 ?
*> 10.201.1.0/24    192.168.30.1          0          32768 ?
*> 10.210.1.0/24    192.168.30.1          0          32768 ?
*> 10.211.1.0/24    192.168.30.1          0          32768 ?
*> 172.16.20.0/24   192.168.30.1          0          32768 ?
*> 172.16.25.0/24   192.168.30.1          0          32768 ?
*> 192.168.30.0     0.0.0.0               0          32768 ?
R3#
```

All the networks are present and correct. If we switch f0/0 on again, then the preferred routes moves back to R1:

```
R3(config)#int f0/0
R3(config-if)#no shut
R3(config-if)#exit
R3(config)#exit
R3#
```

```
%DUAL-5-NBRCHANGE: IP-EIGRP(0) 100: Neighbor 172.16.25.1
(FastEthernet0/0) is up: new adjacency
R3#
%LINK-3-UPDOWN: Interface FastEthernet0/0, changed state to up
%LINEPROTO-5-UPDOWN: Line protocol on Interface FastEthernet0/0,
changed state to up
R3#sh ip bgp | beg Network
   Network          Next Hop           Metric LocPrf Weight Path
*> 10.200.1.0/24    172.16.25.1            0          32768 ?
*> 10.201.1.0/24    172.16.25.1            0          32768 ?
*> 10.210.1.0/24    172.16.25.1            0          32768 ?
*> 10.211.1.0/24    172.16.25.1            0          32768 ?
*> 172.16.20.0/24   172.16.25.1            0          32768 ?
*> 172.16.25.0/24   0.0.0.0                0          32768 ?
*> 192.168.30.0     0.0.0.0                0          32768 ?
R3#
```

It is pretty clear now that lowest AD wins. The route with the lowest AD is the one that is installed in our routing table, and also, if being redistributed into BGP, the route with the lowest AD will be inserted into our BGP table.

Redistribution from BGP into an IGP follows much the same principle. We start by creating our routing protocol (RIP, OSPF, EIGRP or ISIS) and use the command "redistribute bgp <our AS number>" followed by the metrics commands specific to that IGP.

12.2 BGP Backdoors

Using the same network layout as the previous example, we are going to see that sometimes having a lower administrative distance may not actually benefit our routing tables. Routes may be valid, but may not necessarily make the best sense.

If we set up R1 and R2 to have an eBGP peering to R3, and keep the existing EIGRP connection between R1 and R2, but leave out any form of redistribution, we can easily see that sometimes BGP learned routes are not always the best routes.

The configuration is based on the previous section, the only difference is that we have removed all of the OSPF processes, and we are using standard eBGP peerings between R1 and R3 and between R2 and R3. The interfaces and IP addresses are all the same.

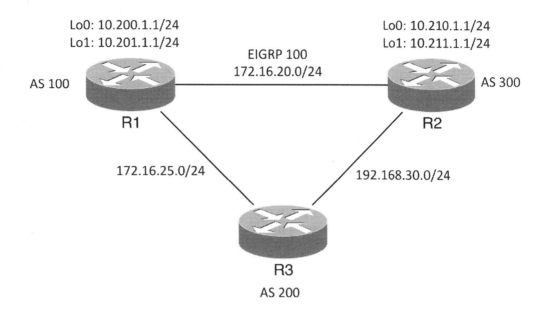

We start by configuring BGP on R1:

```
R1#conf t
R1(config)#router bgp 100
R1(config-router)#bgp router-id 1.1.1.1
R1(config-router)#network 10.200.1.0 mask 255.255.255.0
R1(config-router)#network 10.201.1.0 mask 255.255.255.0
R1(config-router)#neigh 172.16.25.2 remote-as 200
R1(config-router)#exit
R1(config)#exit
```

R1 already knows about R2's loopbacks due to the EIGRP adjacency:

```
R1#sh ip route | beg Gateway
Gateway of last resort is not set

     172.16.0.0/24 is subnetted, 2 subnets
C       172.16.25.0 is directly connected, Fa0/1
C       172.16.20.0 is directly connected, Fa0/0
     10.0.0.0/24 is subnetted, 4 subnets
C       10.201.1.0 is directly connected, Loopback1
C       10.200.1.0 is directly connected, Loopback0
D       10.211.1.0 [90/156160] via 172.16.20.2, 00:02:40, Fa0/0
D       10.210.1.0 [90/156160] via 172.16.20.2, 00:02:41, Fa0/0
R1#
```

Now, we move on to R3 and see the BGP peering establish:

```
R3#conf t
R3(config)#router bgp 200
R3(config-router)#bgp router-id 3.3.3.3
R3(config-router)#neigh 172.16.25.1 remote-as 100
R3(config-router)#
%BGP-5-ADJCHANGE: neighbor 172.16.25.1 Up
R3(config-router)#
```

With our BGP peering fully established, we should start to see the routes in R3:

```
R3#sh ip bgp | beg Network
   Network          Next Hop         Metric LocPrf Weight Path
*> 10.200.1.0/24    172.16.25.1           0             0 100 i
*> 10.201.1.0/24    172.16.25.1           0             0 100 i
R3#sh ip route | beg Gateway
Gateway of last resort is not set

C    192.168.30.0/24 is directly connected, FastEthernet0/1
     172.16.0.0/24 is subnetted, 1 subnets
C       172.16.25.0 is directly connected, FastEthernet0/0
     10.0.0.0/24 is subnetted, 4 subnets
B       10.201.1.0 [20/0] via 172.16.25.1, 00:01:34
B       10.200.1.0 [20/0] via 172.16.25.1, 00:01:34
R3#
```

Now we can create the peering between R3 and R2:

```
R3#conf t
R3(config)#router bgp 200
R3(config-router)#neigh 192.168.30.1 remote-as 300
R3(config-router)#exit
R3(config)#exit
R3#

R2#conf t
R2(config)#router bgp 300
R2(config-router)#bgp router-id 2.2.2.2
R2(config-router)#neigh 192.168.30.2 remote-as 200
R2(config-router)#network 10.210.1.0 mask 255.255.255.0
R2(config-router)#network 10.211.1.0 mask 255.255.255.0
%BGP-5-ADJCHANGE: neighbor 192.168.30.2 Up
R2(config-router)#exit
R2(config)#exit
R2#
```

R3 is learning about both R1 and R2's loopbacks through BGP. No surprises there.

```
R3#sh ip route | beg Gateway
Gateway of last resort is not set

C       192.168.30.0/24 is directly connected, FastEthernet0/1
        172.16.0.0/24 is subnetted, 1 subnets
C          172.16.25.0 is directly connected, FastEthernet0/0
        10.0.0.0/24 is subnetted, 6 subnets
B          10.201.1.0 [20/0] via 172.16.25.1, 00:03:35
B          10.200.1.0 [20/0] via 172.16.25.1, 00:03:35
B          10.211.1.0 [20/0] via 192.168.30.1, 00:00:19
B          10.210.1.0 [20/0] via 192.168.30.1, 00:00:19
R3#
```

So far, this is all very standard BGP behavior. The issues appear when we return to R1 and look at its routing table:

```
R1#sh ip route | beg Gateway
Gateway of last resort is not set

        172.16.0.0/24 is subnetted, 2 subnets
C          172.16.25.0 is directly connected, FastEthernet0/1
C          172.16.20.0 is directly connected, FastEthernet0/0
        10.0.0.0/24 is subnetted, 4 subnets
C          10.201.1.0 is directly connected, Loopback1
C          10.200.1.0 is directly connected, Loopback0
B          10.211.1.0 [20/0] via 172.16.25.2, 00:00:18
B          10.210.1.0 [20/0] via 172.16.25.2, 00:00:18
R1#
```

R1 now prefers the route to R2 through R3, due to the lower AD of eBGP than of EIGRP. Similarly, if we look again at R2's BGP and routing tables, we can see the same issue:

```
R2#sh ip bgp | beg Network
   Network          Next Hop         Metric LocPrf Weight Path
*> 10.200.1.0/24    192.168.30.2                       0 200 100 i
*> 10.201.1.0/24    192.168.30.2                       0 200 100 i
*> 10.210.1.0/24    0.0.0.0               0        32768 i
*> 10.211.1.0/24    0.0.0.0               0        32768 i
R2#sh ip route | beg Gateway
Gateway of last resort is not set

C       192.168.30.0/24 is directly connected, FastEthernet0/1
        172.16.0.0/24 is subnetted, 1 subnets
```

```
C          172.16.20.0 is directly connected, FastEthernet0/0
        10.0.0.0/24 is subnetted, 4 subnets
B          10.201.1.0 [20/0] via 192.168.30.2, 00:01:42
B          10.200.1.0 [20/0] via 192.168.30.2, 00:01:42
C          10.211.1.0 is directly connected, Loopback1
C          10.210.1.0 is directly connected, Loopback0
R2#
```

Clearly this is not the most direct route. We could use route-maps to deny the routes from R1 to R2 and vice-versa, but this would offer no backup in the event that the link between R1 and R2 goes down. We can, instead, instruct BGP to use the IGP learned route, rather then the BGP learned route, with the network "backdoor" command:

```
R1#conf t
R1(config)#router bgp 100
R1(config-router)#network 10.210.1.0 mask 255.255.255.0 backdoor
R1(config-router)#network 10.211.1.0 mask 255.255.255.0 backdoor
R1(config-router)#exit
R1(config)#exit
```

R1 now prefers the more direct route; the EIGRP learned one, to reach R2's loopbacks.

```
R1#sh ip route | beg Gateway
Gateway of last resort is not set

        172.16.0.0/24 is subnetted, 2 subnets
C          172.16.25.0 is directly connected, FastEthernet0/1
C          172.16.20.0 is directly connected, FastEthernet0/0
        10.0.0.0/24 is subnetted, 4 subnets
C          10.201.1.0 is directly connected, Loopback1
C          10.200.1.0 is directly connected, Loopback0
D          10.211.1.0 [90/156160] via 172.16.20.2, 00:00:06, Fa0/0
D          10.210.1.0 [90/156160] via 172.16.20.2, 00:00:10, Fa0/0
R1#
```

Let's do the same for R2:

```
R2#conf t
R2(config)#router bgp 300
R2(config-router)#network 10.200.1.0 mask 255.255.255.0 backdoor
R2(config-router)#network 10.201.1.0 mask 255.255.255.0 backdoor
R2(config-router)#exit
R2(config)#exit
```

Now R2 also prefers the direct route to R1's loopbacks.

```
R2#sh ip route | beg Gateway
Gateway of last resort is not set

C    192.168.30.0/24 is directly connected, FastEthernet0/1
     172.16.0.0/24 is subnetted, 1 subnets
C       172.16.20.0 is directly connected, FastEthernet0/0
     10.0.0.0/24 is subnetted, 4 subnets
D       10.201.1.0 [90/156160] via 172.16.20.1, 00:00:04, Fa0/0
D       10.200.1.0 [90/156160] via 172.16.20.1, 00:00:08, Fa0/0
C       10.211.1.0 is directly connected, Loopback1
C       10.210.1.0 is directly connected, Loopback0
R2#
```

The BGP tables now show the routes with rib failures:

```
R1#sh ip bgp | beg Netw
   Network          Next Hop        Metric LocPrf Weight Path
*> 10.200.1.0/24    0.0.0.0              0         32768 i
*> 10.201.1.0/24    0.0.0.0              0         32768 i
r> 10.210.1.0/24    172.16.25.2                        0 200 300 i
r> 10.211.1.0/24    172.16.25.2                        0 200 300 i
R1#

R2#sh ip bgp | beg Netw
   Network          Next Hop        Metric LocPrf Weight Path
r> 10.200.1.0/24    192.168.30.2                       0 200 100 i
r> 10.201.1.0/24    192.168.30.2                       0 200 100 i
*> 10.210.1.0/24    0.0.0.0              0         32768 i
*> 10.211.1.0/24    0.0.0.0              0         32768 i
R2#
```

If we look at the routes themselves we cannot see any difference, apart from the rib failure

```
R2#sh ip bgp 10.200.1.0/24
BGP routing table entry for 10.200.1.0/24, version 6
Paths: (1 available, best #1, table Default-IP-Routing-Table, RIB-
failure(17))
  Not advertised to any peer
  200 100
    192.168.30.2 from 192.168.30.2 (3.3.3.3)
      Origin IGP, localpref 100, valid, external, best
R2#
```

Using the BGP backdoor command increases the AD of the specified eBGP route to 200, therefore making it less preferred than any of the possible IGPs. There is another alternative, and that is to use the distance command.

12.3 BGP Distance

We already know that the administrative distances for BGP routes are 20 for eBGP and 200 for iBGP, and that, as shown previously, the lower AD value of eBGP to any IGP learned route could cause routers to take a less direct route to a network. We can use the backdoor command to change this, or we can change the distances used by BGP.

We need to remove the backdoor commands we just added:

```
R1(config-router)#no network 10.210.1.0 mask 255.255.255.0 backdoor
R1(config-router)#no network 10.211.1.0 mask 255.255.255.0 backdoor
R1(config-router)#

R2(config-router)#no network 10.200.1.0 mask 255.255.255.0 backdoor
R2(config-router)#no network 10.201.1.0 mask 255.255.255.0 backdoor
R2(config-router)#
```

Let's confirm that R1 and R2 still prefer to go via R3 to see each other's loopbacks:

```
R1(config-router)#do sh ip route | beg Gate
Gateway of last resort is not set

     172.16.0.0/24 is subnetted, 2 subnets
C       172.16.25.0 is directly connected, Ethernet0/1
C       172.16.20.0 is directly connected, Ethernet0/0
     10.0.0.0/24 is subnetted, 4 subnets
C       10.201.1.0 is directly connected, Loopback1
C       10.200.1.0 is directly connected, Loopback0
B       10.211.1.0 [20/0] via 172.16.25.2, 00:00:46
B       10.210.1.0 [20/0] via 172.16.25.2, 00:00:53
R1(config-router)#

R2(config-router)#do sh ip route | beg Gate
Gateway of last resort is not set

C    192.168.30.0/24 is directly connected, Ethernet0/1
     172.16.0.0/24 is subnetted, 2 subnets
D       172.16.25.0 [90/307200] via 172.16.20.1, 00:16:05, Eth0/0
C       172.16.20.0 is directly connected, Ethernet0/0
     10.0.0.0/24 is subnetted, 4 subnets
```

```
B          10.201.1.0 [20/0] via 192.168.30.2, 00:01:02
B          10.200.1.0 [20/0] via 192.168.30.2, 00:01:09
C          10.211.1.0 is directly connected, Loopback1
C          10.210.1.0 is directly connected, Loopback0
R2(config-router)#
```

Because we are using EIGRP, we need to make our eBGP routes AD greater than 90. We do this using the distance command:

```
R1(config-router)#distance bgp 95 200 200
```

Above, 95 is the AD for external routes, 200 is the internal routes AD, and the next 200 is the distance for local routes.

We can add the same commands to R2:

```
R2(config-router)#distance bgp 95 200 200
```

Once we have cleared our BGP peering, we can see that R1 and R2 prefer the more direct route:

```
R1(config-router)#do clear ip bgp *
R1(config-router)#
%BGP-5-ADJCHANGE: neighbor 172.16.25.2 Down User reset
%BGP-5-ADJCHANGE: neighbor 172.16.25.2 Up
R1(config-router)#do sh ip route | beg Gate
Gateway of last resort is not set

     172.16.0.0/24 is subnetted, 2 subnets
C        172.16.25.0 is directly connected, Ethernet0/1
C        172.16.20.0 is directly connected, Ethernet0/0
     10.0.0.0/24 is subnetted, 4 subnets
C        10.201.1.0 is directly connected, Loopback1
C        10.200.1.0 is directly connected, Loopback0
D        10.211.1.0 [90/409600] via 172.16.20.2, 00:00:27, Eth0/0
D        10.210.1.0 [90/409600] via 172.16.20.2, 00:00:27, Eth0/0
R1(config-router)#

R2(config-router)#do sh ip route | beg Gate
Gateway of last resort is not set

C    192.168.30.0/24 is directly connected, Ethernet0/1
     172.16.0.0/24 is subnetted, 2 subnets
D        172.16.25.0 [90/307200] via 172.16.20.1, 00:23:47, Eth0/0
C        172.16.20.0 is directly connected, Ethernet0/0
     10.0.0.0/24 is subnetted, 4 subnets
```

```
D          10.201.1.0 [90/409600] via 172.16.20.1, 00:01:26, Eth0/0
D          10.200.1.0 [90/409600] via 172.16.20.1, 00:01:26, Eth0/0
C          10.211.1.0 is directly connected, Loopback1
C          10.210.1.0 is directly connected, Loopback0
R2(config-router)#
```

We can set this per neighbor as well, even matching to access-lists for granularity:

```
R2(config-router)#no distance bgp 95 200 200
R2(config-router)#distance 95 192.168.30.2 255.255.255.255 ?
  <1-99>       IP Standard access list number
  <1300-1999>  IP Standard expanded access list number
  WORD         Standard access-list name
  <cr>

R2(config-router)#distance 95 192.168.30.2 255.255.255.255
R2(config-router)#do clear ip bgp *
R2(config-router)#
%BGP-5-ADJCHANGE: neighbor 192.168.30.2 Down User reset
%BGP-5-ADJCHANGE: neighbor 192.168.30.2 Up
```

And we can see that this has the same effect, but is more targeted:

```
R2(config-router)#do sh ip route | beg Gate
Gateway of last resort is not set

C       192.168.30.0/24 is directly connected, Ethernet0/1
        172.16.0.0/24 is subnetted, 2 subnets
D          172.16.25.0 [90/307200] via 172.16.20.1, 00:29:18, Eth0/0
C          172.16.20.0 is directly connected, Ethernet0/0
        10.0.0.0/24 is subnetted, 4 subnets
D          10.201.1.0 [90/409600] via 172.16.20.1, 00:06:58, Eth0/0
D          10.200.1.0 [90/409600] via 172.16.20.1, 00:06:58, Eth0/0
C          10.211.1.0 is directly connected, Loopback1
C          10.210.1.0 is directly connected, Loopback0
R2(config-router)#
```

13. Securing BGP

BGP is an obvious target for hackers; if you have control of a BGP router there is the possibility to influence the routing tables of a large number of routers. Obviously the entire Internet cannot be brought down due to one router sending incorrect route advertisements, but certainly damage can be done.

There are, however, standard IOS safeguards that can be implemented, and there are proposals for a much more secure BGP implementation, known as Secure BGP (or S-BGP).

13.1 S-BGP

We will touch on S-BGP briefly, because it is interesting and relevant, but not to dwell on it too much, as it is very much still in the early phases, and large scale rollout will not take place for a very long time.

In early 2003 a draft document was submitted to the IETF (Internet Engineering Task Force), proposing a protocol specification called S-BGP, an extension to the current BGP-4 standard. Because BGP is highly vulnerable to malicious attacks, and lacks any scalable means to identify and validate BGP control traffic, S-BGP proposes a PKI based infrastructure along with IPSec to validate the message and verify the authenticity of the sender. ISPs would be assigned an X.509 certificate, and this would be assigned to the ISPs routers. When another router receives an UPDATE message, the certificate would be checked, and if verified, the router would accept the contents of the UPDATE message.

So far, little has been done with S-BGP in the last ten years. The effort and costs of implementing such architecture on a global scale is enormous. Every ISP would have to update their routers, and questions are asked about what will happen if the PKI infrastructure were to go down. S-BGP sounds good in principle but the uptake will be very slow (if at all). There are some interesting links to S-BGP articles in the further reading chapter.

So, what can we do in the meantime? We have already covered TTL Security, which, to a certain degree, overcomes the issue of hackers changing the TTL value of a BGP UPDATE packet, but, BGP can also use MD5 authentication between peers, which is what we are going to look at next.

13.2 BGP Authentication

We will set up MD5 encryption between R12 and R10, using a password of "BGPPASS". We start with the neighbor command, the neighbor's IP address and the keyword password. If we use the context-sensitive help, we can see options for the encryption type (0-7). If we were copying an encrypted password from another router we would use an encryption type of 7, and paste in the encrypted password.

```
R12(config)#router bgp 65500
R12(config-router)#neighbor 10.4.1.2 password ?
  <0-7>  Encryption type (0 to disable encryption, 7 for proprietary)
```

We can, instead, type in our password:

```
R12(config-router)#neighbor 10.4.1.2 password BGPPASS
R12(config-router)#
%TCP-6-BADAUTH: No MD5 digest from 10.4.1.2(179) to 10.4.1.1(59510)
%TCP-6-BADAUTH: No MD5 digest from 10.4.1.2(179) to 10.4.1.1(59510)
%TCP-6-BADAUTH: No MD5 digest from 10.4.1.2(179) to 10.4.1.1(59510)
%TCP-6-BADAUTH: No MD5 digest from 10.4.1.2(179) to 10.4.1.1(59510)
R12(config-router)#
```

Straight away we will start seeing the above messages being logged. We need to make sure that R10 is also using MD5 encryption, with the same password:

```
R10(config)#router bgp 500
R10(config-router)#neigh 10.4.1.1 password BGPPASS
R10(config-router)#do clear ip bgp 10.4.1.1
R10(config-router)#
%BGP-5-ADJCHANGE: neighbor 10.4.1.1 Down User reset
R10(config-router)#
%BGP-5-ADJCHANGE: neighbor 10.4.1.1 Up
R10(config-router)#
```

R12 continued to log the BADAUTH messages until the peering was reestablished.

The password we specify will be encrypted for us, but only if we use the global command "service password-encryption", otherwise it will be shown in clear-text:

```
R12(config-router)#do sh run | section bgp
router bgp 65500
 no synchronization
 bgp router-id 12.12.12.12
 bgp log-neighbor-changes
```

```
  network 10.3.1.0 mask 255.255.255.0
  network 10.4.1.0 mask 255.255.255.0
  network 172.18.1.0 mask 255.255.255.0
  network 172.18.2.0 mask 255.255.255.0
  redistribute static
  neighbor 10.3.1.1 remote-as 200
  neighbor 10.3.1.1 local-as 300
  neighbor 10.3.1.1 default-originate
  neighbor 10.4.1.2 remote-as 500
  neighbor 10.4.1.2 local-as 300
  neighbor 10.4.1.2 password BGPPASS
  neighbor 10.4.1.2 send-community
  neighbor 10.4.1.2 default-originate
  neighbor 10.4.1.2 route-map 172-18-2-NoExport out
  no auto-summary
R12(config-router)#exit
R12(config)#service password-encryption
R12(config)#do sh run | section bgp
router bgp 65500
 no synchronization
 bgp router-id 12.12.12.12
 bgp log-neighbor-changes
 network 10.3.1.0 mask 255.255.255.0
 network 10.4.1.0 mask 255.255.255.0
 network 172.18.1.0 mask 255.255.255.0
 network 172.18.2.0 mask 255.255.255.0
 redistribute static
 neighbor 10.3.1.1 remote-as 200
 neighbor 10.3.1.1 local-as 300
 neighbor 10.3.1.1 default-originate
 neighbor 10.4.1.2 remote-as 500
 neighbor 10.4.1.2 local-as 300
 neighbor 10.4.1.2 password 7 08036B7E39383624
 neighbor 10.4.1.2 send-community
 neighbor 10.4.1.2 default-originate
 neighbor 10.4.1.2 route-map 172-18-2-NoExport out
 no auto-summary
R12(config)#
```

Instead of specifying the password in clear text on R10, can we use the MD5 hashed version from R12 instead?

If we remove the password:

```
R10(config)#router bgp 500
R10(config-router)#no neigh 10.4.1.1 password BGPPASS
R10(config-router)#do clear ip bgp 10.4.1.1
```

R10(config-router)#

Then R12 starts logging the BADAUTH messages again. We can then clear the peering down and specify the encrypted password:

```
%BGP-5-ADJCHANGE: neighbor 10.4.1.1 Down User reset
R10(config-router)#neigh 10.4.1.1 passw 7 08036B7E39383624
R10(config-router)#do clear ip bgp 10.4.1.1
R10(config-router)#
%BGP-5-ADJCHANGE: neighbor 10.4.1.1 Up
R10(config-router)#
```

The peering is reestablished, and R12 is no longer showing the BADAUTH messages:

```
R12#sh ip bgp neigh | i BGP
BGP neighbor is 10.3.1.1,  remote AS 200,  local AS 300, external
link
  BGP version 4, remote router ID 5.5.5.5
  BGP state = Established, up for 00:50:00
  BGP table version 70, neighbor version 70/0
BGP neighbor is 10.4.1.2,  remote AS 500,  local AS 300, external
link
  BGP version 4, remote router ID 10.10.10.10
  BGP state = Established, up for 00:06:04
  BGP table version 70, neighbor version 70/0
R12#
```

To capture the BADAUTH messages, we need to make sure that "debug ip bgp" is turned on (as it was on R12), but other than that, MD5 authentication for BGP is very straightforward.

14. Tweaking BGP

Once we have a working BGP network, one that is tuned to send the routes we want in the direction that we want, that is redundant and secured through MD5 authentication, what else can we do to tweak it?

In this chapter we will cover BGP timers, next-hop tracking and route dampening. We will be using a very simple topology, R1 and R2, and these are connected using the 10.1.1.0/24 network.

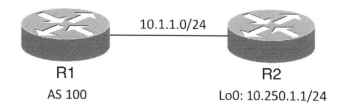

14.1 BGP Timers

BGP uses a number of timers, and these include the Keepalive timer, which we looked at briefly early on, the others are the Hold-Down, Advertisement Interval and the Scan-Timer.

Keepalive and Hold-down

The keepalive timer does exactly as the name suggests; it keeps a peer session alive. The default keepalive interval is 60 seconds, so every 60 seconds a keepalive packet is sent from one peer to another. The keepalive packets are required by the hold-down timer, which is started (at 0), when the peer relationship is formed. The default hold-down timer is 3x keepalives (the default will therefore usually be 180 seconds). Every time the router receives a keepalive, the hold-down timer is reset to 0. If the hold-down timer reaches its limit, and does not receive the requisite number of keepalive packets during the hold-down timer, the neighbor is considered to be down and the routes are flushed out.

Timers are negotiated between peers. We can see the current timers being used between two peers using the "sh ip bgp neighbors" command:

```
R1#sh ip bgp neighbors
BGP neighbor is 10.1.1.2,  remote AS 200, external link
  BGP version 4, remote router ID 2.2.2.2
```

```
     BGP state = Established, up for 00:00:30
     Last read 00:00:30, last write 00:00:30, hold time is 180,
  keepalive interval is 60 seconds
```

These timers can be changed per neighbor (or using peer-groups and templates), using the command "neighbor x.x.x.x timers 30 90". This sets the keepalive timer to 30 seconds and the hold-timer to 90 seconds. Because the timers are negotiated during the BGP session, the session must be cleared for new timers to take effect. If one neighbor has a different set of timers to the other, they will negotiate a peering using the lower of the values of the two peers:

```
R1(config)#router bgp 100
R1(config-router)#neigh 10.1.1.2 timers 40 120
R1(config-router)#
%BGP-5-ADJCHANGE: neighbor 10.1.1.2 Down Peer closed the session
%BGP_SESSION-5-ADJCHANGE: neighbor 10.1.1.2 IPv4 Unicast topology
base removed from session  Peer closed the session
R1(config-router)#
%BGP-5-ADJCHANGE: neighbor 10.1.1.2 Up
%BGP-5-ADJCHANGE: neighbor 10.1.1.2 Down BGP Notification sent
R1(config-router)#
%BGP-3-NOTIFICATION: sent to neighbor 10.1.1.2 1/1 (header
synchronization problems) 0 bytes

R2(config-router)#neigh 10.1.1.1 timers 30 90
R2(config-router)#do clear ip bgp *
R2(config-router)#
%BGP-5-ADJCHANGE: neighbor 10.1.1.1 Down User reset
%BGP_SESSION-5-ADJCHANGE: neighbor 10.1.1.1 IPv4 Unicast topology
base removed from session  User reset
R2(config-router)#
%BGP-5-ADJCHANGE: neighbor 10.1.1.1 Up
%BGP-3-NOTIFICATION: received from neighbor 10.1.1.1 1/1 (header
synchronization problems) 0 bytes
R2(config-router)#
%BGP-5-ADJCHANGE: neighbor 10.1.1.1 Down BGP Notification received
%BGP_SESSION-5-ADJCHANGE: neighbor 10.1.1.1 IPv4 Unicast topology
base removed from session  BGP Notification received
R2(config-router)#
%BGP-5-ADJCHANGE: neighbor 10.1.1.1 Up
R2(config-router)#do sh ip bgp neigh 10.1.1.1
BGP neighbor is 10.1.1.1,  remote AS 100, external link
  BGP version 4, remote router ID 1.1.1.1
  BGP state = Established, up for 00:00:54
  Last read 00:00:00, last write 00:00:00, hold time is 90,
keepalive interval is 30 seconds
```

```
        Configured hold time is 90, keepalive interval is 30 seconds
        Minimum holdtime from neighbor is 0 seconds
```

We can also set a minimum hold-down timer that we are willing to accept; by specifying a minimum value. If the other side tries to peer with a hold-timer lower than our minimum, the session will never establish and we will see errors logged (if we have debug ip bgp all enabled). Here, we will use the same values as above, but will set R1 to have a minimum hold-timer of 120 seconds, and R2 to have a minimum of 90:

```
R1(config-router)#neigh 10.1.1.2 timers 40 120 120
R1(config-router)#
%BGP-5-ADJCHANGE: neighbor 10.1.1.2 Down Peer closed the session
%BGP_SESSION-5-ADJCHANGE: neighbor 10.1.1.2 IPv4 Unicast topology
base removed from session  Peer closed the session
%BGP-3-NOTIFICATION: sent to neighbor 10.1.1.2 passive 2/6
(unacceptable hold time) 0 bytes
R1(config-router)#
%BGP-4-MSGDUMP: unsupported or mal-formatted message received from
10.1.1.2:
FFFF FFFF FFFF FFFF FFFF FFFF FFFF FFFF 0035 0104 00C8 005A 0202 0202
1802 0601
0400 0100 0102 0280 0002 0202 0002 0641 0400 0000 C8
R1(config-router)#
%BGP-3-NOTIFICATION: sent to neighbor 10.1.1.2 passive 2/6
(unacceptable hold time) 0 bytes
R1(config-router)#

R2(config-router)#neigh 10.1.1.1 timers 30 90 90
R2(config-router)#do clear ip bgp *
R2(config-router)#
%BGP-5-ADJCHANGE: neighbor 10.1.1.1 Down User reset
%BGP_SESSION-5-ADJCHANGE: neighbor 10.1.1.1 IPv4 Unicast topology
base removed from session  User reset
%BGP-3-NOTIFICATION: received from neighbor 10.1.1.1 active 2/6
(unacceptable hold time) 0 bytes
R2(config-router)#
```

The two routers will continue to log these messages until they can agree on the hold timer. In this case R2 was then changed to have no minimum hold-down timer.

Advertisement timer

BGP strives for stability; otherwise the Internet would be a pretty flaky place. One of the ways in which stability is set, is using the Advertisement timer, which is the minimum period between neighbor UPDATE messages. The default between eBGP peers is 30 seconds, and 0 seconds between iBGP peers. It's a case of "what you do within your own AS is your business, but let's keep the noise to a minimum for our neighbors".

Scan-Timer

The full BGP table (per peer) now weighs in at around 1Gb, and even a respectably aggregated and default-routed BGP table from an ISP, will still be any where between a few Mb and a couple of hundred Mb, which takes a large chunk of router resources to go through.

It makes sense that the routing table needs to be validated, to ensure that the next-hop for any routes is still valid, or even to check whether a better route exists. Due to the resources this uses (CPU and memory), it should be done periodically, and this is the scan-timer. Originally this was set at 60 seconds, but as of IOS 12.2 it was reduced to 15 seconds.

We can change the default scan-time using the command "bgp scan-time <time in seconds>", or set this per address-family. Below we have a global scan-time of 30 seconds, and a scan-time of 15 seconds for our IPv4 address-family:

```
R1(config)#router bgp 100
R1(config-router)#bgp scan-time 30
R1(config-router)#address-family ipv4
R1(config-router-af)#bgp scan-time 15
R1(config-router-af)#exit
R1(config-router)#exit
R1(config)#
```

Showing the effects of the different scan-timers is actually not as easy as it would seem, and this is due to the next-hop tracking feature.

14.2 Next-Hop Tracking

Next-hop address tracking (NHT) is turned on by default in the recent IOS versions. It is an event-based system to provide faster on-demand convergence, rather than relying on the scan-timer. In fact, NHT actually makes the router ignore any configured scan time commands on the router, forcing it to remain at the system default.

With NHT, the RIB is monitored for changes that would affect the next-hop reachability, for both eBGP and iBGP. This provides a much quicker reaction time to incidents, such as an interface going down, that rely on the 60-second scan-timer.

NHT can be disabled using the command "no bgp nexthop trigger enable". NHT also has a 5 second default delay, in order to prevent the process being swamped by a flapping interface, for example. This can be reduced (but can also lead to instability), or increased in the event of a slow IGP protocol. To configure a different delay timer you use the command "bgp nexthop trigger delay <delay in seconds>".

NHT also opens up the ability for fast session deactivation, which improves BGP convergence time, and means that the router will remove all routes learned from the peer if the session is deactivated:

```
R1(config)#router bgp 100
R1(config-router)#neighbor 10.1.1.2 fall-over
R1(config-router)#
```

We can also use a route-map in conjunction with fast session deactivation, so that in the event that a specific route is no longer available, the peer session will be reset.

We will use this simple topology:

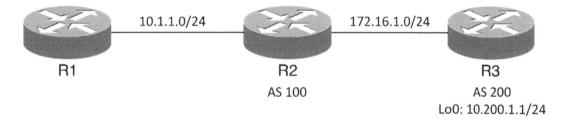

R3 is advertising its loopback interface into BGP, and R2 and R3 have a peering established:

```
R2#sh ip bgp | beg Network
   Network          Next Hop            Metric LocPrf Weight Path
*> 10.200.1.0/24    172.16.1.2               0             0 200 i
R2#
```

At the moment there is nothing unusual about their BGP configurations:

```
R2#sh run | section bgp
router bgp 100
 bgp router-id 1.1.1.1
 bgp log-neighbor-changes
 neighbor 172.16.1.2 remote-as 200
R2#
```

```
R3#sh run | section bgp
router bgp 200
 bgp router-id 2.2.2.2
 bgp log-neighbor-changes
 network 10.200.1.0 mask 255.255.255.0
 neighbor 172.16.1.1 remote-as 100
R3#
```

Our routing table looks like this:

```
R2(config-if)#do sh ip route | beg Gateway
Gateway of last resort is not set

      10.0.0.0/8 is variably subnetted, 3 subnets, 2 masks
C        10.1.1.0/24 is directly connected, FastEthernet0/0
L        10.1.1.2/32 is directly connected, FastEthernet0/0
B        10.200.1.0/24 [20/0] via 172.16.1.2, 00:00:06
      172.16.0.0/16 is variably subnetted, 3 subnets, 2 masks
C        172.16.1.0/24 is directly connected, FastEthernet0/1
L        172.16.1.1/32 is directly connected, FastEthernet0/1
S        172.16.1.2/32 [1/0] via 172.16.1.2, FastEthernet0/1
R2(config-if)#
```

What we will do now is set up tracking on R2, so that in the event that the connection to R1 goes down, then the BGP peering to R3 will immediately go down:

```
R2(config)#track 10 interface f0/0 ip routing
R2(config-track)#carrier-delay
R2(config-track)#exit
R2(config)#ip route 172.16.1.2 255.255.255.255 f0/1 172.16.1.2 track 10
R2(config)#ip prefix-list R3-UP seq 5 permit 172.16.1.2/32
R2(config)#route-map R3-UP permit 10
R2(config-route-map)#match ip address prefix-list R3-UP
R2(config-route-map)#router bgp 100
R2(config-router)#neigh 172.16.1.2 fall-over route-map R3-UP
R2(config-router)#exit
R2(config)#exit
```

The above commands specify that we are to track whether f0/0 is up or not. We attach this track to the static route to R3, so in the even that the link to R1 goes down, we will also remove the routes to 172.16.1.2. We then put this into a route-map and attach it to our peer commands for R3, so that if the route is removed the peering will be torn down immediately.

Now let's turn on BGP debugging, and take down the f0/0 interface:

```
R2(config-if)#do sh clock
*14:47:04.947 UTC Sun Feb 16 2014
R2(config-if)#shut
R2(config-if)#
%LINK-5-CHANGED: Interface FastEthernet0/0, changed state to
administratively down
%TRACKING-5-STATE: 10 interface Fa0/0 ip routing Up->Down
BGP: ses global 172.16.1.2 (0x69B2D150:1) Reset (Route to peer lost).
BGP: nbr_topo global 172.16.1.2 IPv4 Unicast:base (0x69B2D150:1) NSF
delete stale NSF not active
BGP: nbr_topo global 172.16.1.2 IPv4 Unicast:base (0x69B2D150:1) NSF
no stale paths state is NSF not active
BGP: nbr_topo global 172.16.1.2 IPv4 Unicast:base (0x69B2D150:1)
Resetting ALL counters.
BGP: 172.16.1.2 closing
BGP: ses global 172.16.1.2 (0x69B2D150:1) Session close and reset
neighbor 172.16.1.2 topostate
BGP: nbr_topo global 172.16.1.2 IPv4 Unicast:base (0x69B2D150:1)
Resetting ALL counters.
BGP: 172.16.1.2 went from Established to Idle
%BGP-5-ADJCHANGE: neighbor 172.16.1.2 Down Route to peer lost
%BGP_SESSION-5-ADJCHANGE: neighbor 172.16.1.2 IPv4 Unicast topology
base removed from session  Route to peer lost
BGP: ses global 172.16.1.2 (0x69B2D150:1) Removed topology IPv4
Unicast:base
BGP: ses global 172.16.1.2 (0x69B2D150:1) Removed last topology
BGP: nbr global 172.16.1.2 Active open failed - route to peer is
invalid
BGP: nbr global 172.16.1.2 Active open failed - route to peer is
invalid
*Feb 16 14:47:09.747: %LINEPROTO-5-UPDOWN: Line protocol on Interface
FastEthernet0/0, changed state to down
R2(config-if)#
```

Our routing table now looks like this:

```
R2(config-if)#do sh ip route | beg Gateway
Gateway of last resort is not set

      172.16.0.0/16 is variably subnetted, 2 subnets, 2 masks
C        172.16.1.0/24 is directly connected, FastEthernet0/1
L        172.16.1.1/32 is directly connected, FastEthernet0/1
R2(config-if)#
```

If we re-enable the interface, our BGP peering reestablishes very quickly:

```
R2(config-if)#do sh clock
*14:48:16.347 UTC Sun Feb 16 2014
R2(config-if)#no shut
%LINK-3-UPDOWN: Interface FastEthernet0/0, changed state to up
TRACKING-5-STATE: 10 interface Fa0/0 ip routing Down->Up
BGP: nbr global 172.16.1.2 Open active delayed 1024ms (0ms max, 60%
jitter)
%LINEPROTO-5-UPDOWN: Line protocol on Interface FastEthernet0/0,
changed state to up
BGP: 172.16.1.2 active went from Idle to Active
BGP: 172.16.1.2 open active, local address 172.16.1.1
BGP: ses global 172.16.1.2 (0x69B2D060:0) act Adding topology IPv4
Unicast:base
BGP: ses global 172.16.1.2 (0x69B2D060:0) act Send OPEN
BGP: 172.16.1.2 active went from Active to OpenSent
<output truncated>
*Feb 16 14:48:22.223: %BGP-5-ADJCHANGE: neighbor 172.16.1.2 Up
R2(config-if)#
```

Using tracking to control peering provides a much speedier response than waiting for the hold-timer to expire; a peer relationship can be brought down in a matter of seconds, instead of three minutes.

NHT also supports Bidirectional Forwarding Detection (BFD), which is recommended on multipoint interfaces, such as Ethernet, which do not support OAM (Operations, Administration and Management). To use BFD is as simple as using the command:

```
Router(config-router)#neighbor 172.16.1.2 fall-over bfd
```

BFD cannot be used in conjunction with a route-map; it is, however, used with prefix independent convergence.

14.3 Prefix independent convergence and add-path

Protocol Independent Convergence (PIC) borrows the concept of the feasible successor route from EIGRP, to improve convergence in the event that a route is lost, without being dependent on a number of prefixes in order to select the next best path.

This is a relatively new aspect of the IOS and IOS-XE. It did not appear on the v4 exams, and is only on the v5 written exam, not on the lab. As such, and also due to the fact that until VIRL/CML is released it is harder to show working examples, it will only be touched on briefly.

During "normal" operations of BGP, by default only one route to a prefix (the best route) is advertised. If a network failure is experienced then, firstly, BGP will learn of the failure from the IGP, BFD, or interface events. The routes are then withdrawn from the RIB, and subsequently the FIB. BGP then informs its neighbors using a WITHDRAWN message, and calculates the next best path to that prefix. The prefix is then installed into the RIB and the FIB.

This can take several minutes to complete, and can result is large amounts of data loss during the period. We can use two things to, firstly, speed up convergence and, secondly, advertise more than just the best route. In order to speed up convergence PIC installs a backup path, which is the secondary best path. This backup path is also installed in the RIB and FIB, and can reduce convergence to seconds or milliseconds, rather than minutes. The additional paths feature can be used to send and receive the backup path to, or from, other peers.

PIC works with address families (IPv4, IPv6, VPNv4 and VPNv6), and requires a router to be multi-homed and use a fast failure detection method, such as bfd.

In the following scenario, R1 (AS 100) is peered with R2 (AS 200) and R3 (AS 300). R2 is also peered with R3. R3 is advertising the network 10.100.1.0/24, which is configured on its loopback interface.

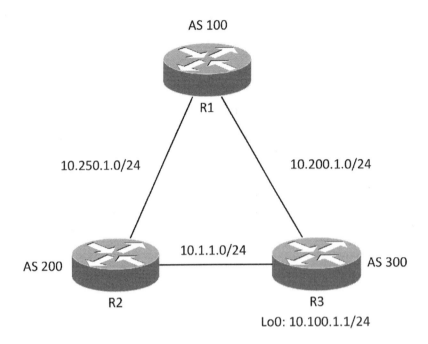

```
R1#sh run | section bgp
router bgp 100
 bgp router-id 1.1.1.1
 bgp log-neighbor-changes
 neighbor 10.200.1.2 remote-as 300
 neighbor 10.250.1.2 remote-as 200
 !
 address-family ipv4
  neighbor 10.200.1.2 activate
  neighbor 10.250.1.2 activate
 exit-address-family
R1#sh ip bgp | beg Network
   Network          Next Hop         Metric LocPrf Weight Path
*  10.100.1.0/24    10.250.1.2                         0 200 300 i
*>                  10.200.1.2            0            0 300 i
R1#
```

We add the commands "neighbor <ip address> fall-over bfd", as well as the commands "bgp additional-paths install" and "bgp recursion host" to activate PIC.

```
R1#sh run | section bgp
router bgp 100
 bgp router-id 1.1.1.1
 bgp log-neighbor-changes
```

```
 neighbor 10.200.1.2 remote-as 300
 neighbor 10.200.1.2 fall-over bfd
 neighbor 10.250.1.2 remote-as 200
 neighbor 10.250.1.2 fall-over bfd
 !
 address-family ipv4
   bgp additional-paths install
   bgp recursion host
   neighbor 10.200.1.2 activate
   neighbor 10.250.1.2 activate
 exit-address-family
 R1#
```

We can now see that the secondary route is selected as a backup route:

```
R1#sh ip bgp
BGP table version is 7, local router ID is 1.1.1.1
Status codes: s suppressed, d damped, h history, * valid, > best, i -
internal,
              r RIB-failure, S Stale, m multipath, b backup-path, f
RT-Filter,
              x best-external, a additional-path, c RIB-compressed,
Origin codes: i - IGP, e - EGP, ? - incomplete
RPKI validation codes: V valid, I invalid, N Not found

     Network          Next Hop        Metric LocPrf Weight Path
*b  10.100.1.0/24    10.250.1.2                        0 200 300 i
*>                   10.200.1.2            0           0 300 i
R1#sh ip bgp 10.100.1.0/24
BGP routing table entry for 10.100.1.0/24, version 25
Paths: (2 available, best #1, table default)
Multipath: eBGP
  Advertise-best-external
  Advertised to update-groups:
     3
  Refresh Epoch 2
  300
    10.200.1.2 from 10.200.1.2 (3.3.3.3)
      Origin IGP, metric 0, localpref 100, valid, external, best ,
recursive-via-connected
  Refresh Epoch 2
  200 300
    10.250.1.2 from 10.250.1.2 (2.2.2.2)
      Origin IGP, localpref 100, valid, external, backup/repair ,
recursive-via-connected
R1#
```

CEF shows this as a repair route:

```
R1#sh ip cef 10.100.1.0/24 detail
10.100.1.0/24, epoch 0, flags rib only nolabel, rib defined all
labels
  recursive via 10.200.1.2
    recursive via 10.200.1.0/24
      attached to Serial0/1
  recursive via 10.250.1.2, repair
    recursive via 10.250.1.0/24
      attached to Serial0/0
R1#
```

Although we have used the fall-over bfd command, we have not actually set up any bidirectional forwarding detection. So, firstly, let's see what happens without it. If we shut down the interface on R3 that connects to R1, how long will it take R1 to detect the failure, and remove the routes from its tables?

```
R1#sh clock
*09:11:21.611 CET Sun Feb 16 2014
R1#
%LINEPROTO-5-UPDOWN: Line protocol on Interface Serial0/1, changed
state to down
%BGP-5-ADJCHANGE: neighbor 10.200.1.2 Down Interface flap
*Feb 16 09:11:54.543: %BGP_SESSION-5-ADJCHANGE: neighbor 10.200.1.2
IPv4 Unicast topology base removed from session  Interface flap
R1#sh ip bgp | beg Network
     Network          Next Hop         Metric LocPrf Weight Path
 *>  10.100.1.0/24    10.250.1.2                          0 200 300 i
R1#
```

It takes about 30 seconds. Now let's see how we can improve on that with BFD. We have already specified the "neighbor fall-over bfd" command in the BGP configurations, what we need to do now is set up the sending and receiving of the packets for BFD, which is done under the interface:

```
R1(config)#int s0/1
R1(config-if)#ip bgp fast-external-fallover permit
R1(config-if)#bfd interval 50 min_rx 50 multiplier 3
R1(config-if)#bfd echo
R1(config-if)#exit
R1(config)#exit
```

We first set our BGP process to use BFD using the "fast-external-fallover" command. The bgp fast-external-fallover command is used to disable or enable fast external fallover for BGP peering sessions with directly connected external peers. The session is immediately reset if the link goes down. Only directly connected peering sessions are supported. If BGP fast external fallover is disabled, the BGP routing process will wait until the default hold timer expires (3 keepalives) to reset the peering session.

Next we set the interval in miliseconds (50), as well as setting the min_rx, which is the Minimum receive interval capability - which acts much like the timers for BGP, and then the mulliplier, which is used to compute the holddown. We then enable the BFD echo. Note that the bfd echo command does not show up in running configuration:

```
R3#sh run int s0/0
Building configuration...

Current configuration : 166 bytes
!
interface Serial0/0
 ip address 10.200.1.2 255.255.255.0
 ip bgp fast-external-fallover permit
 serial restart-delay 0
 bfd interval 50 min_rx 50 multiplier 3
end
```

Once both sides have matching settings, we can confirm that BFD is working using the command "show bfd neighbors":

```
R1#sh bfd neigh

NeighAddr                          LD/RD      RH/RS      State      Int
10.200.1.2                         1/1        Up         Up         Se0/1
R1#
```

We can get even more information, using the detailed version:

```
R1#sh bfd neigh det

NeighAddr                          LD/RD      RH/RS      State      Int
10.200.1.2                         1/1        Up         Up         Se0/1
Session state is UP and using echo function with 50 ms interval.
OurAddr: 10.200.1.1
Local Diag: 0, Demand mode: 0, Poll bit: 0
MinTxInt: 1000000, MinRxInt: 1000000, Multiplier: 3
Received MinRxInt: 1000000, Received Multiplier: 3
Holddown (hits): 0(0), Hello (hits): 1000(198)
Rx Count: 200, Rx Interval (ms) min/max/avg: 9/1002/875 last: 453 ms ago
```

```
       Tx Count: 200, Tx Interval (ms) min/max/avg: 9/1006/873 last: 794 ms
       ago
       Elapsed time watermarks: 0 0 (last: 0)
       Registered protocols: BGP
       Uptime: 00:02:54
       Last packet: Version: 1                  - Diagnostic: 0
                    State bit: Up               - Demand bit: 0
                    Poll bit: 0                 - Final bit: 0
                    Multiplier: 3               - Length: 24
                    My Discr.: 1                - Your Discr.: 1
                    Min tx interval: 1000000    - Min rx interval: 1000000
                    Min Echo interval: 50000
R1#
```

Now let's see this in action. First let's confirm that we have both routes, and have a look at the time. Next we shut down the interface on R3, and then check our routes again:

```
R1#sh ip bgp | beg Network
     Network          Next Hop        Metric LocPrf Weight Path
 *>  10.100.1.0/24    10.200.1.2           0             0 300 i
 *b                   10.250.1.2                         0 200 300 i
R1#sh clock
*09:34:47.564 UTC Sun Feb 16 2014
R1#
*Feb 16 09:34:51.176: %BGP-5-ADJCHANGE: neighbor 10.200.1.2
Down BFD adjacency down
*Feb 16 09:34:51.176: %BGP_SESSION-5-ADJCHANGE: neighbor 10.200.1.2
IPv4 Unicast topology base removed from session  BFD adjacency down
R1#sh ip bgp | beg Network
     Network          Next Hop        Metric LocPrf Weight Path
 *>  10.100.1.0/24    10.250.1.2                         0 200 300 i
R1#
```

Now convergence is reduced to a few seconds, rather than half a minute. This includes the time it took to switch to another terminal window and shut down the interface, so actually the times would have been even quicker than the less than four seconds that is displayed above.

Due to limitations, either in the IOS version being used, or the software in general this is as far as the example can go, but as it is only on the written exam, it is unlikely that this will feature too heavily in the CCIE exam. There are plenty of PDFs from the Cisco Live events, which are listed in the further reading chapter of this book.

In later IOS versions there are additional subcommands for the bgp additional-paths command. These are to send and receive additional paths for inclusion in the BGP table. In the context of the above configuration the commands would be:

```
R1(config)# router bgp 100
R1(config-router)# address-family ipv4
R1(config-router-af)# bgp additional-paths send receive
R1(config-router-af)# neighbor 10.250.1.2 advertise additional-paths best 3
```

This would advertise the three best paths for a prefix, instead of just the singular best bath. Hopefully VIRL/CML will help make this all make sense once it is released.

14.4 Dampening

The Keepalive and Hold-down timers, along with next-hop tracking, do a great job at helping to provide a stable BGP infrastructure. There is, however, another factor that needs to be discussed, and that is BGP dampening. Dampening has a number of values that control how a flapping route is treated, these are the penalty, the suppress limit, the reuse limit, the half-life and the maximum suppress-limit.

When a route flaps it is assigned a penalty, which defaults to 1000, and it is moved into the dampening state "history". Each subsequent flap incurs an additional penalty (again a default of 1000). Once the suppress-limit (default 2000) is reached the route is dampened, and will not be advertised to any peers. If a route has been dampened it will only be advertised again once the penalty has been reduced to be lower than the reuse limit (default 750). Once a penalty has been assigned to a route the half-life timer starts. If the penalty is 1000 and the half-life timer is 15-minutes (which is the default), then after 15 minutes the penalty will be 500, which is lower than the default reuse limit, and will therefore be advertised once again. Once the penalty is below half of the reuse limit (375) the penalty is completely removed.

Let's put this into some perspective, we will use all the default values in this scenario.

A route flaps twice and is assigned a penalty of 2000.
After two minutes the penalty is now reduced to 1933.334, but we have two more flaps. (1000 / 60 = 33.333. 2 x 33.333 = 66.666, 2000 - 66.666 = 1933.334).
The penalty now stands at 3933.334 (2 x 1000 + 1933.334).
The route is stable, and after 15 minutes (the half life). the penalty now stands at 1966.667 (2000 / 2 = 1000, 1933.334 / 2 = 966.667).
Once we reach the next half-life the penalty is 983.3335, which is over the reuse limit (750).

After a further 3 and half minutes the penalty is now lower than the reuse limit, so the route is advertised once again.
After a further 7 minutes the half-life is now below half the reuse-limit, so the penalty is completely removed.

It has taken about 40 minutes for our route to be advertised again. If it had taken longer, such as if the route had flapped a few more times, then we would reach the maximum-suppress limit, which defaults to 60 minutes, and the route would be unsuppressed, so that it is not suppressed indefinitely.

Dampening values can be set in a route-map, or within the BGP configuration. Here, using a route-map, we can set the half-life to 10 minutes, the reuse-limit to 400, the suppress-limit to 1500 and the maximum-suppress to 40 minutes

```
R2(config)#route-map dampener permit 10
R2(config-route-map)#set dampening ?
  <1-45>  half-life time for the penalty

R2(config-route-map)#set dampening 10 ?
  <1-20000>  penalty to start reusing a route

R2(config-route-map)#set dampening 10 400 ?
  <1-20000>  penalty to start suppressing a route

R2(config-route-map)#set dampening 10 400 1500 ?
  <1-255>  Maximum duration to suppress a stable route

R2(config-route-map)#set dampening 10 400 1500 40 ?
  <cr>

R2(config-route-map)#set dampening 10 400 1500 40
```

Or we can make this the default, using a BGP command:

```
R2(config)#router bgp 100
R2(config-router)#bgp dampening 10 400 1500 40
R2(config-router)#exit
R2(config)#exit
R2#
```

There is another value to prevent a route being dampened indefinitely, and this is called the max-penalty. The max-penalty ensures that customized dampening values are valid. The max penalty is calculated using the following formula:

max-penalty = reuse-limit * 2^(max-suppress-time/half-life)

Using the default values this would equate to the following

max-penalty = 750 * 2^(60/15) = 12000

Here, the penalty assigned to a route cannot exceed 12000.

We can check the dampening metrics using the following commands:

```
R2#sh ip bgp dampening parameters
 dampening 10 400 1500 40
  Half-life time        : 10 mins        Decay Time         : 1255 secs
  Max suppress penalty:   6400           Max suppress time: 40 mins
  Suppress penalty    :   1500           Reuse penalty      : 400

R2#sh ip bgp dampening flap-statistics
R2#sh ip bgp dampening dampened-paths
R2#
```

If we quickly shut and then no shut the loopback interface on R3, we can see that the router is now showing "history" on R2:

```
R2#sh ip bgp
BGP table version is 23, local router ID is 1.1.1.1
Status codes: s suppressed, d damped, h history, * valid, > best, i
- internal,
           r RIB-failure, S Stale, m multipath, b backup-path, x best-external, f RT-Filter
Origin codes: i - IGP, e - EGP, ? - incomplete

   Network          Next Hop            Metric LocPrf Weight Path
h 10.200.1.0/24    172.16.1.2               0             0 200 i
R2#
```

This has not been enough to dampen the route though:

```
R2#sh ip bgp dampening flap-statistics | beg Network
    Network          From             Flaps Duration Reuse    Path
*>  10.200.1.0/24    172.16.1.2       1     00:01:15          200
R2#
```

If we do it a few more times and check on R2, we can see that the route is now dampened, and we will have to wait about ten minutes for it to be advertised again:

```
R2#sh ip bgp dampening flap-statistics | beg Network
   Network          From           Flaps Duration Reuse    Path
*d 10.200.1.0/24    172.16.1.2      2    00:02:12 00:00:09 200
R2#sh ip bgp dampening dampened-paths | beg Network
   Network          From           Reuse    Path
*d 10.200.1.0/24    172.16.1.2     00:10:44 200 i
R2#
```

15. Troubleshooting BGP

We have used most of the useful debugging commands already, as we have moved through this book, but they have been out of the context of troubleshooting. Now we will put them in some perspective. We will start by troubleshooting some peering issues, and then move on to issues with networks, such as expected networks not being received by a router. This chapter will make reference to the chapters and sections that cover the commands in deeper detail. Some things will be new topics.

15.1 Troubleshooting peering

If two routers fail to establish a peer session, we need to check a few things.

Troubleshooting Physical issues

We need to start by checking the obvious. It's very easy to jump straight into looking at access-control lists, but this may mean we miss something very obvious.

Is everything plugged in?
Do we have a route to the other peer?
Is the interface we will use for this route up?
Can we ping the other router?
Can we ping the remote peer address from our peering address?

If we can prove that we have connectivity to the other side, then at least one of our physical interfaces will have an IP address.

We can use "sh ip route" and "sh ip int bri" to get the current routing table and confirm that the interface is indeed working.

```
R6#sh ip route 172.20.1.0
Routing entry for 172.20.1.0/24
  Known via "static", distance 1, metric 0
  Routing Descriptor Blocks:
  * 10.7.1.2
      Route metric is 0, traffic share count is 1
R6#sh ip int bri | e down
Interface              IP-Address      OK? Method Status    Protocol
Serial1/0              10.5.1.2        YES NVRAM  up        up
Serial1/1              10.6.1.1        YES NVRAM  up        up
Serial1/2              10.7.1.1        YES NVRAM  up        up
Loopback0              172.26.1.1      YES NVRAM  up        up
```

```
Loopback1              172.26.2.1      YES NVRAM  up      up
Loopback2              172.26.3.1      YES NVRAM  up      up
R6#
```

We can also use the ping command to test connectivity and, if we are not using the nearest physical interface to peer with that router (such as a loopback interface), then we can use an extended ping to specify the source address, where "so" is the shortened version of source-interface, and lo0 is short for loopback0.

```
R6#ping 172.20.1.1
Type escape sequence to abort.
Sending 5, 100-byte ICMP Echos to 172.20.1.1:
!!!!!
Success rate is 100 percent (5/5)
R6#ping 172.20.1.1 so lo0
Type escape sequence to abort.
Sending 5, 100-byte ICMP Echos to 172.20.1.1:
Packet sent with a source address of 172.26.1.1
!!!!!
Success rate is 100 percent (5/5)
R6#
```

The MTU (or maximum transmission unit) controls how large a packet can be before the router fragments it. The MTU size on both sides of a peering should match. This is done using the command "ip mtu <bytes>" command, such as "ip mtu 1500".

Holding a large number of routes uses memory on a router. A router will display a number of issues if the memory is exhausted, such as not being able to telnet into it, or commands which should return a result (such as "sh run") not returning anything. If memory is an issue the following error will be seen: "%SYS-2-MALLOCFAIL". If this is the case, then the router either needs a memory upgrade, or, if it is caused by the number of BGP routes, then the number of incoming routes needs to be limited, which we can do through outbound route filtering (8.8) or distribute lists (8.9).

If we can prove we have physical and IP connectivity, then we also know that we have at least one physical IP address that BGP can use as its router-id. Recall from section 4.4 a router without a BGP router-id cannot start the BGP process. If all is well at this stage we can move on.

Troubleshooting Ports

BGP requires port 179 and a random port over 1023 in order to establish a session. The router with the highest BGP router-id will end up listening on port 179. We need to ensure that this port is open.

We can check our routers configuration to make sure that port 179 is not explicitly referenced in any access-lists using the following:

```
R6#sh run | i 179
R6#
```

Also check for access-lists using a range of ports.

If we are not blocking the ports we need then we can move on.

Troubleshooting BGP Configuration issues

This is probably where most of the issues will arise. The things to look out for here are peering to the wrong AS and peering to the wrong IP address.

If we take a very simple two-router example, we can look at these types of issues.

If we get R1 in AS 100, to peer with R2, which is in AS 200, but we will, incorrectly, place it in AS 300, then will see these kinds of errors:

```
R1(config-if)#router bgp 100
R1(config-router)#neigh 10.250.1.2 remote-as 300
R1(config-router)#
%BGP-3-NOTIFICATION: sent to neighbor 10.250.1.2 active 2/2 (peer in wrong AS) 2 bytes 00C8
%BGP-4-MSGDUMP: unsupported or mal-formatted message received from 10.250.1.2:

R2(config)#router bgp 200
R2(config-router)#neigh 10.250.1.1 remote-as 100
```

```
R2(config-router)#
%BGP-3-NOTIFICATION: received from neighbor 10.250.1.1 passive 2/2
(peer in wrong AS) 2 bytes 00C8
```

The binary to hex conversion chart looks like this:

Decimal	Hex	Binary
0	0	0000
1	1	0001
2	2	0010
3	3	0011
4	4	0100
5	5	0101
6	6	0110
7	7	0111
8	8	1000
9	9	1001
10	A	1010
11	B	1011
12	C	1100
13	D	1101
14	E	1110
15	F	1111

In binary the numbers would be 0000 0000 1100 1000. Using standard binary to decimal conversion tables this would be:

128	64	32	16	8	4	2	1

| 1 | 1 | 0 | 0 | 1 | 0 | 0 | 0 |

128 + 64 + 8 = 200

If we correct the AS number but change the IP address:

```
R1(config-router)#neigh 10.250.1.3 remote-as 200
R1(config-router)#do debug ip bgp
BGP debugging is on for address family: IPv4 Unicast
R1(config-router)#
```

We can see that, obviously, the host is not responding:

```
R1(config-router)#
BGP: 10.250.1.3 active went from Idle to Active
BGP: 10.250.1.3 open active, local address 10.250.1.1
BGP: topo global:IPv4 Unicast:base Scanning routing tables
BGP: topo global:IPv4 Multicast:base Scanning routing tables
BGP: 10.250.1.3 open failed: Connection timed out; remote host not responding
BGP: 10.250.1.3 Active open failed - tcb is not available, open active delayed 13312ms (35000ms max, 60% jitter)
```

So we would need to make sure that we have the correct IP address to peer with.

If we are peering with a router, we need to make sure that they are expecting us to peer from the correct interface, as we can see if we switch to using loopback interfaces:

```
R2(config)#int lo0
R2(config-if)#ip add 10.250.2.1 255.255.255.0

R1(config-router)#ip route 10.250.2.0 255.255.255.0 gi 1/0
R1(config)#router bgp 100
R1(config-router)#neigh 10.250.2.1 remote-as 200
R1(config-router)#

R2(config-router)#do debug ip bgp
BGP debugging is on for address family: IPv4 Unicast
R2(config-router)#
BGP: 10.250.1.1 active went from Idle to Active
BGP: 10.250.1.1 open active, local address 10.250.1.2
BGP: 10.250.1.1 open failed: Connection refused by remote host
R2(config-router)#
```

It's important to note that even with "debug ip bgp all" turned on, R1 is not showing any errors. The errors are all being shown on R2, so, if possible, check both routers for issues, but here we can see that our local address needs to be modified:

```
R2(config-if)#router bgp 200
R2(config-router)#neigh 10.250.1.1 update-source lo0
R2(config-router)#
```

At this stage, BGP will still not form a peer relationship between R1 and R2, and this is because the loopback interface on R2 is more than one hop away from R1:

```
R1(config-router)#neigh 10.250.2.1 ebgp-multihop 2
R1(config-router)#
%BGP-5-ADJCHANGE: neighbor 10.250.2.1 Up
R1(config-router)#
```

So, if we are using loopback addresses, then we need to make sure that we tell BGP that it is more than one hop away, also refer back to section 6.3 where we looked at the differences between ebgp-multihop and TTL security, as both sides need to match their settings. If a bgp router is expected to peer through a firewall to another router the number of hops must therefore be increased.

If we are using address-families we need to make sure that we activate our neighbor using the "neighbor <ip address> activate" bgp command (section 10).

If we are using BGP authentication it must be set up on both sides (section 13).

If we are looking at a neighbor that previously had an established peering we need to make sure that the peer has not been dampened due to a flapping interface (section 14.4).

Keepalive and hold timers should be correct. Although they will synchronize to the lowest number, make sure that the minimum hold timer (if set) will allow the routers to talk to each other (14.1).

A router can be instructed to allow a maximum number of prefixes from a peer, here we are setting the maximum number or prefixes to be 5, and the router should warn us when it reaches 80% of that number. If there are more than five routes the peering will be torn down.

```
R1(config-router)#neigh 10.250.2.1 maximum-prefix 5 80
```

On R2 we create five additional loopback interfaces, and advertise the first four of these into BGP

```
R2(config-router)#int lo1
R2(config-if)#ip add 10.211.1.1 255.255.255.0
R2(config-if)#int lo2
R2(config-if)#ip add 10.212.1.1 255.255.255.0
R2(config-if)#int lo3
R2(config-if)#ip add 10.213.1.1 255.255.255.0
R2(config-if)#int lo4
R2(config-if)#ip add 10.214.1.1 255.255.255.0
R2(config-if)#int lo5
R2(config-if)#ip add 10.215.1.1 255.255.255.0
R2(config-if)#
R2(config-if)#do sh ip int bri | e unas
Interface            IP-Address      OK? Method Status      Protocol
GigabitEthernet1/0   10.250.1.2      YES manual up          up
Loopback0            10.250.2.1      YES manual up          up
Loopback1            10.211.1.1      YES manual up          up
Loopback2            10.212.1.1      YES manual up          up
Loopback3            10.213.1.1      YES manual up          up
Loopback4            10.214.1.1      YES manual up          up
Loopback5            10.215.1.1      YES manual up          up
R2(config-if)#router bgp 200
R2(config-router)#netw 10.211.1.0 mask 255.255.255.0
R2(config-router)#netw 10.212.1.0 mask 255.255.255.0
R2(config-router)#netw 10.213.1.0 mask 255.255.255.0
R2(config-router)#netw 10.214.1.0 mask 255.255.255.0
R2(config-router)#
```

R1 has received the first four routes:

```
R1(config-router)#end
R1#sh ip bgp | b Netw
   Network           Next Hop         Metric LocPrf Weight Path
*> 10.211.1.0/24     10.250.2.1            0             0 200 i
*> 10.212.1.0/24     10.250.2.1            0             0 200 i
*> 10.213.1.0/24     10.250.2.1            0             0 200 i
*> 10.214.1.0/24     10.250.2.1            0             0 200 i
R1#
```

We can advertise the next loopback into BGP, and see the warnings on R1

```
R2(config-router)#netw 10.215.1.0 mask 255.255.255.0
R2(config-router)#
```

```
R1#
%BGP-4-MAXPFX: Number of prefixes received from 10.250.2.1 (afi 0)
reaches 5, max 5
R1#
```

Adding another loopback on R2 and advertising it, will force R1 to drop the BGP peering to R2:

```
R2(config-router)#int lo6
R2(config-if)#ip add 10.216.1.1 255.255.255.0
R2(config-if)#router bgp 200
R2(config-router)#net 10.216.1.0 mask 255.255.255.0
R2(config-router)#
%BGP-5-ADJCHANGE: neighbor 10.250.1.1 Down Peer closed the session
%BGP_SESSION-5-ADJCHANGE: neighbor 10.250.1.1 IPv4 Unicast topology
base removed from session  Peer closed the session
R2(config-router)#

R1#
%BGP-3-MAXPFXEXCEED: Number of prefixes received from 10.250.2.1 (afi
0): 6 exceeds limit 5
%BGP-5-ADJCHANGE: neighbor 10.250.2.1 Down BGP Notification sent
R1#
```

For the moment, let's fix this by removing the maximum-prefix command:

```
R1(config)#router bgp 100
R1(config-router)#no neighbor 10.250.2.1 maximum-prefix 5 80
R1(config-router)#
```

If a route is missing from an iBGP peer, we should check to see whether synchronization turned on. It is disabled by default, but if it is turned on a BGP router will not install an iBGP learned route into the routing table, unless it is able to validate it by the IGP (5.2).

If the route is coming from an iBGP neighbor we need to make sure that the next hop is valid, remember that iBGP peers do not change the next hop address, and must have the bgp neighbor command next-hop-self configured (5.2).

If all of the above are correct, then your peers should form relationships.

Troubleshooting route advertisement

Assuming that we have two established peers, then we might have to troubleshoot missing routes.

If we have access to the sending peer we can use the command "*sh ip bgp neighbor <ip address> advertised-routes*", to see all the routes that are being advertised to that peer.

If we are limited to the local router we can see what a peer is sending us, and what we are receiving, using the command "*sh ip bgp neighbor <ip address> received-routes*". This requires route-refresh to be enabled (using the bgp command "neighbor <ip address> soft-reconfiguration inbound" from section 6.5), or we can use the command "sh ip bgp neighbor <ip address> routes" command:

```
R1#sh ip bgp neigh 10.250.2.1 routes | b Net
   Network          Next Hop         Metric LocPrf Weight Path
*> 10.211.1.0/24    10.250.2.1            0             0 200 i
*> 10.212.1.0/24    10.250.2.1            0             0 200 i
*> 10.213.1.0/24    10.250.2.1            0             0 200 i
*> 10.214.1.0/24    10.250.2.1            0             0 200 i
*> 10.215.1.0/24    10.250.2.1            0             0 200 i
*> 10.216.1.0/24    10.250.2.1            0             0 200 i

Total number of prefixes 6
R1#
```

Using the above commands, we can see whether a route that we are expecting has been aggregated into a larger prefix, or, if we are using the network command, that we haven't accidentally tried to advertise the classful network, instead of networks that we can advertise.

We can use the command "sh ip route" to see a list of our own prefixes

```
R2#sh ip route | b Gate
Gateway of last resort is not set

      10.0.0.0/8 is variably subnetted, 16 subnets, 2 masks
C        10.211.1.0/24 is directly connected, Loopback1
L        10.211.1.1/32 is directly connected, Loopback1
C        10.212.1.0/24 is directly connected, Loopback2
L        10.212.1.1/32 is directly connected, Loopback2
C        10.213.1.0/24 is directly connected, Loopback3
L        10.213.1.1/32 is directly connected, Loopback3
C        10.214.1.0/24 is directly connected, Loopback4
L        10.214.1.1/32 is directly connected, Loopback4
C        10.215.1.0/24 is directly connected, Loopback5
L        10.215.1.1/32 is directly connected, Loopback5
C        10.216.1.0/24 is directly connected, Loopback6
L        10.216.1.1/32 is directly connected, Loopback6
```

```
C           10.250.1.0/24 is directly connected, GigabitEthernet1/0
L           10.250.1.2/32 is directly connected, GigabitEthernet1/0
C           10.250.2.0/24 is directly connected, Loopback0
L           10.250.2.1/32 is directly connected, Loopback0
R2#
```

Currently we are advertising the loopback addresses

```
R2#sh run | sec router bgp
router bgp 200
 bgp log-neighbor-changes
 network 10.211.1.0 mask 255.255.255.0
 network 10.212.1.0 mask 255.255.255.0
 network 10.213.1.0 mask 255.255.255.0
 network 10.214.1.0 mask 255.255.255.0
 network 10.215.1.0 mask 255.255.255.0
 network 10.216.1.0 mask 255.255.255.0
 neighbor 10.250.1.1 remote-as 100
 neighbor 10.250.1.1 update-source Loopback0
R2#
```

If we remove the loopbacks from our BGP configuration and instead advertise the classful 10.0.0.0 network, we can see that we are not advertising anything to R1:

```
R2(config)#router bgp 200
R2(config-router)#no network 10.211.1.0 mask 255.255.255.0
R2(config-router)#no network 10.212.1.0 mask 255.255.255.0
R2(config-router)#no network 10.213.1.0 mask 255.255.255.0
R2(config-router)#no network 10.214.1.0 mask 255.255.255.0
R2(config-router)#no network 10.215.1.0 mask 255.255.255.0
R2(config-router)#no network 10.216.1.0 mask 255.255.255.0
R2(config-router)#net 10.0.0.0
R2(config-router)#do sh ip bgp neigh 10.250.1.1 advertised-routes

Total number of prefixes 0
R2(config-router)#
```

This shows that we need to advertise matching routes properly:

```
R2(config)#router bgp 200
R2(config-router)#no network 10.0.0.
R2(config-router)#network 10.211.1.0 mask 255.255.255.0
R2(config-router)#network 10.212.1.0 mask 255.255.255.0
R2(config-router)#network 10.213.1.0 mask 255.255.255.0
R2(config-router)#network 10.214.1.0 mask 255.255.255.0
R2(config-router)#network 10.215.1.0 mask 255.255.255.0
```

```
R2(config-router)#network 10.216.1.0 mask 255.255.255.0
R2(config-router)#do sh ip bgp neigh 10.250.1.1 advertised-r | b Netw
   Network          Next Hop         Metric LocPrf Weight Path
*> 10.211.1.0/24    0.0.0.0               0         32768 i
*> 10.212.1.0/24    0.0.0.0               0         32768 i
*> 10.213.1.0/24    0.0.0.0               0         32768 i
*> 10.214.1.0/24    0.0.0.0               0         32768 i
*> 10.215.1.0/24    0.0.0.0               0         32768 i
*> 10.216.1.0/24    0.0.0.0               0         32768 i

Total number of prefixes 6
R2(config-router)#
```

If we are redistributing from an IGP into BGP, we need to make sure that we are aware of the effects of auto-summarisation. We will stop advertising the loopback addresses of R2 in BGP, and advertise the first four through RIP v2.

```
R2(config-router)#no network 10.211.1.0 mask 255.255.255.0
R2(config-router)#no network 10.212.1.0 mask 255.255.255.0
R2(config-router)#no network 10.213.1.0 mask 255.255.255.0
R2(config-router)#no network 10.214.1.0 mask 255.255.255.0
R2(config-router)#no network 10.215.1.0 mask 255.255.255.0
R2(config-router)#no network 10.216.1.0 mask 255.255.255.0
R2(config-router)#exit
R2(config)#router rip
R2(config-router)#version 2
R2(config-router)#auto-summary
R2(config-router)#net 10.211.1.0
R2(config-router)#net 10.212.1.0
R2(config-router)#net 10.213.1.0
R2(config-router)#net 10.214.1.0
R2(config-router)#exit
R2(config)#router bgp 200
R2(config-router)#redistribute rip
```

R1 now sees all of the loopback interfaces advertised from R2:

```
R1#sh ip bgp | b Net
   Network          Next Hop         Metric LocPrf Weight Path
*> 10.211.1.0/24    10.250.2.1            0             0 200 ?
*> 10.212.1.0/24    10.250.2.1            0             0 200 ?
*> 10.213.1.0/24    10.250.2.1            0             0 200 ?
*> 10.214.1.0/24    10.250.2.1            0             0 200 ?
*> 10.215.1.0/24    10.250.2.1            0             0 200 ?
*> 10.216.1.0/24    10.250.2.1            0             0 200 ?
r> 10.250.1.0/24    10.250.2.1            0             0 200 ?
```

```
r> 10.250.2.0/24      10.250.2.1              0           0 200 ?
R1#
```

If we still have the maximum-paths command configured on R1's neighbor statement for R2, this would have caused the peering to be torn down. Clearly, we only advertised four of the loopback networks into BGP, but because of auto-summarisation RIP has advertised all of its networks to R1 through redistribution.

```
R2(config-router)#do sh run | sec router rip
router rip
 version 2
 network 10.0.0.0
R2(config-router)#
```

We can be missing routes for a number of reasons. We could have a filter-list in place, preventing the router becoming a transit AS, outbound route filtering or a prefix-list blocking certain networks; routes may have been suppressed, or conditionally advertised. If the fault is on our own router then it is usually due to a neighbor statement attaching a route-map or prefix list for example. The quickest way to ascertain whether this is the issue is to use the command "sh run I i neighbor", which we will do as we return to our main topology:

```
R9#sh run | in neighbor
 bgp log-neighbor-changes
 neighbor 10.10.1.1 remote-as 11100
 neighbor 10.10.1.1 inherit peer-session R8
 neighbor 10.10.1.1 capability orf prefix-list receive
 neighbor 10.10.1.1 inherit peer-policy R8
 neighbor 10.11.1.1 remote-as 12000
 neighbor 10.11.1.1 inherit peer-session R11
 neighbor 10.11.1.1 inherit peer-policy R11
R9#
```

Assuming that R9 is missing a route, using this command we would see there is outbound route filtering on routes being received, and also, the neighbors are controlled by peer policy and session templates. Therefore, we would need to look into the orf prefix-list, and the templates.

If we are seeing that different routes are preferred to ones we would expect, the same command as above will show us what routes-maps are assigned to different neighbors:

```
R5#sh run | i neigh
 bgp log-neighbor-changes
 neighbor 10.3.1.2 remote-as 300
```

```
  neighbor 10.3.1.2 route-map set-R12-localpref in
  neighbor 10.5.1.2 remote-as 400
  neighbor 10.5.1.2 route-map set-R6-routes in
  neighbor 172.16.1.1 remote-as 200
  neighbor 172.16.1.1 update-source Loopback0
  neighbor 172.16.1.1 next-hop-self
  neighbor 172.17.1.1 remote-as 200
  neighbor 172.17.1.1 update-source Loopback0
  neighbor 172.17.1.1 next-hop-self
  neighbor 172.17.1.1 route-map R3-PEER in
R5#
```

We can use the command "sh route-map" to look at the contents of all our route-maps, or limit this down to particular route-map:

```
R6#sh route-map
route-map AS300-prefix, permit, sequence 10
  Match clauses:
    ip address prefix-lists: 172-18-2-prefix
    community (community-list filter): 1
  Set clauses:
  Policy routing matches: 0 packets, 0 bytes
route-map 172-26-to-AS200, permit, sequence 10
  Match clauses:
    ip address prefix-lists: lo-prefix
  Set clauses:
  Policy routing matches: 0 packets, 0 bytes
route-map set-R5-172-18-weight, permit, sequence 10
  Match clauses:
    ip address prefix-lists: 172-18
    as-path (as-path filter): 5
  Set clauses:
    weight 100
  Policy routing matches: 0 packets, 0 bytes
route-map set-R5-172-18-weight, permit, sequence 20
  Match clauses:
  Set clauses:
  Policy routing matches: 0 packets, 0 bytes
route-map set_community, permit, sequence 10
  Match clauses:
    ip address prefix-lists: 172-18
    as-path (as-path filter): 5
  Set clauses:
    community 19661300
    weight 100
  Policy routing matches: 0 packets, 0 bytes
route-map set_community, permit, sequence 20
```

```
    Match clauses:
    Set clauses:
        community 19661300
    Policy routing matches: 0 packets, 0 bytes
R6#

R5#sh route-map R3-PEER
route-map R3-PEER, permit, sequence 10
    Match clauses:
        community (community-list filter): 1
    Set clauses:
        local-preference 150
    Policy routing matches: 0 packets, 0 bytes
route-map R3-PEER, permit, sequence 20
    Match clauses:
    Set clauses:
    Policy routing matches: 0 packets, 0 bytes
R5#
```

We can also look at what as-path access-lists we are using as well:

```
R6#sh ip as-path-access-list
AS path access list 5
    permit _500_
R6#

R9#sh ip as-path-access-list
AS path access list 1
    permit ^[11100]+$
    permit ^$
R9#
```

There really isn't a right way and wrong way to troubleshoot. There are preferred methods, but troubleshooting is a quite personal thing - what works for one person may not necessarily work for another person. Yes, it makes sense to start with the basics (make sure its plugged in), before working towards looking at access lists and the like, however experience will always dictate strategy. Certainly someone who is studying for their CCNA may see the output from some error and start from the beginning and work their way through it, whereas someone who is CCIE level will be able to skip to the most pertinent parts and formulate cause and effect quicker. Hopefully this chapter will help all levels of ability.

16. This book and the CCIE v5

Unlike the CCNP exams, which require a valid CCNA certification, there are no requirements for taking the CCIE exams. The exams come in two parts, the 2-hour written exam, and the 8-hour lab exam.

The v5.0 blueprint lists the following topics that are required for BGP (2.7 in the Lab exam and 3.7 in the written exam). Along side it is the section or chapter that you will find this covered in. 3.7.i is for the written exam only:

Written	Lab	Title	In this book
3.7.a	2.7.a	**Describe, implement and troubleshoot peer relationships**	
3.7.a [i]	2.7.a [i]	Peer-group, template	9.2
3.7.a [ii]	2.7.a [ii]	Active, passive	6.2
3.7.a [iii]	2.7.a [iii]	States, timers	4.3, 14
3.7.a [iv]	2.7.a [iv]	Dynamic neighbors	9.1
3.7.b	2.7.b	**Implement and troubleshoot IBGP and EBGP**	
3.7.b [i]	2.7.b [i]	EBGP, IBGP	4 & 5
3.7.b [ii]	2.7.b [ii]	4 bytes AS number	2.5
3.7.b [iii]	2.7.b [iii]	Private AS	2.5, 7.3
3.7.c	2.7.c	**Explain attributes and best-path selection**	11
3.7.d	2.7.d	**Implement, optimize and troubleshoot routing policies**	
3.7.d [i]	2.7.d [i]	Attribute manipulation	11
3.7.d [ii]	2.7.d [ii]	Conditional advertisement	8.6
3.7.d [iii]	2.7.d [iii]	Outbound route filtering	8.8
3.7.d [iv]	2.7.d [iv]	Communities, extended communities	7.1

Written	Lab	Title	In this book
3.7.d [v]	2.7.d [v]	Multi-homing	8.6
3.7.e	2.7.e	**Implement and troubleshoot scalability**	
3.7.e [i]	2.7.e [i]	Route-reflector, cluster	6.4, 6.7
3.7.e [ii]	2.7.e [ii]	Confederations	6.6
3.7.e [iii]	2.7.e [iii]	Aggregation, AS set	8.2, 8.3
3.7.f	2.7.f	**Implement and troubleshoot multiproctocol BGP**	
3.7.f [i]	2.7.f [i]	IPv4, IPv6, VPN address-family	10
3.7.g	2.7.g	**Implement and troubleshoot AS path manipulations**	
3.7.g [i]	2.7.g [i]	Local AS, allow AS in, remove private AS	6.8, 7.2, 7.3
3.7.g [ii]	2.7.g [ii]	Prepend	11.8, 11.9
3.7.g [iii]	2.7.g [iii]	Regexp	11.2
3.7.h	2.7.h	**Implement and troubleshoot other features**	
3.7.h [i]	2.7.h [i]	Multipath	11.13
3.7.h [ii]	2.7.h [ii]	BGP synchronization	5.2
3.7.h [iii]	2.7.h [iii]	Soft reconfiguration, route refresh	5.2
3.7.i		**Describe BGP fast convergence features**	
3.7.i [i]	n/a	Prefix independent convergence	14.6
3.7.i [ii]	n/a	Add-path	14.6
3.7.i [iii]	n/a	Next-hop address tracking	14.5

17. Further Reading

Although BGP gets updated pretty frequently BGP books do not. Most are at least a few years old, but still very worth reading. Here are a few additional books and links.

General

There are a number of books on BGP such as:

Internet Routing Architectures (2nd Edition), Sam Halabi, 2000
Cisco BGP-4 Command and Configuration Handbook, Parkhurst, 2001
Routing TCP/IP, Volume II, Doyle, 2001

Secure BGP

http://www.cisco.com/web/about/ac123/ac147/archived_issues/ipj_6-3/securing_bgp_s-bgp.html
http://www.ir.bbn.com/sbgp/
http://www.ir.bbn.com/sbgp/draft-clynn-s-bgp-protocol-01.txt

PIC and Additional Paths

http://www.cisco.com/c/en/us/td/docs/ios-xml/ios/iproute_bgp/configuration/12-2sr/irg-12-2sr-book/irg-bgp-mp-pic.html#GUID-FEC7102C-D49D-4D29-8308-FC31D1AFF691

http://www.cisco.com/c/en/us/td/docs/ios-xml/ios/iproute_bgp/configuration/xe-3s/irg-xe-3s-book/irg-additional-paths.html

Troubleshooting

http://www.cisco.com/c/en/us/support/docs/ip/border-gateway-protocol-bgp/22166-bgp-trouble-main.html

BGP Looking glasses

BGP looking glasses are publicly accessible servers (mainly run by ISPs), which anyone can use to do BGP lookups and run a number of commands.

There is a large list published at http://www.bgp4.as/looking-glasses.

Although they do not offer anything different to what we have seen during this book, they do give a good insight into real-life BGP, and you can easily test using your own IP address. Some will even let you test regexp commands, such as http://lg.alsysdata.net/.

Made in the USA
San Bernardino, CA
29 February 2016